PRIMITIVE SEMITIC RELIGION
TO-DAY

PRIMITIVE SEMITIC RELIGION TO-DAY

A RECORD OF RESEARCHES, DISCOVERIES AND STUDIES IN SYRIA, PALESTINE AND THE SINAITIC PENINSULA

BY
SAMUEL IVES CURTISS D.D.
PROFESSOR OF OLD TESTAMENT LITERATURE AND INTERPRETATION
CHICAGO THEOLOGICAL SEMINARY

Wipf & Stock
PUBLISHERS
Eugene, Oregon

Wipf and Stock Publishers
199 West 8th Avenue, Suite 3
Eugene, Oregon 97401

Primitive Semitic Religion Today
A Record of Researches, Discoveries and Studies
in Syria, Palestine and the Sinaitic Peninsula
By Curtiss, Samuel I.
ISBN: 1-59244-600-0
Publication date 3/17/2004
Previously published by Hodder and Stoughton, 1902

TO THOSE MISSIONARIES AND TO
ALL OTHERS IN SYRIA AND PALESTINE WHO HAVE
BEEN MY COMPANIONS IN TRAVEL
HAVE RECEIVED ME INTO THEIR HOMES
OR AIDED ME IN ANY WAY
THIS VOLUME IS
GRATEFULLY DEDICATED

TABLE OF CONTENTS

		PAGE
I.	INTRODUCTORY	17
II.	SKETCH OF PRELIMINARY TRAVELS, 1898-1899	22
III.	SPECIAL RESEARCHES, SUMMERS OF 1900, 1901	34
IV.	SOURCES OF PRIMITIVE SEMITIC RELIGION	49
V.	MODERN SEMITES	56
VI.	CONCEPTIONS OF GOD	63
VII.	THE LOCAL DIVINITIES	75
VIII.	THE DEIFIED MEN	96
IX.	PHYSICAL RELATION OF MAN TO GOD	112
X.	MORAL RELATION OF MAN TO GOD	124
XI.	THE HIGH PLACES AND SACRED SHRINES	133
XII.	PRIESTS AND "HOLY MEN"	144
XIII.	VOWS AND ANNUAL FESTIVALS	156
XIV.	THE INSTITUTION OF SACRIFICE	170
XV.	THE USE OF BLOOD	181
XVI.	REDEMPTION, AND "THE BURSTING FORTH OF BLOOD"	194
XVII.	THE SIGNIFICANCE OF SACRIFICE	218
XVIII.	THE PLACE OF SACRIFICE	229
XIX.	CONCLUSION	238

APPENDICES

A.	QUESTIONS ON THE SURVIVALS OF ANCIENT RELIGION IN BIBLE LANDS	247
B.	OUTLINE OF JOURNEYS IN SYRIA, PALESTINE, EGYPT, AND THE SINAITIC PENINSULA	249
C.	THE SEVEN WELLS AT BEERSHEBA	255
D.	THE PROSE VERSION OF THE STORY OF 'ARJA	257

TABLE OF CONTENTS

		PAGE
E.	HIGH PLACES AND SACRED SHRINES	260
F.	THE SAMARITAN PASSOVER	264
G.	ALTARS AND SACRIFICES IN THE PRIMITIVE ART OF BABYLONIA. BY THE REV. W. HAYES WARD, D.D., LL.D.	266

INDICES

	PAGE
NAMES	279
SUBJECTS	282
LIST OF ARABIC AND OTHER SEMITIC WORDS	285
SCRIPTURE REFERENCES	286
QUOTATIONS FROM THE KORAN	288

LIST OF ILLUSTRATIONS

	PAGE
WELL AT BEERSHEBA	36
UNOPENED WELL AT BEERSHEBA	37
GADIS FROM THE EAST	38
SACRED GROVE AT THE "MOTHER OF PIECES"	44
PLATFORM OF THE "MOTHER OF PIECES"	45
PART OF THE "CHAIR OF THE LEADERS"	46
SHRINE OF AARON ON MOUNT HOR	79
CENOTAPH OF AARON	81
MAR RISHA AT KARYATEN	85
THE ROCK OF JOB AT SHEIK SA'D	86
SACRED TREE HUNG WITH RAGS	91
SHRINE OF NUSAIRIYEH AT DER MARIA	143
PRIEST OR MINISTER OF THE MEZAR AT JAFAR	146
SHRINE OF NEBI DAUD, JERUSALEM	157
GRAVE OF HOLY MAN NEAR MEDEBA	179
SHRINE IN THE LAND OF AMMON	185
SHRINE OF ST. GEORGE	187
BLOOD MARKS OF ARABS ON THE SHRINE OF ABU OBEIDA	193
GREAT WATER-WHEEL AT HAMATH	198
SACRED TREES AND ROCK ALTAR AT YAZUZ	234
DOLMEN-ALTAR WITH HOLLOWS FOR BLOOD	234
DOLMEN NEAR ZERKA MAIN	235
SPECIMEN OF ALTAR AT THE GIZEH MUSEUM	235
GENERAL PLAN OF HIGH PLACE AT PETRA	236
ANCIENT PLACE FOR SLAUGHTERING SACRIFICE AT PETRA	237
SIXTEEN CUTS AND THREE HALF-TONES ILLUSTRATING THE ARTICLE ON ALTARS AND SACRIFICES IN THE PRIMITIVE ART OF BABYLONIA, IN APPENDIX G, BY THE REV. WILLIAM HAYES WARD, D.D., LL. D.	267-276

PREFACE

Every new book must demonstrate its right to be. The publisher and the circle of readers for which it is designed may well ask, "Why should you claim our attention? What are you? Do you give any new or important information? Are you interesting?"

These are all legitimate questions, to which I shall attempt a brief answer. In the preparation of the following pages, I have not thought of any special class of readers except those who may be interested in the study of primitive religious customs. Earnest students of the Bible, as well as those of comparative religion, may perhaps find in this treatise new materials for thought and investigation.

My chief interest in the subject is as an interpreter of the Old Testament, who after four years of preparation with the late Professor Franz Delitzsch, of the University of Leipzig, and twenty years of teaching and lecturing in Chicago Theological Seminary, at last spent fourteen months in tours throughout the length and breadth of Syria and Palestine, not to speak of a visit to Egypt and the Sinaitic Peninsula. In that period, largely devoted to travel, I had the opportunity to see these countries as perhaps few have seen them. To carry out my purpose involved anxieties, struggles, and victories, which I have sketched as an encouragement to those who might wish to engage in a similar undertaking. Aside from Chapters II and III, and the Itineraries contained in Appendix B, I have not attempted to describe these travels in detail.

The first journeys, including my sojourn at such centers as Beirut, Jerusalem, and Damascus, requiring more than a twelvemonth, were supplemented by two others, covering fully five months, in the summers of 1900 and 1901. The last two were conducted in the interest of a particular investigation, namely, to discover from personal interviews with natives in different parts of the country who had not come in contact with European civilization, and who were but slightly influenced by Islam, what was the primitive religion of the ancient Semites; for it is not to the Hebrews, to the Assyrians, or to the Babylonians that we are to go for this primitive picture. They have indeed retained many traces of primitive religious customs, but these have been modified from the original type through outside influences. If, then, we wish to discover the ancestor of Semitic religions, whose lineaments are to be found in the beliefs and usages of Assyria, Phœnicia, and Israel, we shall pursue our investigations among Syrians and Arabs, who observe the same religious rites as did their progenitors from the earliest dawn of history. We shall find among them many individual examples of religious customs, of which perhaps only one or two may be seen among the Assyrians and the Hebrews. Thus, through many illustrations discovered among Syrians and Arabs, a religious custom observed among the Assyrians or Hebrews which almost escapes our attention, or which we might suppose to be primitive among them, comes out in its true bearing as something which they have inherited from a primeval source.

A book which contains many examples of vows, of blood-sprinkling, of sacrifice, should be of interest to all who desire to know what was the foundation on which the religion of other ancient Semitic peoples was built.

PREFACE 13

It may seem that it is an unwarrantable assumption to claim that among such modern Semites as Arabs and Syrians we have the sources of primitive Semitic religion. But to my mind, this assumption becomes an indisputable fact when we once recognize the power of custom in the East, which persists throughout the millenniums without change when untouched by outside influences.

The basis for my treatment of primitive Semitic religion is in my own researches, some of which, considering their number and significance, may have the value of original discoveries. It may well be that those who are familiar with the literature of the subject, or with the countries traversed, may recognize isolated facts as already known to them, and see their bearing on the discussion after a large number of examples have been presented, and so be tempted to claim that in all that follows there is little that is new. But from my knowledge of the literature, and as the result of interviews with numerous missionaries, I am persuaded that there are many new facts which have enabled me to put the subject in a new light. While I refer to some of the most important works bearing on this discussion, I am not dependent upon them, but have relied almost altogether on personal investigation.

It has been my effort to trace the characteristic features of the primitive religion of the Semites: their conceptions of the being who has for them the value of God, their ideas of sin; to describe their places of worship, their priesthood, and to discuss the nature as well as the significance of their sacrifices. I have not sought to establish any theory, only to give the facts, so far as I apprehend them. The discussion is based on unpublished personal journals of my travels and observations, to which constant reference is made in the notes.

With respect to my position as an Old Testament interpreter, I see in the Bible a record of many divine revelations, each adapted to a particular age and condition of God's people, beginning with a disclosure of himself, made with infinite condescension, to the child-age of the world, hence simple, elementary, and pictorial. Forms of speech and modes of thought belonging to primitive Semitism have been adopted as a medium of communication, without which the Semites could not originally have understood the divine message. I have given a few illustrations of such a use of primitive Semitic conceptions and modes of thought as are found in the Scriptures.

While it seems to me that we find abundant evidences of development in the Old Testament, from very simple concrete representations of God to those which are profoundly spiritual, I am not able to account for this development on naturalistic principles. In it I see God at all times and everywhere co-working with human instruments until the fullness of the time should come.

The messages which we find in the Old Testament seem all the more divine to me because of the great gulf which is fixed between primitive Semitic conceptions of God, and the noble, spiritual views of Him set forth under divine illumination by an Isaiah. The great prophet is a product of many ages of divine revelation and teaching, and cannot be accounted for as a natural representative of his age and people.

In my investigations I have been indebted to many, especially to the Rev. J. Stewart Crawford, of the Irish Presbyterian Mission in Damascus and the Syrian Desert—the nature of this indebtedness I shall mention later. At my earnest solicitation I have received from the Rev. W. Hayes Ward, LL.D., editor of The Independent, a valuable paper on Altars and Sacrifices in the Primitive Art of Babylonia, with many illustrations, the result of years of study, which I have added as Appendix G. In the revision of my manuscript, I have enjoyed many kindly and helpful suggestions from my colleague, the Rev. William Douglas Mackenzie, D.D.; in reading the proof I have had the valued assistance of our librarian, Mr. Herbert Wright Gates. No attempt has been made to indicate the quantity of the syllables of Arabic words, or the mode of their pronunciation. Such transcription is difficult on account of the many ways of pronouncing Arabic among the Arabs themselves and the many kinds of transliteration employed by English and German scholars. So far as the English dictionary affords a standard for the spelling of Arabic names it has been followed, otherwise essentially the transliteration of Baedeker's Syria and Palestine has been adopted, though with some modifications, except the spelling of Arabic words occurring in various quotations, which has not been changed.

A large proportion of the photographs were taken at my suggestion, by my companions in travel, and serve to illustrate the special themes discussed.

PRIMITIVE SEMITIC RELIGION TO-DAY

CHAPTER I

INTRODUCTORY

This book is the outgrowth of three journeys during the years 1898–1901, in which Syria was visited three times, Palestine twice, and the Sinaitic Peninsula once. It was on my first journey to northern Syria, in the autumn of 1898, that my attention was drawn to this subject. During a tour made with Rev. F. W. March, and Rev. W. S. Nelson, D.D., both missionaries of the American Presbyterian Board, a sacred grove and high place were recognized at Beinu. In the further course of the journey to Safita, many others were visited. Greeks, Maronites, Moslems and Nusairiyeh were interviewed as to the use of the shrines found in connection with the groves, the missionaries acting as interpreters.

As a result of the information received the question at once arose whether there was in these shrines a survival of ancient Semitic worship. The elucidation of this question gradually opened up a whole vista of usages, antedating the Israelitish codes and presupposed by them.

It was a fascinating investigation, continued for three years and constantly growing in interest to the end of my journey last summer. Hints became positive information, conjectures developed into certainties, facts, obscurely apprehended at first, often came out as the result of many interviews with natives into clearness. These investigations covered the whole round of sacred places, seasons, persons, and rites.

Important information had been expected from some of the missionaries in Syria and Palestine. It seemed as if they must know, by virtue of a long residence in the country and by an unconscious absorption, many things that ought to be gathered before they should pass away. And yet I had been warned by one of the most eminent authorities on manners and customs, Rev. George E. Post, M.D., of the Syrian Protestant College in Beirut, that not much new material could be expected from this source. Such has largely proved to be the case. Missionaries are so fully occupied with their pressing duties that they cannot easily turn aside to get information which would be within their reach if they were prepared to conduct researches, which would reveal the primitive beliefs of the people. In general, such an investigation was characterized by Dr. Post as likely to be almost fruitless, since every essential fact that could be gathered was already in print. All that could be looked for would simply be a restatement of these old facts in a new dress. A careful examination of the literature of the subject, and various contributions solicited from those who had been long in the country, appeared to confirm this view.[1] Nevertheless, it seemed that if no new facts about ancient religious customs were to be discovered, those already published would possess a new value if grouped and discussed by an Old Testament interpreter. It will be

[1] In all I sent out several hundred circulars, from London in the autumn of 1900, and again from Beirut in the summer of 1901, with respect to the manners, customs, and religious usages of Syrians and Bedouin. Very few replies were received. For the second set of questions see Appendix A.

INTRODUCTORY 19

found, however, as the result of my researches, that a mass of new material has been unearthed, and that some institutions are proved to exist, the presence of which had not been described by any previous traveler, or even by missionaries who had resided for years in the country. I have not merely recorded the facts which came to me—I have been on the lookout for them.

It might be natural to suppose that the orthodoxy of Islam as well as that of ancient Christianity must have had power to suppress such usages of ancient Semitism as were clearly contrary to them. Reasoning on this basis, a well-known physician in Jerusalem declined to analyze a substance from a Moslem shrine that looked like blood. The assurance of eminent Moslems in Jerusalem, that the use of blood would be impossible in connection with any Moslem shrine, was assigned by him as a sufficient reason for not making what he deemed a useless investigation. The following pages will show the real state of the case.

Heretofore there has been much difficulty in gaining information on such points. Some of the most learned scholars in Great Britain, for example, working under the auspices of the Palestine Exploration Fund, had prepared six pamphlets, of about forty-five pages each,[1] containing an elaborate series of questions regarding the manners, customs, and religious practices of various sects and classes of people. But aside from articles by Mr. Philip Baldensperger in The Quarterly Statement,[2]

[1] The titles of those at hand are as follows: Questions on the Bedawin; Questions on the Fellahin; Questions on the Ismailiyeh and Anseiriyeh; Questions on the Yezids.

[2] Peasant Folklore of Palestine, 1893, pp. 203-219; Religion of the Fellahin of Palestine, ibid., pp. 307-320; Orders of Holy Men in Palestine, 1894, pp. 22-38; Morals of the Fellahin, 1897, pp. 123-134; Woman in the East, 1899, pp. 132-160.

there has been very little response to these inquiries. Each one who had made an investigation seemed like the man with the one talent, ready to hide it in a napkin. Then there was the difficulty of securing trustworthy information, for in the kindness of his heart the Oriental is often ready to give the traveler just the knowledge he desires, while intelligent natives have looked upon such investigations as "unworthy of a serious-minded man."

I believe I have been able to overcome most of these difficulties. My method was to avoid asking leading questions, and to pursue my inquiries in such a way as to get the exact facts in a given inquiry. I was able to have interviews with large numbers of persons widely distant from each other. The frankness with which natives answered my interrogatories was a delightful surprise. Undoubtedly the openness of the replies was often due to the confidence which the natives felt in my companions, the missionaries and their helpers. Information partially gained at one point was supplemented and made clear by further interviews in other parts of the country.

While Burckhardt, in his travels among the Arabs, found it impracticable to write any notes in their presence, because those who have had but little contact with civilization fear writing as if it were a black art, in every interview, thus far, I have been able to take down information from the lips of the interpreter.[1] In this way a mass of material has been gathered about the ancient religious customs of the people, such as has never been published before. For help in getting this information, I am indebted to Mr. A. Forder, of Jerusalem, mission-

[1] The Arabs at one of the encampments in the South Country (*Negeb*), when they saw me taking notes, said: "He is writing down our names so as to report to the Sultan at Stambul (Constantinople) whether or not he has been well treated."

ary among the Arabs, with whom I traveled during the summer of 1900, and pre-eminently to the Rev. J. Stewart Crawford, of the Irish Presbyterian Mission, Damascus, who was born in Syria, who speaks Arabic like a native, who entered into every investigation with the keenest interest, and who, in addition to a brief tour in the Syrian Desert in the autumn of 1898, was, during the summer of 1901, an almost constant companion and interpreter.

Although much valuable material is scattered through the volumes of travelers, especially of Burckhardt and Doughty, and through the learned monographs of Trumbull, I am not aware of any systematic attempt to gain information regarding ancient religious usages from Syrians and Arabs to-day. W. Robertson Smith, in his Religion of the Semites, has drawn on Arabic literature for a masterly treatise, but the field of special investigation into the primitive religious customs of modern Semites, which this volume enters, is entirely new. May it prove of service to students of the Old Testament, as well as to those of Comparative Religion.

CHAPTER II

SKETCH OF PRELIMINARY TRAVELS
1898-1899

When I sailed from New York for Naples, the 21st of May, 1898, on the steamship Aller, of the North German Lloyd, I could not forecast what would be the final outcome of my studies and investigations. I knew it would not be easy for a private individual, with no society behind him, to open up a new field of research, owing to the great contributions which have been made to the knowledge of Palestinian geography by the Palestine Exploration Fund. I did not feel disposed to add another book to the delineation of a country which had been so often described by so many competent travelers.

But for many years I had desired to visit Palestine. This was the goal of my expectations when I first set sail from New York, in May, 1872, with the hope of devoting a considerable period to study and travel. The realization of this hope seemed near when, in the winter of 1877, the late Professor Philip Schaff, LL.D., of Union Theological Seminary, New York, kindly invited me to join his party for a tour in Palestine and the Sinaitic Peninsula. Much as I desired to accept his invitation, I was dissuaded from undertaking a journey at that time by Professor Franz Delitzsch, of the University of Leipzig, who with fatherly kindness had supervised my Semitic studies for three years. As I was then engaged in translating Bickell's Outlines of Hebrew Grammar, it did not seem wise to him that I should undertake the journey at that time.

SKETCH OF PRELIMINARY TRAVELS 23

Later I entertained the hope of spending one or more summers in Lebanon, but became so involved in various forms of work in Chicago that it proved impossible, as I thought, to visit the land toward which my heart had repeatedly turned.

It was not until I had served as Professor of Old Testament Literature and Interpretation in the Chicago Theological Seminary for twenty years that the opportunity came, through the great kindness of the directors of the seminary, for a leave of absence, which was to extend over sixteen months.

While planning for this journey, I entertained the view held by most travelers in Syria and Palestine, so far as I am aware, which is emphasized in their travels and in guide-books, that there are only about three months each year suitable for traveling in these countries, owing to the excessive heat of summer, and the consequent danger of Syrian fever and to the rains falling at intervals between the middle of November and the beginning of April. Not contemplating any other seasons for travel than those laid down in the guide-books, and desiring to make the most careful and effective preparation possible for my journey, I debated with friends and myself whether I should spend the months preceding the autumn in preliminary study at the British Museum, and under the advice of the officers of the Palestine Exploration Fund, or whether I should spend the time at Berlin, or should proceed at once to Beirut and avail myself of the admirable facilities to be found in the library of the Syrian Protestant College. I therefore addressed a letter of inquiry to the Rev. Daniel F. Bliss, D.D., president of that college, from whom in due time I received a type-written list of many excellent books on the countries I was to visit, and a very cordial invitation to pursue my studies at the college. This letter was decisive. I determined to journey at once to Beirut. My voyage was accomplished in nineteen days from New York, by the way of Gibralter, Naples, and Port Said, on three different lines of steamers. I arrived in Beirut the 9th of June, where through the great kindness of President Bliss, I was soon established in one of the rooms in the main college building overlooking the Lebanon and St. George's Bay. I at once began the study of modern Arabic, and made such use of the library as I could.

The charm of the changing colors which rested on the bay, sometimes becoming deep as indigo, and rivaling the beauty of the Bay of Naples, the soft light which fell on the mountain sides, bringing out every configuration in the landscape and shedding a glory upon it, baffle my powers of description. For five weeks my eyes rested on these scenes, and on such peculiarities of Oriental life as may still be observed in the most European city of Syria, only to be fascinated by them. I think I felt something of the saying attributed to Mohammed, when he is said to have withheld his foot from entering Damascus, lest he should not afterwards desire the joys of paradise. I am well aware that many a traveler is grievously disappointed in Syria and Palestine; the filth and the squalor are so present to the senses that he can neither see nor feel the beauty that surrounds him.

My surprise was great when I learned that instead of traveling in Syria and Palestine for only about three months, there would be no very serious barrier to continuing my journeys almost throughout the year. I had provided the means for three months of travel and for nine months of study, how then could I find the resources involved in this change of plans without incurring a burdensome debt? It seemed certain that if I would find a more economical way of traveling than that pursued by the ordinary tourist, I must become able to communicate with natives and muleteers so as to dispense with the services of a dragoman, and that besides I must try, if possible, to make some money in a literary way.

I had studied classical Arabic in Leipzig. Indeed I passed an examination on it as a minor, when I was a candidate for the degree of doctor of philosophy. But it was evident that I could not undertake a journey in the country five weeks after entering it with such slight knowledge as I had, and where at every step I was liable to be imposed on. I therefore labored in vain for some time to secure the services of a student as dragoman for a tour of three months. His demands were quite beyond my means. But through the kindly interest of Professor Robert H. West; the Rev. George C. Doolittle, of Der el-Kamar; the Rev. W. S. Nelson, D.D., of Tripoli; the Rev. William Jessup, of Zahleh; the Rev. W. K. Eddy, of Sidon; the Rev. Henry H. Jessup, D.D., of Beirut; and of Professor George Post, M.D., doors that had seemed closed, opened, and insuperable difficulties vanished. The first gentleman named was my trusted counselor, and lent me his Damascus tent, Mr. William Jessup hired my muleteers, Dr. Jessup and Dr. Post prepared an itinerary for a journey to Baalbek and in the Lebanon, and the other gentlemen were companions in travel, offering me missionary fare and their unexcelled knowledge of the country at a minimum. I shall never cease to be grateful to them, nor to the missionaries all through Syria, Palestine, and Egypt, who refreshed me by their counsel and sympathy, and who in no small degree contributed to the success of my journeys.

I can merely allude to these, for I could easily

fill more than one volume with incidents of travel in uncommon sections of country seen in an uncommon way.

My first journey to Baalbek and the Cedars from the home of Mr. William Jessup at Zahleh, began July 19, 1898, and lasted eighteen days. Anis Masud, a member of the senior class, was my dragoman and Jirjis, of the culinary department in the college, was cook. I had the loan of two tents and had two muleteers. I traveled in great comfort at an expense of about five dollars a day. I do not know of a more delightful and inspiring journey in the East than one beginning at Baalbek. There is an indescribable glamor about the ruins, rising fairy-like in their beauty, near the Litani, and having the highest of the white-capped mountains of Lebanon as their distant background. I cannot even enumerate the attractions of such a journey. It is one delightful memory, full of novel adventure, and the enjoyment of grand and beautiful scenery. From beginning to end it was romantic, refreshing, and inspiring.

Then came a rest for a week at Brummana, the seat of the Friends' Mission. It is about two hours and a half from Beirut by carriage. The view of that city and of the Bay of St. George is wonderful. There I attended the first general conference held by missionaries of Syria and Palestine, and was greatly instructed by many admirable papers.

During the latter part of August and until about the end of October I joined various missionaries, already named, in their tours of travel. Who that has seen Der el-Kamar and the surrounding country will think I exaggerate when I write of the joy I experienced in the company of Mr. George C. Doolittle, now of Zahleh, who then had his home in this gem of the Lebanon, with whom I went on one of his missionary tours to a neighboring village?

This was preliminary to my joining Mr. W. K. Eddy, for the ascent of Mount Hermon. Attended part of the way to Jezzin by a native, I rode over the remainder of it quite alone. Accompanied by three of Mr. Eddy's children, we traveled over the road to the mission station at Jedaideh, whence we could see the surrounding country. How grand was Mount Hermon! How soft and lovely the afternoon light which rested like a halo on the hills of Naphtali! How enticing the blue waters and malarial marshes of Huleh—when seen from afar! How varied and interesting the ascent of the mountain, under the guidance of one who had made it twelve times before; who knew and could explain so many points of interest; who could tell of exposure to death, when for thirty hours on that lonely height with a faithful companion, almost without food and drink, he had sunk down in exhaustion; who could speak of perils of robbers, and adventures with bears!

It was a grand view that greeted our eyes from the summit of Hermon; a wide prospect reaching far away and revealing the anatomy of the country in the clear light of the afternoon. A little before sunset there was the shadow of the mountain rising higher and higher above the eastern horizon, and the illusion of a polar sea on the western. After my return to Jedaideh, I visited all the sources of the Jordan.

But I did not find my vocation as a traveler until I began my journey in northern Syria with Messrs. March and Nelson, of the American Presbyterian Mission, the 11th of September, of the same year. It was in that northern country, once the stronghold of the ancient Canaanites, and now, as there is reason to think, inhabited by their descendants, that I recognized the sacred groves and high places for the first time. These had been seen and described by missionaries, but I do not know of any one who had previously made an investigation of the facts connected with them. My former classmate, the Rev. F. W. March, was a constant and faithful interpreter. Visiting many shrines on the way from Beinu to Safita, we heard substantially the same story at each, as to the vows made, the sacrifices paid, and the feasting which followed. We had also interviews with Protestant congregations, who had much to tell. The recognition of these groves, and the researches which I at once instituted with respect to them, gave me an aim which I have followed with increasing interest to the present time. I have already alluded to W. Robertson Smith's Religion of the Semites. It seemed to me that studies and investigations which had been made mostly in the domain of Semitic literature could also be profitably pursued into the life of the people. Indeed I could not resist the conjecture that ancient institutions had been transmitted from the remotest past to the present day.

The information which I received on this journey with these missionaries was supplemented and the inspiration was augmented by the next tour which I made in the Syrian Desert, with the Rev. J. Stewart Crawford, of the Irish Presbyterian Mission, who resides at Nebk. If I could have spent all of my time with such companions, and have followed the method which I adopted in the summer of 1901, the results would have been much greater. But I was still like one groping in the dark. I did not yet know the field, nor how to conduct my investigations, nor could I find one capable of aiding me. Both my helper and myself needed time for study, and a much wider experience. However, as a Bible interpreter, without any hope or expectation of authorship, but desiring that I might be a more useful teacher of students, I sought to see the land thoroughly, from the entering in of Hamath to the South Country (*Negeb*) and the Sinaitic Peninsula. The question of ways and means was still a perplexing one, though the directors of the seminary had made liberal provision for me. But it became necessary to earn as well as to save money. With the hope of increasing resources, I visited Jerusalem when the German emperor was there at the dedication of the Church of the Redemption, and wrote a description of his visit, which was published in one of the magazines. With the hope of saving money I went to Damascus, where I engaged in the study of colloquial Arabic, that I might get on without the services of a dragoman. While there I experienced great kindness from the veteran missionary, the Rev. John Crawford, D.D., and from others. I had my home in two small chambers on a Syrian housetop. It was a unique experience. Dimitri, one of the native teachers of the Irish Presbyterian Mission, gave me two lessons a day during December and January, one at eight o'clock in the morning, the other at eight o'clock in the evening. Life under such circumstances was novel and full of variety. Damascus is the most interesting Oriental city I have seen, surpassing Cairo in its presentation of various forms of Oriental life. None could have been kinder than my Syrian hostess, nor could I have found a more willing maid than her daughter. The absence of sons and brothers in a foreign land warmed their hearts toward a stranger. They were applying the principle of the Golden Rule, which in their minds ran something like this: "As we would that strangers should do to our sons and brothers, so we do to you." At the same time there was a suggestion of the ancient homage which woman pays to man in the East, which Sarah exhibited when she called Abraham lord.

These two months were a most profitable, most enjoyable season, in which I was practising Arabic, reading books from the college library, and was frequently cheered by the sympathy and kindness of the missionaries. I often gazed with joy at Hermon, completely enveloped in snow, white and glistering in the sunlight. My last visit to Jebel Kasiun, one hour west of Damascus, whither I went to bid adieu to Anti-Lebanon and Hermon and all of the plain of Damascus, might have had serious consequences, for I was surrounded by five or six robbers. Previously instructed by Mr. Crawford concerning the law of blood revenge, which prevails among Orientals at the present day, I did not attempt to defend myself with a revolver. Barring a trifling loss of money and valuables, I suffered no serious injury.

On the 6th of February, 1899, I left Beirut for Egypt and the Sinaitic Peninsula. At Cairo I experienced much kindness from the Rev. Dr. Watson, of the American Mission, and at Luxor from the Rev. Mr. Murch. I continued my journey to Assuan at the first cataract. The journey to Mount Sinai, which I undertook after my return to Cairo, was in every way successful. I enjoyed it to the full, and was able to make the ascent of Jebel Katherin and of Jebel Musa; and from Ras Sufsaf to look out on the great plain Er-Raha. I spent two and a half days in camp near the monastery of St. Catharine. It was on this journey that I first discovered there were annual festivals in connection with certain shrines. It was a strange contrast to former experiences in the life of the desert, after meeting many an Arab in a soiled shirt and with an abba of rusty black, to see one morning men and women clad in clean, white undergarments with abbas of fresh black, looking as if they had been at some festival. I found they had been in attendance on an annual feast of one of their saints.

On my return journey I reached Beirut the last of March, where I was delayed for a week, as the rainy season was not yet over, and was delightfully entertained at the home of my friends, Dr. and Mrs. Graham. The rain ceased on the 5th of April so that I could go to Sidon, to the house of my friend, the Rev. W. K. Eddy, who had promised to prepare me for my tours in Palestine, which were to continue until the middle of August. I had secured Peter (*Butrus*), of Safita, in northern Syria, who had been trained in the Protestant school, as cook and muleteer. In the autumn of 1898, during my journey in northern Syria, and again in the Syrian desert, he had been of my company, so we were in no sense strangers. I owed much in the journeys that followed to his good sense, his coolness, and fearlessness in danger. I do not refer to those mock attacks which dragomen sometimes institute in collusion with Arabs for the diversion of tourists, that they may have something to tell, but to those perils which become dangers in lawless countries, if not promptly and resolutely met. He never failed me, when others were on the point of open rebellion, or even deserted me, and was always faithful to my interests, and sought to promote the economies that I found necessary.

The first two days out, I tried a camel for the transportation of my baggage, but found him too slow and uncertain. Shut off from speaking my own tongue, and entirely dependent upon the natives for social intercourse, with but a very imperfect knowledge of Arabic, I found the first two days out quite disappointing, and began to count up the time I must practise endurance.

But the spirit of travel soon possessed me, the charm of the scenery prevailed, the love of adventure, the joy of receiving light on the Bible so inspired me that every day became a satisfaction, and I could have gone on alone to the end. But friends suggested there were loss and danger involved in travel where I was cut off from English-speaking companionship. What if I should fall ill? Who, then, would minister to my needs? After five weeks of touring, in which I had visited many important points between Sidon and Jerusalem, by a series of zigzags, I reached the Holy City, where I made arrangements with Professor Gilroy, of the Semitic department of the University of Aberdeen, Scotland, to make the rest of our journeys together. While this arrangement was pleasant, it necessitated the employment of another muleteer, at the scale of prices current in Jerusalem, and created considerable dissatisfaction among the men I had hired in Syria at a cheaper wage. My expenses had been three dollars and sixty cents a day, after this they averaged four dollars apiece, including such difficult journeys as those to Beersheba, Kerak, and the Hauran, an amount which was not excessive.

I had carried out all these journeys without malaria and without the loss of a single day through illness, except a slight indisposition in Jerusalem, at the end of my tours, which hindered me from a visit to Mar Saba and the cave of Adullam. In the months reviewed I had visited the most important places from Hamath to Beersheba on the west side of the Jordan, and from Karyaten in the Syrian desert on the east, to Kerak on the south; had passed up the sea coast from Beirut to Tripoli, and in the opposite direction to Haifa; and from Carmel to Jaffa, had seen Gaza and all the cities of the Philistine Plain, including a visit of two days with Dr. Fred Bliss at Tell es-Safi, who afterwards showed me the line of his excavations in Jerusalem. I had scaled the most important mountains, such as Jebel Mahmal, Sunnin, Keneiseh, Hermon, Jermak; the hills back of, Nazareth, Carmel, Tabor, Little Hermon, Osha, Jebel Neba, and Shihan. I had traversed the most important rivers, from the Orontes down; had visited most of their principal sources; had seen the lakes, from Kadesh near Homs, and Lake Yammuneh in Lebanon, to Huleh, Galilee, and the Dead Sea, all, through God's goodness, without serious accident or mishap, thus adding greatly to my knowledge and appreciation of the Old Testament. However, the best results of travel were still to come. A list of tours will be found in Appendix B.

CHAPTER III

SPECIAL RESEARCHES
SUMMERS OF 1900 AND 1901

For years I had been impressed with the importance of realism in the interpretation of the Old Testament—of being able to reproduce the life of the people as it was when lawgivers rendered their decisions, when prophets preached, when psalmists sang, and wise men uttered proverbs. It was in the hope that I could enter more truly into the flesh and blood of the Old Testament that I planned the second journey for the summer of 1900. It seemed to me, as I have already indicated, that treasures of knowledge were possessed on the subject of manners and customs by missionaries which must pass away with the passing of those missionaries who had been longest in the country. But how to get that after which I was groping I could hardly tell; where to go and what to do, what companions I should choose was not clear.

I had completed my travels the year before with two regrets. One was that on account of the great expense of the journey, as I could not secure a companion, it had been impossible to visit Gadis,[1] as it is known among the natives, though commonly called Ain Kadis, in the works on geography—the Kadesh Barnea of Trumbull[2] and

[1] Gădîs is the pronunciation indicated by the natives. In vain we inquired for 'Ain Kadis; finally Gadis was suggested. As is well known by Arabic scholars, the Egyptians and some Bedouin tribes pronounce *kaf* like a hard g. This is the pronunciation recorded by Professor Palmer, The Desert of the Exodus, New York, 1872, pp. 282-287, though he uses the term 'Ain Gadis. The Arabs with whom we conversed spoke simply of Gadis.

[2] Kadesh-Barnea, New York, 1884.

others. The few who have visited this place have journeyed by the way of the Sinaitic Peninsula and Nakhl.[1] They have found it difficult of approach and have been compelled to pay heavy blackmail by the Arabs.[2] The other regret was that I had been foiled in my attempt to visit the Druse Mountains.[3]

Reaching Jerusalem the 15th of June, 1900, I found Mr. A. Forder, missionary among the Arabs, ready to accompany me. He had lived in Kerak as the head of an independent English mission more than five years. He had traveled repeatedly and successfully in various parts of Syria and Palestine, especially over the more difficult routes. He has quite recently made an extensive tour in Arabia. He bears on his body the marks of stripes from Arabs, who on one occasion beat him unmercifully and left him almost naked. In the gray

[1] Edward L. Wilson, editor and proprietor of the Photographic Magazine, failed to find it, as did Professor Schaff. Père Lagrange of the Dominicans, Jerusalem, who approached it by the way of Nakhl, said: "The Arabs pretended utter ignorance of Ain Kedeis," Revue Biblique, July, 1896. This Review contains a caustic criticism of Trumbull's Description of Gadis, as he derived it from Guthe, Zeitschrift des Palestina Vereins, Vol. VIII., p. 182, ff. Père Lagrange writes, after giving particulars of that which Trumbull described with great enthusiasm, "the deception was so great, the disenchantment so profound, that I threw myself on Sheik Suleiman, crying that he had deceived us. He gravely lifted his hand toward heaven, swearing by the Prophet that there was no other Ain Kedeis."

[2] A professor of one of the American theological seminaries was compelled to pay ninety dollars blackmail to the Arabs in order to visit Gadis.

[3] I copy the following from Journal V., Jerusalem, July 11, 1899: "I have been waiting here ten days in hope that the restriction laid by the Governor of Damascus on my traveling in the Leja and the Jebel el-Druse might be removed, and have incurred no little expense in telegraphing both to Mr. Ravndal, the Consul at Beirut, and to Mr. Oscar Straus, the Minister at Constantinople, but it was all in vain. Mr. Straus saw the Grand Vizier at Constantinople last Saturday, who portrayed the dangers of the journey so effectively that Mr. Straus telegraphed I should not go."

morning he stole, with a piece of sack around his loins, to the house of Mr. Murray, in Hebron, where he secured a suit of clothes.

I had been told that it was possible to approach Gadis from the northeast by way of Beersheba.[1] Mr. Forder had never visited the place, but did not fear to attempt the journey. We set out on the 18th of June from Jerusalem, and spent the first night at Mar Saba in the wilderness. Thence we went to Hebron, visited Main and Kurmul, the scene of David's history when he guarded the sheep of the churlish Nabal, and when he afterwards took Abigail to wife.[2] We visited Juttah, supposed by some to be the birthplace of John the Baptist,[3] and passed the night at Dahariyeh. Thence we went to Beersheba, a second time. On my first visit, in the summer of 1899, I found that there were four wells, the Arabs were then engaged in reopening the fourth. On my second visit there were five, and I was shown the place where the sixth and seventh were to be found.[4]

We passed on through the South Country, which derives its water supply from wells only. People bring all their flocks and herds a distance of three or four hours for their supplies of water. It is a great sight to visit such wells as those at Khalasa or at Biren, and to see from five to seven hundred and fifty sheep and goats, three hundred camels, and numerous asses—the flocks attended by

[1] This information came from Dr. Sterling, who was then missionary of the Church Missionary Society at Gaza. It seems that some travelers had made the journey from Gaza, as Mrs Patterson of Hebron told me she had met three Americans who had visited Gadis, going by way of Gaza.

[2] 1 Sam. xxv. 40-43.

[3] "The Juttah of Joshua, xv. 55, and perhaps also the 'City of Judah,' of Luke i. 39."—Baedeker, Palestine and Syria, Leipsic 1898, p. 199.

[4] See Appendix C.

WELL AT BEERSHEBA, WITH GROOVES WORN IN THE STONES BY ROPES.

UNOPENED WELL AT BEERSHEBA.

women, the camels and asses by men—and to reflect that for millenniums, just such scenes have been enacted at these wells as one may behold to-day.

At a tradesman's tent in Khalasa we made friends with a sheik of the Azazimeh, who had been collecting taxes for the Turkish government and was returning home. After much hesitation he decided to go with us to Gadis. Accompanied by a clansman of his we set out about four o'clock in the morning. Though my thermometer had registered ninety-two degrees Fahrenheit in my tent about half-past two P. M. the day before, it had fallen to fifty-nine degrees at four o'clock A. M., and was so cold that I was glad of the abba of my friend. Every now and again we passed by flocks of goats in the wilderness under the care of a shepherdess, for in that country, as well as in the Sinaitic Peninsula, girls attend the flocks, like Rachael and Zipporah[1] in the days of old. Each one started to her feet at the sound of our horses' hoofs to watch the travelers.

We wound around wadis, where there were small fields of wheat with strong and luxuriant stalks, and where the soil was kept from being washed away in the rainy season by a succession of low, retaining walls. We saw threshing-floors, where camels were treading out the grain. Presently we left the country of the Azazimeh and came to that of the Teyahah. A man greeted us savagely, asked us whither we were going, and assured us if we kept on in our course to the spring, the people there would cut off our heads. We were not dismayed.

About noon we came to a very deep and wild ravine, where the path was so precipitous that we had to dismount. We saw large flocks of goats in the distance, and after about half an hour, we suddenly came on

[1] Gen. xxix. 9; Ex. ii. 16-21.

Gadis. Rather a small stream of water ran through the lowest part of the wadi. On the right, as we entered it, was a succession of springs, or places in the ground where there was water, perhaps from ten to fifteen. I was unable to make careful observations on account of the threatening attitude of the men and boys, who charged me with trying to bewitch a spring. There were from three to five hundred goats, scores of donkeys, and some camels. Many women were engaged in watering their flocks and in filling water-skins. Gadis is equivalent to Kadesh, and this is connected with a root in the Semitic family of languages which signifies holy. The spring was also called En Mishpat, or spring of judgment. As we shall see, such a place might be conceived of as the residence of a spirit to whom the people came for judicial decisions.[1] This may have been the site of the famous Kadesh Barnea. At least no place has yet been discovered which so well fulfils the conditions of the problem. There is good sweet water in considerable abundance for the wilderness, so that Gadis is in marked contrast to the rest of the South Country, which is dependent, as we have seen, on wells.

As I cannot do more in the present work than to sketch travels which were of wide extent, I must not delay on details, which were most interesting, such as a night at Kurnub, where there are ruins and an ancient dam across the wadi. We had hoped to cross the southern end of the Dead Sea at this point on the way to Petra, but deceived by the Arabs as to our ability to reach an encampment and to secure food for our animals, we spent an anxious night in the wilderness, full of the sons of the desert, who might have massacred us and none would

[1] W. Robertson Smith, Lectures on the Religion of the Semites, New York, 1889, p. 165.

GADIS (KADESH BARNEA) FROM THE EAST.

have been the wiser. Indeed at midnight I heard footsteps near my bed, out under the stars, and springing to my feet saw an Arab advancing with his long gun. My outcry put him to flight. The next day we reached an Arab encampment on the way to Hebron, where there were five Turkish horsemen collecting taxes. A more courteous, hospitable sheik than Salem, of the Zulam tribe of Arabs, whom we met there, I have never seen. He was tastefully dressed, was elegant in manners, and graceful in every gesture.

After returning to Jerusalem and resting for a few days we set out for Petra, on the 2d of July, by the way of Jericho, Medeba,[1] the hot springs of Callirrhoe, Machærus, Kerak, Tafileh (Tophel), famed for its springs and olive groves, and Shobek. It is a most interesting journey. At certain points there are magnificent views of the southern end of the Dead Sea. We passed Busera in Edom, supposed to be ancient Bozra, to which allusion is made in a passage of Isaiah.[2] I was surprised to find how cold it was at Shobek in the summer-time. I was glad to fold my blankets at night so that there were four thicknesses.[3]

Others have described Petra. I cannot attempt to do so in this work. But to me it is one of the most fascinating places I have ever visited. The Treasury of Pharaoh, which you behold almost at once after riding twenty minutes through a narrow cleft in the rock the walls of which rise in some places one hundred and fifty feet, might seem to be one of the creations of Aladdin's lamp. It is cut out of the solid rock, which is suffused with a light carnation-pink, and seems as fresh as if it had been hewn yesterday.

By keeping our purpose a profound secret, we eluded

[1] Deut. i. 1.   [2] Is. lxiii. 1.   [3] Appendix B.

our mounted horsemen, and made the steep ascent to the traditional tomb of Aaron at Mount Hor, along the path which in many places passes over bare rock. None saw us, and so we were not prevented from visiting the shrine. On our return in the early evening our horses went flying; Musa our guide first, I next, and Mr. Forder last, as he observed, "just as if all the sprites were after us."

The next journey was to Palmyra and the Druse Mountains. On account of quarantine, we were not able to go by Jaffa and Beirut, so had to take our journey overland, one day from Jerusalem to Nablus, one from Nablus to Beisan, one from Beisan to Irbid, where, as we failed to find the Jisr el-Mujami, we forded the Jordan in the wake of a caravan of camels, and one by the way of Muzerib and the railroad to Damascus.

The journey to Palmyra, for which we set out the 31st of July, had no especial bearing on my researches, but I had deeply regretted that when I was within less than a day of Tadmor in the desert, eighteen months before, I had not visited it. We drove all the way from Damascus to Palmyra in a victoria. We were accompanied by a single horseman from Karyaten whom I had secured with no small difficulty, as the twenty-five mounted soldiers were otherwise engaged and he had brought the mail from a solitary fort in the desert,[1] about five hours from Palmyra. Naturally he had set his heart on enjoying some of the pleasures of civilization for a day or two, and was most reluctant to return at once. Off we drove at night over what seemed like the trackless ocean of the desert, guided by our horseman and drawn by three horses. Early in the morning we reached Beda, consist-

[1] The term Syrian Desert is partly a misnomer. In March it is carpeted with verdure, and gay with flowers, even between Karyaten and Palmyra, as the Rev. John Crawford, D.D., of Damascus assured me.

SPECIAL RESEARCHES

ing only of a fortress by a deep well where four soldiers were stationed. There we rested about nine hours, and then pushed on. In the early evening we reached Palmyra. The ruins are extensive and magnificent. Baalbek, Jerash, Petra, Palmyra, who that has seen them can be the same person any more? Each has a fascination of its own, and awakens thoughts and emotions which become a lifelong possession.

On our return from Palmyra, we undertook a tour to the Druse Mountains under the most favorable circumstances. This time I did not seek the permission of the government, as I had been thwarted in my endeavor to visit this district the year before. Mr. Forder had secured the services of a Druse who was familiar with the country, and who was highly esteemed by his coreligionists.

We stole out of Damascus, the 13th of August, by one of the side streets, so that none might inquire concerning our destination, or be inclined to stop us. Toward evening, we reached a point where we met several caravans of camels during half an hour. I had fallen behind. My horse, in his efforts to overtake my companions, dropped my saddle-bags containing my notes of all the preceding journeys of that summer. Our Druse guide, when he learned what had happened, slipped from his camel, took my horse, and at once galloped after the last Arab caravan, which had just passed us. There, off in the wilderness, Mr. Forder and I stood waiting in the gloaming. They were anxious moments, because almost a constant stream of dark, wild men of the desert were passing us, and more than all, because these precious records might be lost for good. In due time our Druse appeared with the bags and everything intact. They had been appropriated by a cameleer.

At ten o'clock at night, wrapped in our abbas, we passed the military station, on the frontier at Brak, where a guard of one hundred soldiers were peacefully sleeping. On we went to the first house of entertainment (*medayfeh*), with which every considerable village is supplied. Thus for nine days we traveled without tents in the country of the Druses, enjoying a delightful hospitality.

I had my bed, but with the exception of the last night, when my Druse had lain on it, I had escaped the pests of the country. On this tour I saw some most interesting evidences of blood-sprinkling and of other curious customs. I had the pleasure of spending Sunday at the home of our Druse guide. He had desired we should take his photograph. I had stipulated that when it was taken his wife should be in the group. He had seemed to accede to this condition, but when the time came for the picture to be taken, he discovered that it would be a "shame" to have any woman in the group. His wife, a sweet-faced woman, was compelled to be content to stand at a corner of the house with her babe in her arms, shyly looking on while the lords of creation were being photographed.

These journeys seemed rich in their fruits. On reaching London I published several hundred circulars of inquiry regarding the manners and customs of the peoples of the East.[1] These I sent quite widely to missionaries. I received less than a dozen answers, some of these, however, were valuable.

On my return to my work at the Chicago Theological Seminary, I prepared a course of ten lectures on the Manners and Customs of the Peoples of Bible Lands,

[1] For the questions on the religious life of the people see Appendix A.

SPECIAL RESEARCHES

during the second period of our year; and during the third, another course on the Survivals of Ancient Semitic Religion To-day. This latter sketch proved to be of great value in preparation for the researches I was to make in the summer of 1901, the results of which have far exceeded anything I had gained before.

The preceding summer I had arranged with the Rev. J. Stewart Crawford to be my companion and interpreter. I had supplied him with a copy of the list of questions prepared in London. He had seen but little light on the subject of my inquiries during most of the year, but in the spring of 1901, a series of floods at Nebk revealed religious beliefs of which he had never dreamed. In the prosecution of his inquiries he had the assistance of two native teachers, Selim and Suleiman, both men of much intelligence and of great caution. He told them, in their interviews with natives, never to ask leading questions, but to get all the information possible. They had regarded with disdain "the old wives' fables" which so abound in Syria, but under his encouragement they undertook the task with great success.

I landed in Beirut to spend my fourth summer in Syria, the first day of June, 1901. I had been expecting to begin my travels at once, but Mr. Crawford was waiting for the arrival of a surrey from America, which we expected to use on our journey for four days from Damascus to Mehardeh by Nebk, Homs, and Hamath. While waiting until the 20th of June, I had the opportunity to make some investigations which were of the rarest interest. I shall never lose the fascination of the first interview which I had with the priest of a shrine, of whose existence the missionaries had not dreamed, though Doughty must have seen it without recognizing its significance.[1] This first interview, in the information and suggestions gained, was most inspiring, and was of happy augury for others which were to follow.

Between the Lebanon and the Anti-Lebanon is the famous plain of the Buka, in which rise the sources of the Orontes and the Litani, and in which are the magnificent ruins of Baalbek.

Parallel to the first range of the Anti-Lebanon is a second east of it, and between these ranges is a large valley, though of far less extent in length and width than the Buka, the southern part of which is known as the Plain of Zebedani. In this valley rises the Barada, commonly supposed to have been the Abana, to which Naaman refers.[2] It is also traversed by the railway from Beirut to Damascus.

The observant traveler, after leaving the station of Zebedani, on his way to Damascus, may notice, a little past the village of Bludan, a grove of oaks, covering several acres on one of the foothills of the second range of Anti-Lebanon. It has long been known among the missionaries as the "Mother of Pieces" (*Umm Shakakif*) from the custom of breaking jars in fulfillment of a vow, though the legends connected with the name were first ascertained by Mr. Crawford and myself on

---

[1] Travels in Arabia Deserta, Cambridge, 1888, Vol. I., p. 450. "In the W. Barada, near Damascus, where certain heathenish customs do yet remain amongst the Moslemîn, I have visited two groves of evergreen-oaks, which are wishing-places for the peasantry. If the thing fall to them for which they vowed, they will go to the one on a certain day of the year to break a crock there; or they lay up a new stean in a little cave which is under the rock at the other. There I have looked in and saw it full to the entry of their yet whole offering-pots; in that other grove you will see the heap of their broken potsherds. [The groves are in the valley coast westward above the village of Zibidany.]" He should have said eastward above the village.—C.

[2] 2 Kings v. 12.

SACRED GROVE AT THE "MOTHER OF PIECES."

PLATFORM OF "MOTHER OF PIECES."

SPECIAL RESEARCHES

the 18th of June, and are now published, in another connection, for the first time.

Such a grove, which would be common enough in other countries, easily suggests to the student of the religious customs of Syria a sacred grove. Such groves, aside from some religious use, are comparatively rare in Syria and Palestine, as the temptation is very great to use the wood for charcoal or for some other purpose.

On visiting a hillside, which slopes rather abruptly, one finds a rectangular plot of ground, or platform, composed of earth, which is supported on two sides by retaining walls, meeting at right angles at the southwest corner. The wall in front, running nearly north and south, is thirty-five feet long, the other, running nearly east and west, is forty-four feet. The highest part of the front wall is six feet eight inches. There are no evidences of cement between the stones, which are of their natural size, except they have been broken so as to give a rough face. Back of the first platform there are traces of a second, on which I discovered the remains of a lintel, with a hollow for a hinge, such as is common in the buildings of the country. The presence of this stone seemed to indicate that a building once existed here. Whether we have in this platform the remains of an ancient high place cannot be determined, though it does not seem unlikely.

At a considerable distance farther on, about a third of the way up the mountain, are other oaks, and a prominent rock, described by some missionaries as having the shape of a natural altar, though the top of it has been artificially smoothed. On visiting it, the 11th of June, with a muleteer, who is a nominal Christian, I learned that it was called "Rock of the Chair" (*Kalat el-Kursi*). It was on this visit I discovered that there was a weli underneath the base of the monolith, which is superimposed upon two projections of the ledge below, thus forming a little cave, in which I found a small banner of cotton cloth, with an Arabic inscription on it, beginning in the usual way, "In the name of God, the merciful, the compassionate," etc. There were some bits of matting about the size of door-mats laid over each other and water-jars, perhaps designed for oil. Two other visits were made later with Mr. Crawford. The first on the 18th of June, when we learned from the care-taker, or minister,[1] that it was called among the Moslems "Chair of the Leaders" (*Kursi el-Aktab*).

The situation of the "Chair" is one of rare beauty and grandeur. To the south is Hermon, usually striped with snow before it has dissolved under the fierce Syrian sun; to the northwest is the highest summit of Lebanon. Below is the lovely valley of Zebedani, with its rich meadows, covered with grain, its tall green poplars, its vineyards, and in general a profusion of foliage, which is in sharp contrast to much of the barren scenery in Syria. The thoughts of the ancient worshipers, mounted on this rock, whatever their cult, as they gazed on this grand and beautiful scene, must have been of an inspiring character.

The "Chair," which resembles a great natural altar, rises thirty-two feet, fronting toward the valley. Its width near the base, northwest by west and southeast by east, is about twenty feet. The dimensions of the top, which is perfectly flat and rectangular, are fourteen feet six inches in length, running nearly north and south, by eleven feet three inches running nearly east and west. It is, therefore, in the shape of a rough monolith. The

[1] I had visited the place June 10, and did so again August 3, 1901, when I took as exact measurements as possible.

PART OF THE "CHAIR OF THE LEADERS."
THE DARK OPENING IS A SMALL CAVERN USED AS A SHRINE.

appearance of this rock on the brink of a precipice at least sixty feet in depth, with sacred oaks all around it, about a third of the way up the mountain, is commanding. There can be no doubt that from the earliest times it has been set apart for some sacred use. It may be that altar-fires have been kindled on its summit. It may have been a favored place for the adoration of the sun. The rites now observed are doubtless different from what they once were, but their existence testifies to the sacred character of the rock in ancient times. It is impossible to determine whether it was put in its present place by human hands or by some convulsion of nature. The latter seems more probable.

For prudential reasons I cannot enter into details of the journeys undertaken during the summer of 1901, in giving names and the circumstances of each interview. They are all in my journals, and were taken down with the utmost care. Each day was a surprise, with reference to the people with whom I had interviews. I do not see how I could have been more favored had I been gifted with the power to summon whom I would, for I conversed, through Mr. Crawford, with men familiar with distant parts of the Arab world, who had traveled widely and observed many curious customs.

There were Arabs and men who had lived with Arabs; there were Bedouin; there were Moslems, including those who held official positions in mosques and at shrines; there were representatives of sects who had been initiated, whose disclosures, if known, might have meant death to them. The statements of Suleiman of Adana were confirmed, and an interesting manuscript was found. Almost every day was a revelation and a delight, for the information received was beyond the most sanguine expectations, and often came from sources, and on occasions least expected. Mr. Crawford was much surprised, for we were hearing about matters concerning which the veteran missionaries of the country had no clear and connected knowledge. We experienced a joy and intoxication like men who have found a treasure. So far as it was possible for us, we were careful in receiving our information and in testing it.

Our first journey, which lasted from the 21st of June to the 19th of July, covered the following chief points: Nebk, Homs, Hamath, Mehardeh, Ain Kurum, Ladikiyeh, Jendairieh, Dibbash, Behammra, Baniyas, Musyaf, and the return was over Mehardeh, Hamath, Homs, Nebk, and so back to Damascus. Besides, we visited Rasheya, Mount Hermon, and Nebi Safa.

I also had the privilege of attending the second missionary conference at Brummana, and of visiting Abbas Effendi, the head of the Babites at Acre.

The value of the researches which I was enabled to make must stand the test of criticism. I am aware that at certain points they are incomplete. But I hope to continue my travels and researches, and in my efforts to receive further information shall welcome criticism and suggestions, and shall hope for the co-operation of those who can add anything which may enforce or correct the positions taken, or shed new light upon them.

CHAPTER IV

THE SOURCES OF PRIMITIVE SEMITIC RELIGION

The student of early Semitic religion is at once confronted with the question of the sources to which he shall go for investigation. There are two chief methods of approach, one is to take the religious literature, as far as it exists, in the great branches of the Semitic peoples, the other is to study the customs and beliefs of modern Semites.

There should be abundant materials for the former among the clay tablets of the ancient Babylonians. How suggestive and fruitful these are may be seen from such a work as that of Zimmern.[1] There are also plentiful materials in the Old and New Testaments, especially in the Old Testament, and in the literature of the ancient Arabs. The results of researches in this latter domain were brought most clearly to light in W. Robertson Smith's Religion of the Semites.

It is perhaps the most natural assumption that the form of Semitic religion, which is most ancient in years, is most ancient in fact, and comes nearest to revealing the primitive form of Semitic religion. If this be so, we shall turn to the records of the Babylonians, written in a Semitic language, for they reach back several thousand years before Christ. But such a method is open to this objection, that we may not be able to reach primitive conditions by the use of it, since there was a high degree of civilization in ancient Babylonia, and civilization is a

[1] Beiträge zur Kenntnis der Babylonischen Religion, Leipzig, 1901.

disturbing element in the study of primitive forms of religion.[1] If we really wish to learn what the original religious conceptions were, we shall study those peoples and those usages which have been least affected by civilization, so that a people living to-day may present more that is primitive in their religious ideas and customs than the most ancient record can afford.

For a similar reason, while we shall find much of greatest value for the discussion of this subject in the Bible, we must remember that original pictures of primitive conditions have been seriously affected in that book by later developments in religious teaching and history; in other words, by the influences which they have received outside of the primitive life of the people, or through Divine revelation. But the student who has once recognized the constituent elements of primitive Semitic religion, from whatever source he may have derived them, will find abundant suggestions of their survival and influence in shaping and giving expression to religious conceptions among the Assyrians and the Hebrews, which otherwise would have appeared in a different form.

On the other hand, the accounts of the ancient Arabs, as used by Wellhausen and W. Robertson Smith, in their

[1] W. Robertson Smith, Religion of the Semites, New York, 1889, pp. 14, 15, well says, after remarking that "the preponderating opinion of Assyriologists is to the effect that the civilization of Assyria and Babylonia was not purely Semitic..... If this be so, it is plain that the cuneiform material must be used with caution in our inquiry into the type of religion characteristic of the ancient Semites. That Babylonia is the best starting-point for a comparative study of ancient beliefs and practices of the Semitic peoples is an idea which has lately had some vogue and which at first sight appears plausible on account of the great antiquity of the monumental evidence. But in matters of this sort, ancient and primitive are not synonymous terms; and we must not look for the most primitive form of Semitic faith in a region where society was not primitive. In Babylonia, it would seem, society and religion alike were based on a fusion of two races and so were not primitive but complex."

SOURCES OF PRIMITIVE SEMITIC RELIGION 51

investigations, probably afford the most trustworthy guide in the study of primitive religion, and the most trustworthy representation of its original character, aside from the sources which we may find to-day among the peoples who have transmitted primitive institutions from a remote antiquity.

If we turn to the literature of Islam, we are presented with a problem similar to that found in the Old Testament. There is an abundance of original Semitic ideas and usages, but these have been considerably distorted through the medium of Judaism, and to some extent through Christianity, which have exercised an influence upon the teachings of Mohammed, the founder of Islam.[1] The student who begins his study with the Koran cannot be certain as to that which is original in Semitic religion and that which is not.

Where, then, are the sources of primitive Semitic religion to be found, aside from the accounts which we have of the ancient heathen Arabs? Shall we not follow essentially the same method in this study as has been used so successfully by Mr. Andrew Lang in his Making of Religion; by Frazer in his Golden Bough; and others? Whence do these writers derive the materials for their conceptions of primitive religion, of which primitive Semitic religion is but a subdivision? Is it not mainly from studies in the life of primitive peoples as they were found and may still be found among the American Indians, among the aborigines of Australasia and of Africa, and among the ignorant and simple-minded of civilized peoples? It is to such that they have gone for their materials.

---

[1] Geiger, Was hat Mohammed aus dem Judenthume Aufgenomen? Bonn, 1833; Nöldeke, Geschichte des Qorans, Göttingen, 1860.

If, then, we follow their example, we shall conduct our investigations among those Semites who have been least affected by Judaism, Christianity, or Islam. There are multitudes of these who have preserved the most antique ideas and customs. The tenacity with which the Oriental mind if left to itself, holds that which has always been, and turns to it as unerringly as the needle to the pole, has been often observed, and is our guaranty that we may find primitive religious conditions among people with whom, if we approach them in the right way, we may hold intercourse to-day.

The educated among them may be ignorant of such customs because they deem them beneath their notice, and so unworthy of their observation, or through shame that their people should be so superstitious and ignorant they may deny the existence of such customs, but patience and the right method will bring out the truth.

The best results in the study of primitive religion may be found through direct investigation at many different points in Syria and Palestine. Elements will be found which may be traced in other manifestations of Semitic religion, as seen among the Babylonians, the Phœnicians, the Moabites, the Hebrews, the Moslems, and all other Semites who have left any monuments of their religious beliefs and practices. But our conception of primitive Semitic religion is to be gained by an induction from facts and phenomena found among the modern Semites. Of this primitive Semitic religion, when once we have recognized its characteristic features, we shall find hints, suggestions, and examples in the historic religions of the ancient Semitic literatures. Each of them has been built upon these primitive foundations or to use another illustration, each displays traits derived from this common ancestor.

The temptation is, indeed, very great to suppose that the religion which is most ancient in years must be nearer the primal sources than anything we may find to-day, when in fact, if civilization has come in, or a process of development, it may be much farther away. The question is not when a man left a certain road, but whether he has left it at all; not when he changed his religious beliefs and usages, but whether he has really changed them. Hence the simple, modern Semite who has remained untouched by the world's progress may represent a primitive religion which was in existence before the ancient Babylonian empire began to be, or was even thought of. From this point of view, the thousands of years by which Babylonian civilization was measured do not count, for the purposes of our investigation they are but one day.

I emphasize this point because we are otherwise in danger of being seriously misled. Zimmern seems to me to indicate this tendency when he urges that the Assyrian word *kuffuru* (to atone, or expiate), as used in the Babylonian Ritual of Atonement, which is identical with *kipper*, of the Old Testament, as a technical term in the priests' language for atonement, is primitive; that the Hebrews derived it from the Babylonians; the Aramæans from the Hebrews; and the Arabs received the word from the Aramæans. Evidently he is impressed by the extreme age of the Babylonian religion. But is it not probable that this word, which is found among simple, ignorant Arabs to-day, may be from the primitive Semitic stock, from which Assyrians, Hebrews, and Aramæans have derived it? I think that any one who reads the definitions of *kafara* and its derivatives in Lane's Arabic English Lexicon must be persuaded that he is dealing with a primitive Arabic word, from which the technical sense was naturally derived.

Zimmern finds more than hints of a use of blood, which remind him of the sprinkling of blood in connection with the Passover.[1] He does not argue that the Hebrews derived this rite from the Babylonians, though he might be tempted to do so.[2] We shall see, however, that we are dealing with a primitive Semitic institution, or one, even if we look into other literatures, which is found among other peoples. It will be clear, I think, that the Babylonians derived the word *kuffuru* from a language kindred to that of the Semitic forebears, from whom Hebrews, Aramæans, and Arabs have sprung.

Zimmern does not call special attention to the sacrifices for houses, though he alludes to them, but in one of the tablets there are clear indications of such sacrifices.[3] Here, again, it might be supposed that a custom very prevalent among the ignorant Arabs had been derived

---

[1] Ex. xii. 7.

[2] Op. cit., p. 127: "The exorcist shall to the .... gate go out, a sheep in the gate of the palace he shall offer, with the blood of this lamb the lintel .... and post right and left before the gate of the palace." ....
Zimmern supplies the word *askuppati*.

[3] Op. cit., pp. 147-149.

" To the house thou shalt take them.
Upon a pedestal shalt thou place them. †
To direct their eyes to the rising sun, to bring them bowls of consecrated water of incense and torches.
As soon as the sun goes down thou shalt the house .... shalt prepare a sacrifice for Marduk, shalt offer a lamb thou shalt place four altars, shalt sacrifice four sacrifices of lambs, shalt remove the preparation for the sacrifices.
For ....
Thou shalt place three altars for the house god, the house goddess and the house demon, three sacrifices of lambs shalt thou sacrifice."

* "This and the following texts have to do with the preparation and service of the images as household gods, as protecting deities against demons, witches, etc., which are brought in at the gate of the house." Zimmern Note.

† "Meaning the prepared images of the protecting deities." Ibid.

SOURCES OF PRIMITIVE SEMITIC RELIGION 55

from the Babylonians, but no one who has the facts before him, as they appear later in our discussion, will have the hardihood to make such an assumption.

It is our object to apply the touchstone of primitive Semitic religion thus found to the Semitic religions of ancient literature. I cannot attempt anything more in my investigation than to indicate some of the lineaments and characteristics of this primitive Semitic religion which have been described by W. Robertson Smith, and of which, as I have indicated in the introductory chapter, I have gathered fresh examples, and new materials have been discovered for other conclusions regarding that religion.

I cannot even attempt, at this stage of my investigation, from the standpoint of an Old-Testament interpreter, to give any systematic, much less exhaustive, treatment of the subject. I can simply show the way.

But of this I am assured, that while the peculiarities of this ancient Semitic religion were in nowise necessary for a divine revelation, that revelation, through God's gracious condescension and in His divine wisdom, has taken not a little of its form and color from primitive Semitic religion, should it be found too much to affirm that it furnished the historical starting-point for the religion of the ancient Israel.

CHAPTER V

MODERN SEMITES

Professor Sayce and others have described the difficulty which is found in making an accurate definition of the Semites.[1] It is hardly practicable to consider those who speak a Semitic language and those in whose veins flows Semitic blood as coextensive.[2] It is clear from various points of view, even from those furnished by Arabs themselves, that while theoretically they derive their pedigree from one ancestor,[3] their tribes are made up of diverse elements, which have been incorporated by covenant, or as slaves. Even on the face of the Old Testament record there are more than hints of the infusion of outside elements among the progenitors of ancient Israel.

In the representations of patriarchal life, Abraham appears as an emir, with a trained band of three hundred and eighteen men.[4] As each of these men must have had a wife and at least one or more children, there must

---

[1] Races of the Old Testament. London, 1891, pp. 69, ff.
Cf. an interesting and learned discussion of the subject by Barton: A Sketch of Semitic Origins, Social and Religious. New York, 1902, pp. 1 ff.

[2] Sayce, op. cit., p. 70. "The ancient population of Babylonia was a mixed one, and it is probable that the predominant element in it remained non-Semitic to the end, although it had learned to speak a Semitic idiom. It is questionable whether the Phœnicians or Canaanites were of purely Semitic ancestry, and yet it was from them that the Israelites learned the language which we call Hebrew."

[3] W. Robertson Smith, Kinship and Marriage in Early Arabia, Cambridge, 1885, pp. 3 ff. I have heard various examples from the Arabs of a similar sort.

[4] Gen. xiv. 14.

have been an encampment of three hundred and fifty tents and a population of twelve hundred. While these are not reckoned in the Bible as the tribe of Abraham, among both ancient and modern Semites they would be thus reckoned, as if they were of his own flesh and blood.

It is true that this retinue of servants disappears in the account that is given of the twelve patriarchs, who go down to Egypt as individuals,[1] but we read of a mixed multitude who follow the children of Israel out of Egypt.[2] The blood of these original tribes could not be kept pure, when "blood brotherhood" through covenant constitutes a closer tie among Orientals than brotherhood through descent,[3] and those who are gathered under one leader are considered as belonging to the same tribe.

Dr. Henry Clay Trumbull gives an interesting illustration of the fact that people, not at all related to each other, are reckoned in the East as members of the same family. He writes:[4]

"My two traveling companions were young men, neither of them being a relative of mine. This fact was well understood by our Egyptian dragoman, but when we first met old Shaykh Moosa, who was to convey us from Cairo to Sinai, the three were presented to him as 'Mr. Trumbull and his two sons.' At this I touched the dragoman and said, quietly, 'Not my sons, but young friends of mine.'

" 'That's all right,' said the dragoman. 'He wouldn't understand anything else.'

"Then I found that each traveling party was known as a 'family,' of which the senior member was the father.

[1] Gen. xlvi. 1-27.
[2] Ex. xii. 37-38.
[3] Trumbull, The Blood Covenant, Philadelphia, 1893, p. 11.
[4] Studies in Oriental Social Life, Philadelphia, 1894, p. 238.

So it was simply a choice in our case, whether I should be called the young men's father, or one of them should be called mine; one of us must stand for the father of the other two. In view of this alternative, I, from that time on, passed as the father of the 'family,' until the desert was crossed.''

While, therefore, it would be of the utmost interest if we could unwind the strands which have been twisted together in tribal life, and trace the modern Bedouin back to the ancient Bedouin and Arabs, known as the Midianites and all the children of the East,[1] this is not necessary for our purpose. Those who live in Semitic lands, and who use Semitic forms of speech, have also retained Semitic customs.

Semitic speech and Semitic territory conjoined, even if we could prove that radical changes have been made in the population, would be found more powerful for sustaining ancient customs than alien blood in obliterating them. Whatever ignorant Oriental people might take up their abode in northern Syria, if we could suppose that the present inhabitants could come under subjection to them, would soon become converts to the worship of the high places. The seats of ancient Canaanitish heathenism had power to master the Israelitish conquerors of Canaan, who had from the very beginning been accustomed to a worship which was not dissimilar to that of the conquered; and any Oriental people coming into the same country to-day would fall under the spell of ancient heathenism and superstition. The conquered people allied with the high places and seats of primeval worship become the conquerors in religion. The little maid of Naaman's wife had power to set in

[1] Cf. George Adam Smith, The Historical Geography of the Holy Land, New York, 1895, p. 8.

motion a train of influences which led the proud Syrian to humble himself, so that he sought healing from the prophet of the despised Israelites, and at last turned from the bright waters of his beautiful Damascus to wash in those of the turbid Jordan.[1]

Again, in modern times there is a well-attested instance of the same principle in a servant being able to induce an intelligent English woman to yield to superstition.[2] The story goes that there was the wife of an English officer in India, well advanced in years, who was childless. Her Hindustani maid knew of a temple to which barren Hindoo women had recourse, which was a place of phallic worship so common in India.[3] The Hindustani maid firmly believed that if her mistress could be induced to go thither and take her seat in the prescribed manner she would become a mother. Her English mistress, perhaps partly through curiosity, and partly to please her maid, repaired to the temple and took the seat as directed; in due time, as in so many other cases of a similar sort,[4] she had a son.

This, then, illustrates the proposition, that the conquered race allied with high places and seats of primeval worship can maintain themselves against every Oriental conqueror. If we establish this point, we may, for all practical purposes, consider the whole domain of Syria and Palestine as the proper field of investigation for survivals of ancient Semitic religious customs.[5] The

[1] 2 Kings v. 2-14.

[2] Daniel Z. Noorian of New York, trusted dragoman of Rev. W. Hayes Ward, LL. D.

[3] Testimony of Rev. J. F. Loba, D.D., a member of the Deputation of the American Board to India.

[4] There are many well-attested instances of barren women having children after the performance of superstitious rites.

[5] George Adam Smith, op. cit. pp. 10, 11: "The population of Syria has always been essentially Semitic. There are few lands

Sinaitic Peninsula, Arabia Deserta, the entire region of Mesopotamia, of ancient Babylonia, and of Asia Minor are valuable for comparative purposes. But the chief seat of investigation is, after all, to be found in the country known as Syria and Palestine, so far as we desire to find apposite illustrations of Semitic usage in the Old and New Testaments, though Asia Minor is said to afford a fruitful field. Such usage is not confined to the Old Testament. There are abundant examples in the New. The demonology which we find there resembles strongly the teaching which appears among modern Arabs concerning the jinn, nor need we suppose it to be essentially different from the beliefs which made witchcraft possible and profitable in Old Testament times.

In all these studies we are encroaching on the larger domain of comparative religion, as will be abundantly clear from the comparison of any good book on the subject[1] with the results of such investigations. But there is a distinct gain in limiting our researches to those who, by virtue of descent, by territory, or by language, may be reckoned as Semites.

However, as the subject has been suggested, "Who are the modern Semites?" we may pursue it a little farther, remembering that anything like certainty is impossible.

In northwestern Syria are the Nusairiyeh and Ismailiyeh, thought by many to be descendants of the ancient Canaanites. An intelligent Syrian has suggested that

into which so many divers races have come; as in ancient times Philistines and Hittites; then in very large numbers, Greeks; then with the Crusades a few hundred thousand Franks; then till the present day more Franks, more Greeks, Turks, Khurds, and some colonies of Circassians. But all these have scarcely even been grafted on the stock, and the stock is Semitic."

[1] Jevons, An Introduction to the History of Religion: Frazer, op. cit.

they are of the ancient Hittite stock, who failed to be dislodged from their mountain fastnesses by the storms of invading armies.[1] Certain it is that when they had once taken their place in their mountains no foe could dislodge them, nor can to-day, until roads are constructed by the government. However, in general terms, we may consider them as of the ancient Canaanitic race, but speaking a language then, as they speak a language now, of Semitic origin. Israel, the Phœnicians, the Philistines, the Moabites, Ammonites, and other ancient Semites, all spoke a kindred tongue[2] as is the case with the modern Semitic peoples to-day.

In the Syrian Desert and in northeastern Syria are the Aramæans. Their speech is still preserved in the ritual of the Jacobites, of the Syriac church, of the Maronites, and in three villages, including Malula,[3] where Syriac is still spoken. These, excepting perhaps the Maronites, are Semites. Various races entering Palestine on the western side of the Jordan have caused an admixture of blood, and the introduction of foreign elements, which no man can determine.

It has been suggested by a writer in the Encyclopædia Britannica on the Druses that they may be of Chinese extraction.[4] It is a singular and interesting fact, however it may be explained, that their heaven is in China, where they claim to have a thousand cities. When a man of some distinction dies among them there is said to be an antiphonal service consisting of a

[1] Mr. Jabur of Nebk.
[2] Cf. Stade, Lehrbuch der Hebräischen Grammatik, Leipzig, 1879, pp. 1-22.
[3] Dr. F. J. Bliss, Malula and its Dialect, Palestine Exploration Fund, London, 1890, pp. 74-98.
[4] Mr. H. A. Webster, but he does not commit himself to this view.

chorega and chorus, all of whom are women. The leader sings:

"Oh man who has been a chief for two centuries,
We congratulate the people of China on receiving your soul."

The chorus repeats these lines.[1] This is curious, and while it is not enough to prove that the Druses in Lebanon and in the Druse Mountains are of Chinese extraction, it seems to indicate at least that they are of foreign elements.

Nor are the Syrians of pure stock. One may often see fair faces and golden hair, inclining to red,[2] among the children, which may well point back to some Crusading sire. It is certain that the soldiers from Britain and European countries who could not return and who did not die would find Syrian wives; hence a fair skin and a cast of features are often found among Syrians which betray a European origin.

The swarthy inhabitants of the Jaulan, the Hauran, of Moab, Edom, and the South Country (*Negeb*), even when they dwell in towns, except where Circassians have taken their place among certain ruins, betray their Arab origin. But from whatever loins they may have sprung, all the inhabitants of Syria and Palestine, except Protestant Christians, who have been mostly shamed out of the ancient beliefs, are for the purposes of our investigation, modern Semites. Even in towns which have been most fully Europeanized there are traces of ancient superstitions and usages coming down from primitive Semitism.

[1] This and other information about the Druses was given me by a Syrian physician who has lived among them and is a graduate of the Syrian Protestant College at Beirut.

[2] Cf. Sayce, op. cit. p. 74; George Adam Smith, op. cit. p. 11. I have seen such fair faces and golden locks in many parts of the country.

CHAPTER VI

CONCEPTIONS OF GOD

Dr. W. L. Thompson, of the American Board,[1] says, that "the Tongas have a hazy idea of God, as the first cause, but the worship of spirits and ancestors is more of a power in their lives."[2]

The same statement is true of those modern Semites who have not been affected by the teaching of Islam, or by that of ancient Christianity. These are to be found, as we have seen, among ignorant peasants in Syria and Palestine, as well as among various tribes of Arabs.[3]

---

[1] Of Mount Silinda, East Central African Mission.

[2] Personal interview, Journal, summer of 1901.

[3] While the words Arab and Bedouin, in their application, practically mean the same thing, there is a clear difference in signification indicated by Lane (see his Arabic-English lexicon) as well as in usage. Lane defines *el-Arab* as "Those who have alighted and made their abode in the cultivated regions, and have taken as their homes the Arabian cities and towns or villages, and others also that are related to them . . . . an appellation of common application [to the whole nation] . . . . [and in the lexicon . . . . applied to the desert Arabs of pure speech]." Hence this term is frequently used, not only of those Arabs who have begun to cultivate the fields, but also of those who live in towns. It may be used of the inhabitants of the desert, or pure nomads, but not exclusively so. On the other hand, *Bedawi*, according to the same eminent authority, signifies: "Of, or belonging to, or relating to, the *bedw* or desert: and used as a subst., a man, and particularly an Arab of the desert." The Bedouin never live in towns, never cultivate the soil, but gain their livelihood by raids; and they regard with unspeakable disdain those who have forsaken the nomad life to live even in part by the tillage of the soil. The term *Fellahin*, which signifies ploughman, is used of the peasant class. It is among the Fellahin and the Bedouin, as least affected by Islam that we should expect the largest results in these investigations with respect to the survivals of ancient Semitic religion.

In conducting our investigations it is not easy to discover whether the conceptions of God, which exist to-day among them, however shadowy, have come from the instruction of Moslem sheiks, who often teach the Bedouin, at least for a brief period, the tenets of Islam,[1] or whether we have the same phenomenon among them as that which has been pointed out by Mr. Andrew Lang, in his Making of Religion,[2] where the worship of God, and of inferior deities, without the influence of "positive religion,"[3] exists side by side. Nor can we determine whether the conceptions of God, now found among the Bedouin, are evolutions from the conditions of tribal life, so that God is but a superhuman sheik. This is a domain in which further investigations are necessary. The opinions and reports of travelers are too fragmentary to supply adequate data for an induction.

It must be remembered that the modern Semite does not reason with respect to religious matters. By nature,

---

[1] It was the testimony of Habeeb Yadji, of Mehardeh, who is remarkably familiar with the customs of the Arabs from personal observation, that "there are scarcely any religious sheiks among the Bedouin. If they have no religious sheik they send for one to attend a funeral. He has seen the Arabs come to Karyaten, in the Syrian Desert, for such a sheik."
On the other hand, the chief of the Rawaein, a small tribe that migrate east of Palmyra, affirm that "every body of Arabs has a religious sheik." Journal XII., summer of 1901. This latter statement is improbable. Lady Blunt, Bedouin Tribes of the Euphrates, London, 1879, Vol. II., p. 217, testifies: "The Shammar alone of all the noble tribes we visited possessed a mollah, and his duties with them were in no way of a priestly character."

[2] Pp. 178, ff.

[3] W. Robertson Smith, Lectures on the Religion of the Semites, New York, 1889, p. 1: "Judaism, Christianity, and Islam are positive religions—that is, they did not grow up like the systems of ancient heathenism, under the action of unconscious forces, operating silently from age to age, but trace their origin to the teachings of great religious innovators, who spoke as the organs of a divine revelation, and deliberately departed from the traditions of the past."

imaginative and impressionable, his ideas regarding the Divine Being are rather pictures left on his mind than the result of any philosophical reflection, since he does not philosophize. He is not at all affected by views which are inconsistent, hence mutually exclusive.[1] He will admit, that according to the tenets of Islam he should be a fatalist, whose life cannot be prolonged by prayers, tears, or sacrifices; one day, after the limit decreed has expired, he will confess his belief in fatalism, and then will justify a usage entirely inconsistent with such a belief by naïvely saying, "This is according to the simplicity of our minds."[2] The simplicity of the Semitic mind accounts for the survival of ancient customs which have been handed down from the remotest antiquity, notwithstanding the teachings of Islam or Christianity.

To the Arab or Syrian, custom is mightier than right; indeed custom is the only right he knows. Both morality and religion depend upon it. The heavens might sooner fall than custom be set aside. If we can get at the usage of the Semite we shall know what his religion is.

Another principle which we must remember is deeply

[1] Palgrave, Narrative of a Year's Journey through Central and Eastern Arabia, London, 1865, Vol. I., p. 68: "The Arabs are, generally speaking, rather a believing than a religious nation . . . . Men who readily grant an abstract belief to everything are not unlikely to reconcile, in a practical way, the many contradictions thus admitted into their theory by acting on nothing. Christian, Jewish, Mahometan or Pagan creeds and forms—the Arab, when left to himself, does not see why they should not all be equally true, equally estimable."

[2] The Servant of the "Chair," a shrine near Zebedani, which will be described later, after saying, "Every building must have its death—man, woman, child, or animal. God has appointed a redemption for every building through sacrifice. If God has accepted the sacrifice he has redeemed the house"—added, "this is according to the simplicity of our minds, of course every man dies when his time comes." Journal X., summer of 1901. This expression recurred in different forms a number of times, showing that the Arab or Syrian was conscious of the contrast between ancient usage and the tenets of Islam.

ingrained in their view of the divine as well as the human economy, is the belief that might makes right. In the words of another, "God makes right by edict."[1] In the same category belongs the conviction that God can be bought; that is, that he is bribable. This is the experience which every Oriental has had of human government, he naturally has the same view of the divine.

From the foregoing it is easy to see that the modern Semite has no ethical conception of God as holy, or as just, hence we shall find that his views of sin are entirely deficient, and do not possess a moral quality. He is not afraid to take God's name in vain, or to swear falsely by him,[2] or to use it in the most shameful connections.[3] It is certain that such a conception of God has no power to affect the life of the Syrian or Bedouin. Nor need we find it at variance with the representations which have been given of him by most travelers.

It may well be that Palgrave is right when he claims that, "A general belief in the Supreme Being, author of all, and ruler of all, has from time immemorial prevailed throughout Arabia."[4] Nor does such a belief serve to cloud their hopes of the future life, or check a spirit of cheerful bravado, when brought to think of appearing before a God who is neither just nor holy. Mr. Henry G. Harding, of the Church Missionary Society, for twelve

---

[1] "The Oriental has not the same idea of abstract right and wrong as the Occidental. He thinks God makes right and wrong by edict."—Interview with the Rev. George E. Post, D.D., of the Syrian Protestant College, Beirut, Journal IX., summer of 1900.

[2] Of this there are abundant examples, as is affirmed everywhere; and see Doughty, Travels in Arabia Deserta, Cambridge, 1888, Vol. I., p. 266.

[3] Lane, An Account of the Manners and Customs of the Modern Egyptians. London, 1896, pp. 286, 287.

[4] Op. cit. Vol. I., p. 249.

years missionary in the East, including a residence in Tripoli, Africa, and in Kerak, now of Gaza, testifies in the same strain: "The idea of God is very vague, but seems to be mainly an enlarged edition of a Bedouin sheik; that is, of a beneficent but capricious despot. I have never met with any one who had a notion of the character of God."[1] "God is for them a chief, residing mainly, it would seem, in the sun, with which indeed they in a manner identify him . . . . somewhat more powerful, of course, than their own head man . . . . but in other respects of much the same style and character."[2]

Lady Blunt's characterization of the Bedouin's relation to God gives no disclosure of him as a just or holy being, but rather as one possessed of superior power: "A belief, then, in God certainly exists among the Bedouins, though the only active form of it is a submission to the Divine will. It stands in singular correspondence with the religion of the ancient patriarchs. At the present day, no doubt, it is but a vague reflection of ancient faith, and depends as much upon custom as every other belief or prejudice of the Bedouin mind."[3]

Perhaps an exceptional consciousness of sin and a religion that is beautiful—and it would almost seem exceptional among the sons of the desert, as observed among the Towarah in the Sinaitic Peninsula—is indicated in some Bedouin prayers, overheard and reported by Professor Palmer. The following is a specimen of one at sunset: "O Lord, be gracious unto us! In all that we hear or see, in all that we say or do, be gracious

[1] From answers furnished by Mr. Harding to questions, winter of 1901.

[2] Palgrave, ibid. p. 33.

[3] Lady Anne Blunt, Bedouin Tribes of the Euphrates, London, 1879, Vol. II., p. 220.

unto us! Have mercy upon our friends who have passed away before us. I ask pardon of the great God. I ask pardon at the sunset, when every sinner turns to Him. Now and forever, I ask pardon of God. O Lord, cover us from our sins, guard our children, and protect our weaker friends!"

Again, at sunrise, they pray: "I seek refuge with the great God from Satan accursed with stones. Deliver me from evil, provide for me and for my brethren the faithful. . . . . O Lord, uncover not our inmost faults, protect our children and our weaker friends. O Lord, provide for me, Thou who providest for the blind hyena!"

These higher and better conceptions of God may well have been inspired by the teachings of Islam. This seems likely from the formula with which they preface every prayer: "I desire to pray and to seek guidance from God; for good and pure prayers come from God alone. Peace be upon our Lord Abraham and our Lord Mohammed."[1] Besides they are able, from memory, to recite certain sections of the Koran, as I was assured, at one of their festivals.[2]

It is doubtless true that among the majority of the Fellahin and Arabs their conceptions of God have been modified by their habits and condition, if we may not affirm that they have been derived from them. Hence to them God is the author of good and evil.[3] No sheik with whom they have had to do, no emir, or sultan, of whom they have ever heard, is the author of good alone.

[1] The Desert of the Exodus, New York, 1872, pp. 86, 87.

[2] Journal IV, spring of 1899, in the Sinaitic Peninsula.

[3] Lady Blunt, op. cit., Vol. II., pp. 216, 217: "God is the fate to which all must bow, the cause of the good and of the evil in life . . . . of the fertility of their flocks, and of the murrains which sometimes afflict them." The Moslems think that evil is directly from the Devil by the permission of God. Journal X. Nebk.

CONCEPTIONS OF GOD 69

This is an old Semitic conception which we find illustrated in the Old Testament. Job says, with respect to the appalling calamities which have befallen him in the loss of property and children, "What? shall we receive good at the hand of God, and shall we not receive evil?"[1] So it is "an evil spirit from the Lord" that troubles Saul.[2] Thus "The anger of the Lord was kindled against Israel, and he moved David against them, saying, go, number Israel and Judah."[3] The same fear of numbering the people among the modern Semites is partially chargeable for the absence of any correct statistics as to the population of Oriental cities and towns. It is interesting to note that the theology of later Judaism has amended the passage to read, "And Satan stood up against Israel and moved David to number Israel."[4] Amos speaks from the old point of view, when he asks, "Shall evil befall a city, and the Lord hath not done it?"[5]

Closely connected with this is the thought, that God may lead astray. Thus Suleiman, a teacher in a school of the Irish Presbyterian Church in Nebk, who made most careful investigations for me during more than two months, interviewing Moslems and Christians, Fellahin and Bedouin, at the suggestion of Rev. J. Stewart Crawford, said, as the result of many interviews with many kinds of people: "Their view is that God is the creator of heaven and earth, the maker of all men, the giver of good to all. He may also lead astray. The ignorant know up to this point."[6] This is evidently a survival of an ancient Semitic conception, which we find gives coloring to certain Old Testament passages, as for

[1] Job ii. 10.
[2] 1 Sam. xvi. 14-16, 23; xviii. 10.
[3] 2 Sam. xxiv. 1.
[4] 1 Chron. xxi. 1.
[5] Amos iii. 6.
[6] Journal X., Syrian Desert.

example, when the Lord is represented as saying of Pharaoh: "I will harden his heart,"[1] and Isaiah represents God as bidding him, "Make the heart of this people fat, and make their ears heavy, and smear their eyes, lest they should see with their eyes, and hear with their ears, and perceive with their heart, and should convert and be healed."[2] I do not, of course, believe that these passages teach that God leads man astray, but they are certainly colored by this idea. Another passage, read literally, expresses the view, that God makes the enemies of his people guilty—I refer to Ps. v. 11., where the psalmist prays, according to the Hebrew idiom, "Make them guilty, O God," which the Revisers well translate, "Hold them guilty, O God," or perhaps better, "Declare them guilty, O God"; that is, "Let them suffer the consequences of their guilt." We have an illustration of this meaning in passages parallel to God's hardening Pharaoh's heart, where it is said: "Pharaoh hardened his heart."[3] But the thought that God leads man astray is original in the Semitic mind. So ingrained is the ancient idea, through millenniums of oppression, that any one in power is responsible for the failure of an inferior, that it sometimes appears to-day in a very amusing way. The following incident, which illustrates this point, came under my notice when I was spending five weeks at the Syrian Protestant College in Beirut. A student failed to pass his examination in French. He therefore wrote a very indignant letter to the French professor, in which he asked the question, in Arab-English, "Why did you fail me?" By this he did not mean, "Why did you declare that my examination was a failure?" but "Why did you cause me to fail?" This was

[1] Ex. iv. 21, cf. ix. 12, x. 20, 27; xi. 10; xiv. 4, 8, 17.
[2] Is. vi. 9, 10.   [3] Ex. viii. 15, 32.

evidently his meaning from the tenor of his letter, in which he claimed that he had done excellent work in French. The belief that God leads men astray has a very important bearing on their notion of sin, as we shall see, when we come to consider the moral relation of man to God.

The people, judging from experience, regard God as a jealous being, upon whose help they may rely at any given crisis of their lives, if they make him a satisfactory present. The late Rev. John Zeller, for more than forty years missionary in Palestine, who knew much of the working of the native mind, said: "The sacrifice of a sheep may have a vicarious character, in so far as it is thought to appease a jealous God who is not willing to have any one too prosperous."[1] It seems as if one of the earliest representations of man's approach to God was through a gift, as that is the proper rendering of *minha*, the term used to describe the present which Cain and Abel are represented as bringing to God.[2] This is the simplest conception of sacrifice. They bring a present to God as a man would bring a gift to an emir, and would consider it "singularly impertinent to go empty-handed."[3] Men, realizing too well their experiences with earthly potentates, and fearing their jealousy, bring their gifts. It is this ancient idea which appears in an utterance of David, when he has a parley with Saul: "If it be the Lord that hath stirred thee up against me, let him smell an offering."[4] The account of the confusion of tongues seems almost to suggest the belief of the writer that God was jealous because of an achieve-

[1] Journal VIII. Jerusalem, summer of 1900.
[2] Gen. iv. 3, 4 (Hebrew).
[3] Interview with the Rev. G. M. Mackie, D.D., Beirut, Journal X.
[4] 1 Sam. xxvi. 19, Rev. Ver. Margin.

ment, which might indicate that in time men, if permitted to live together unchecked, might become "too prosperous" and endanger the supremacy of God himself.[1] There are other illustrations of the same conception of God. There are numerous examples in the Old Testament which show that the ancient writers have been led in their choice of expressions and manner of representation, by beliefs and modes of thought current in their times, and which still exist among Syrians and Bedouin to-day.

There seems to be abundant evidence that ignorant people think of God as one of themselves,[2] as having a human organism.[3] He and St. George, the most powerful of the saints, are considered by some as brothers. The implications of such a view are far-reaching, as we shall see when I come to speak of the physical relation of man to God.

We have Old Testament examples, where the form of the narrative has been borrowed from old Semitic ideas, although the truth taught has not been dominated by them. Such is a class of passages which are not adequately explained by affirming that they are anthropo-

[1] Gen. xi. 6.
[2] Mr. Henry Harding, made the following statement: "Ordinary people would think of God as like themselves. They would expect God to deal with them as they would deal with one another. The idea of God is very vague. The welis and spirits are much nearer." Journal XIII. Brummana, summer of 1901.
[3] Suleiman, the Protestant teacher at Nebk, asked a man, "Who is God?" Ans. "The existing one." "Has he eyes?" Ans. "Certainly." "Has he ears?" Ans. "Certainly." There is an expression in Nebk, if a man is very tall, that he can reach to certain parts of the body of the deity. Even the women of the same place will say, when vexed, "Get out, for the sake of the back parts of our Lord!" At the village of Dibbash in the Nusairian Mountains, occupied by Greek Christians, we were told that the people "think of God as made in the image of man," Journal XI. summer of 1901.

morphic; they are really more than that, for they betray conceptions of God at a stage when his omniscience and omnipresence were not apprehended in any such sense as other writers apprehend them. For example, God is represented in one of the most ancient Old-Testament documents as walking in the garden in the cool of a tropical day, the safest and most agreeable time for man to walk abroad, and so the safest time for God, here conceived of by the writer as needing to avoid the burning sun. He, too, like one of his creatures, needs to call the man who, with his wife, has hidden himself among the trees of the garden, else He might not find him.[1] Most antique is the representation of God smelling the sweet savor of Noah's sacrifice, and pleased as much as any man could be with a gift, and promising in his heart, because of this satisfaction, that he will not curse the ground again because of man.[2] We know that this is an ancient Semitic conception, inasmuch as we have a grotesque and polytheistic form in the ancient Babylonian tradition.[3] But it is also clear from this parallel account, that while the Jehovistic writer is so naïve in his descriptions, he has been kept by the Divine Spirit from making unworthy representations of God; for these children's pictures of God acting like a man, are not unworthy of the child age of the world. Indeed, they are wonderfully adapted to the conceptions of that age. When Jehovah

[1] Gen. iii. 8-10.
[2] Gen. viii. 21.
[3] Parallel Accounts of Noah's Sacrifice.

Babylonian iii. 49-50.
"The gods smelt the savor; the gods smelt the good savor; the gods like flies over the sacrificer gathered." Sayce-Smith Chaldean Account of Genesis, New York, pp. 286, 287.

Jehovistic (Gen. viii. 21).
"And the Lord smelled the sweet savor."

goes down to see the city and tower of Babel on a visit of inspection,[1] or when he proposes to make a personal examination of Sodom,[2] and permits Abraham to beat him down, as if they were on the same plane, just as is the custom in Syria at the present day, and when he suffers Jacob to wrestle with him all night until the breaking of the morning,[3] we are moving, indeed, in the domain of ancient Semitic conceptions, but conceptions of which there are survivals to-day.

Some may be inclined to put the words of Jotham's parable in a different category, "Should I leave my wine which cheereth God and man?"[4] as if it were less of the essence of Scripture than the passages quoted. But this position cannot be well established, for there are many more illustrations which might be cited showing how certain institutions go back to human conceptions of God, as for example, "the shewbread that was taken from before the Lord to put hot bread" in its place.[5] Such bread, according to the Priests' Code, was placed on a table, for God was conceived of as humanlike, having a table.[6] The sixteenth psalm indicates that there are "drink offerings of blood" which the heathen god was thought of as drinking. With reference to these representations of God as a man with a man's appetites, the psalmist quotes him as saying in another place: "Will I eat the flesh of bulls or drink the blood of goats?"

We may be sure that in the conceptions of God, which the ignorant Arab or Fellahin entertains to-day, we have men at the same stage as when God began to reveal himself in terms which the childhood of the ancient Semites could understand.

[1] Gen. xi. 5.
[2] Gen. xviii. 20, 21.
[3] Gen. xxxii. 24–30.
[4] Judg. ix. 13.
[5] 1 Sam. xxi. 16.
[6] Ex. xxv. 30.

CHAPTER VII

THE LOCAL DIVINITIES

Among most sects of Moslems and Christians, including Bedouin as well as Syrians, the worship of saints exists. In the popular imagination they exercise a power far above that of God. Men fear lightly to break oaths made at their shrines, or to use obscene language, so prevalent in the East, when going into their presence.[1]

It is true that orthodox Moslems insist that the saints are only mediators, that the worshiper asks his weli to intercede for him with God,[2] but this is not the type of religion as it is found among the ignorant, whose usage corresponds most closely to that of antiquity. The antinomy between doctrine and practice came out in a conversation with a religious sheik, an orthodox Moslem, at Nebk, in the Syrian desert, about vows, concerning which he said: "If a vow is made, it is made to God, not to the saint, but it is made by the grave of the saint, to honor him and to please God. . . . . However, a simple person would say, that the vow was given to the weli, thus making him a lord, which is an error. I am an educated person, therefore I give you the right account."[3]

---

[1] "They are very particular on the road (to the shrine) not to speak foul language." Journal XI. Behammra among the Nusairiyeh, summer of 1901.

[2] Cf. my article, "Ancient Shrines in northern Syria," The Independent, Vol. L., p. 1448, "God is almighty . . . I ask the weli, and the weli asks God." The same idea was brought out in other interviews with Moslems.

[3] Journal X., Nebk, summer 1901.

The general designation used among the Christians for these beings who are practically treated as divine, is the Aramaic word, *mar* (lord, or saint), while that used among Moslems is *weli* (which signifies protector, patron, nearest of kin). In the Arabic version of the American Press, Job appeals to God as his weli, to be his avenger,[1] and Ruth confides in Boaz, as her weli or nearest of kin, who is under obligations by that relationship to marry her.[2]

In the Koran the term weli is used many times, both in the singular and plural. It is almost always translated by Professor Palmer as "patron." The singular is mostly applied to God. Thus we read: "God is the patron of those who believe,"[3] or "of the believers."[4] The taking of other patrons besides God is condemned in the strongest terms. There is no place in all this teaching for the worship of the welis, and there is good reason for the opposition to their worship on the part of the Wahabites, the most orthodox sect of Islam, who sought as resolutely to crush out the sacred shrines[5] as King Josiah attempted to stamp out the worship of the

---

[1] Job xix. 25. } In both these passages weli is used in the Arabic
[2] Ruth iii. 12. } version as the rendering of the Hebrew *goel*.
[3] ii. 258.
[4] iii. 61.
[5] Burckhardt, Notes on the Bedouin and Wahabys, London, 1830, pp. 280, 281.

"The Wahabys declared that all men were equal in the eyes of God; that even the most virtuous could not intercede with him; and that it was consequently sinful to invoke departed saints, and to honor their mortal remains more than those of any other persons. Wherever the Wahabys carried their arms they destroyed all the domes and ornamented tombs; a circumstance which served to inflame the fanaticism of their disciples, and to form a marked distinction between them and their opponents. . . . The destruction of cupolas and tombs of saints became the favorite taste of the Wahabys."

THE LOCAL DIVINITIES

high places.[1] In the call to prayer we were told that *ulia*, the plural of *weli*, is used,[2] but this seems most unlikely, certainly in the sense of "patrons."

The term *mar* is employed among the Christians as a title, St. George being known in Syria as Mar Jirjis, but the Moslems designate their saints by the special term of *nebi* (prophet), if they may be considered Biblical characters, or as sheik, if they belong to post-Biblical times. The term *weli* is general, and applies both to the saint and to his tomb.

These saints are really departed spirits, connected with some particular shrine, chosen because they revealed themselves there in times past, and where they are wont to reveal themselves now to those who seek their favor.

While our previous examination shows[3] that the Semitic conception of God to-day degrades him, that which we are about to make concerning the saint will prove that he is exalted to the place of deity, at least among the ignorant.

We must recognize a close connection between the ordinary spirit of the departed and that of the saint who is supposed to possess superior sanctity and power. Indeed we shall find that conceptions which might be held with respect to the disembodied spirit are held of the saint and may be held of God.

Frazer has well said: "The notion of a man-god, or of a human being endowed with divine or supernatural powers, belongs essentially to that earlier period of religious history in which gods and men are still viewed as beings of much the same order, and before they are

[1] 2 Kings xxiii. 8-13.
[2] "In the regular call to prayer there is a mention of all the ulia, first the Prophet, then all the other prophets, then the ulia." Journal XI., Mehardeh, summer of 1901.
[3] P. 72.

78   PRIMITIVE SEMITIC RELIGION TO-DAY

divided by the impassable gulf, which to later thought, opens out between them."[1] Such a notion still exists among the most ignorant of the modern Semites, and the impassable gulf has not yet been fixed between them.

It is evident from an examination of numerous passages in the Koran, where the term weli is used as relating to God, that an application of the term weli to a saint, as has been suggested, is contrary to the Koran[2] and to Moslem law;[3] but even good Moslems affirm that a man who does not believe in a weli does not believe in God.[4] There are also said to be ascriptions of praise rendered to the welis, among the Nusairiyeh, a heretical sect, far beyond those rendered to God.[5]

Every shrine, of whatever sort, theoretically presupposes a weli or saint. He may have lived within the memory of the generation that does him honor, and many tales may have been preserved in regard to him. Or he may be a mythical character about whom a profusion of folk-lore has sprung up. It may be that he has little objective existence in the thought of the people beyond his name and shrine. They cannot tell much regarding his life and his achievements. Indeed there is sometimes a clear indication of skepticism on the part

---

[1] The Golden Bough, London, 1900, Vol. I., p. 130.

[2] See Flügel, Concordantiae Corani Arabicae, Lipsiae, 1842, *sub voce*.

[3] Journal, Hama, summer, 1901: "There rises before the company, when they arrive at the shrine, one who recites a poem. The subject of the poem is praise to God, or the Prophet, or the weli. The praise of the weli is a very prominent part of it. But this is all contrary to Mohammedan law." Cf. Burckhardt, Notes on the Bedouin and Wahabys, London, 1830, p. 279.

[4] Declaration of a Moslem peasant, Journal XI., Nebk.

[5] Rev. James S. Stewart of Ladikiyeh, testifies: "I have read in their books (of the Nusairiyeh) ascriptions of glory and praise greater than any they ascribe to God."

SHRINE OF AARON ON MOUNT HOR.

THE LOCAL DIVINITIES 79

of the people with respect to the origin of such shrines.[1] But to the heated imaginations of some of their servants, they appear in bodily form.[2] Theoretically they are worshiped in connection with the God of all the world; practically many people know no other god. In this respect the worship of the saints is like that of the ancient Baalim. They are the deities whom the people fear, love, serve, and adore.

Remembering that the saints are spirits, once living, we shall find it of interest to consider some of the ways in which they reveal themselves. One of the most famous shrines is that of Aaron on Mount Hor. Whether his body was ever buried on that height which tradition assigns to him is of no moment in this investigation. As will be seen from the following dialogue with Musa, an Arab guide at Petra, it is evident that Aaron is thought of as having existence, and as coming to his shrine during two days of the week:

Question. Is there a yearly festival?

Answer. No.

Q. Why do the people visit the prophet's tomb?

A. Because he is a great prophet, out of honor to him.

[1] See the Rev. H. H. Jessup, D.D. The Women of the Arabs, London, 1874, pp. 269-272.

[2] Sheik Yuseph el-hagg, of Nebk, says, with respect to the saint who has charge of the streams at Nebk, and whose name is Mohammed el-Ghuffary, that he appears in various forms: "Sometimes as an old man, sometimes as a young man in white, but always in human form; some see him at night, others see him by day, some see him in dreams, only those who have the light in their hearts see him."

Another Moslem, by the name of Abu Ali, from the same village, who works himself at times into a frenzy, and sometimes makes a frightful noise when engaged in prayer, testified: "I have seen his spirit because I love the saint and he loves me. He appears to me by day and by night like a middle-aged man wearing a green robe. I speak to him and we converse together." Journal X., Nebk, summer of 1901.

Q. What benefits do they expect to receive from such a visit?

A. If any one has a son or friend ill, he goes and asks the prophet to intercede for him [with God] and promises in case of recovery to visit the tomb once a year.

Q. Do they vow they will give the prophet anything in case of recovery?

A. Yes; it is not necessary that they should go to the top of the mountain to make a vow. They may pile up a heap of stones anywhere in sight of the mountain, as a witness [*meshhad*].[1] They may kill the animal they have vowed anywhere.

Q. Do they consider the animals they have vowed, and which they eat, sacrifices?

A. Yes.

Q. How can they be sacrifices when they eat them? Does the prophet partake of them?[2]

A. The prophet is dead, how could he eat of them? We would not throw them away after we had killed them.[3]

Q. Is the prophet dead?

A. Prophets never die. The prophet [Aaron] is alive to-day. We ask him to intercede for us.

Q. Do the people ever make any use of the blood of the sacrifice?

A. No, they throw it away.

Q. Why do the people put *semn* [Arab butter] in the lower room of the shrine?

---

[1] These heaps of witness (Cf. Gen. xxxi. 48) are very common in sight of shrines which are difficult of access.

[2] This question was asked to see if there was any trace of the critical theory that God is the host at sacrificial meals. Musa did not seem to conceive of the Prophet Aaron in any such capacity.

[3] This is certainly a very important statement in connection with the use made of the flesh in sacrifices, and would seem to indicate that the sacrifice does not consist in eating it.

CENOTAPH OF AARON.

THE LOCAL DIVINITIES

A. It is customary to have a lamp burning Thursdays and Fridays, so they use semn for this purpose.

Q. Why is the light burning only on Thursdays and Fridays?

A. Our books[1] say that the prophet comes only on Thursday and Friday. The rest of the time he is with his brother Moses, and with their friend [God]. He comes down only on these two days.[2]

The alleged birthplace of Abraham at Berzeh, near Damascus, affords Moslems a reason for seeking the patriarch, by vows and prayers, as the place of his revelation, since his mother is said to have given him birth in a hole of the rock. She remained with him three days, and then putting his finger in his mouth, left him. There he abode, according to the legend, seven years. The shrine, which affords a dwelling for the minister on the same court, is especially interesting, because on a sheet of paper posted on the wall, all visitors who are in trouble are invited to make known their sorrows to the weli. "Advice to people who visit this place, where is Abraham, father of Isaac, the sacrificed, the grandfather of the prophets! Come, tell him all your adversities and hardships, and he will help you."[3] It will be noticed that nothing is suggested as to his intercession with God for them. The people are bidden to come to him as the sole source of their comfort.

Of quite another sort is the weli at an ancient plat-

[1] Unlettered Moslems frequently refer to their books for statements which they make. As they cannot read, the allusion to such books must be taken with a great deal of allowance. Friday is the ?oslem Sunday, hence a favorite day for saints to visit their ₋rines.

[2] Journal VIII., Petra, summer of 1901.

[3] This was translated by Rev. Anis Nasif Sellum of Damascus, into Arab-English, which I have retained. Journal XII., Berzeh, summer of 1901.

form, surrounded by several acres of oak-trees, known as the "Mother of Pieces" (*Umm Shakakif*). It was my good fortune to learn the story of this shrine for the first time, and in two forms, one in poetry, from the servant of another shrine, about an hour and a quarter south, the other in prose from the servant of the shrine itself. Both are interesting specimens of folk-lore. I give the former here as briefer, reserving the one in prose for Appendix D.

The story goes that there were four maidens, each of whom was under the protection of a particular saint. The heroine of the shrine was known, according to one story, as 'Arja, or the lame one; according to the other, as Fatima. She was lame, blind of an eye, bald, poor, and almost naked. Accompanied by her three friends she went to the fountain to draw water, where the four saints, the respective patrons of these girls, were seated. Each of 'Arja's companions let down her water-jar, in turn, and it came up full of water, and each set out on her way home. When 'Arja had lowered her jar, instead of coming up brimming, she drew up only the handles. Her patron, whom she had served faithfully, had shattered it. Urged to desert him and choose another, she affirmed her unalterable fidelity to him. Touched by her devotion, he bade her give him the handles. In a few moments she drew up her jar, more beautiful than ever, full of water. On this the following dialogue took place:

Saint to 'Arja. Go join your companions.

'Arja. I am your servant, you see I am lame.

He healed her.

Saint. Go join your companions.

'Arja. I am your servant, you see I am blind.

He cured her.

Saint. Go join your companions.

'Arja. I am your servant, you see I am bald.

He gave her long hair.

Saint. Go join your companions.

'Arja. I am your servant, you see I am naked.

He clothed her.

Saint. Go join your companions.

'Arja. I am your servant, you see I am poor.

Saint. Raise up the carpet, and you will find silver and gold.

She did so.

Thus, through her obedience and faith, a poor, blind, bald, and lame girl became the object of worship, and the place where she is reputed to be buried is still the place of blessing. Vows are made of jars of pottery, which are broken on the ancient platform.

In direct contrast with the legends which have grown up around the "Mother of Pieces" is a Druse Shrine, about two and a half hours west of Rasheya, known as Nebi Safa.[1] While they say that the Prophet Safa is descended from Jacob, and that his people lived in the direction of Jerusalem and Hebron, they do not know how he came to be there, or to die there. "The honorable body is there, and the spirit is always to be found there. Any day that a man seeks him he will find him, it depends on his faith." The people charged with the care of the shrine could tell wonderful stories, indicating the exercise of supernatural powers, but nothing shedding any real light on the history of the one exercising them.

The most famous saint in the Christian calendar is St. George, or Mar Jirjis, who killed the dragon at Beirut, after whom the bay is named. The monastery is said to

[1] Journal XIII., Nebi Safa, summer 1901.

be placed on the spot where St. George used to reveal himself.[1] He is known among the various sects of Islam as Khuddr. While his most famous shrine is near Kalat el Hosn, west of Homs and near Safita, in northern Syria, he is associated with more places than any other saint. His shrines are found in all parts of the country, both in buildings originally erected for him as well as in ancient Greek churches in the Druse Mountains,[2] which, during their occupation by Christians, may have been sacred to the worship of St. George. At each of these shrines there is a tomb, or the representation of one, and at all these he is thought to reveal himself.

Such a self-revelation of the saints also takes place in connection with sacred stones.[3] These stones are not of the sort with which one troubled with any ailment rubs his back or head,[4] in which case they are used as charms, and are supposed to belong to some saint, as at Berzeh; nor are they of the same sort as at the shrine of St. Rih, which is reverenced by all sects, where there is a round stone like a heavy ring, weighing five or six pounds—large enough to go over the wrist. The saint, by means of this stone, manifests his power. There are two pillars, between which a bastard cannot pass,[5] at Ezra in the Hauran, and upright stones, between which bridal couples must walk, as at a village in the Druse

[1] Journal I., Safita, autumn of 1898.

[2] Journal VI., Negran, Tell Shaf, Smed., summer of 1900.

[3] Among the Tongas there is a "natural stone about nine feet high, called the stone that is not to be pointed at; people would not point at it on any account." Journal X., W. L. Thompson, M. D., spring of 1901.

[4] Journal XI., Hamath, summer of 1901: "At Sheik Mustafa, in the center of the makam, is a stone made smooth by rubbing. The sick man uses it for his back. He does not vow to it but to the weli. The stone belongs to the weli, he is not in it. God blesses it."

[5] Journal XIII., Mr. Faris L. Khuri, Damascus, summer of 1901.

MAR (ABU) RISHA AT KARYATEN.

THE LOCAL DIVINITIES 85

Mountains,[1] and stones which receive the sacrificial blood, as in the Sinaitic Peninsula.[2]

The stones used in healing are evidently not regarded as the places where the saints reveal themselves, but there are others which are more or less clearly considered as being the place of divine revelation. Abu Ali, a devout Moslem, said:

"No one knows where the saints really are, but they know where they have appeared. There is a saint who appears near my house; his name is Abu Zed. At Asal there is a stone, into which my own patron saint entered."

"At Sphene, in northern Syria, there is a Maronite shrine of Mar Yehanna, which consists only of an ancient stone, about three feet high by fourteen inches wide, in the shape of a panel, standing on a hill under a grove, near a modern church. The other sides are triangular. [It is probably part of the lid of a sarcophagus]." A man said of the remains of incense which were in front of the stone, that the incense had been offered to the weli. His expression seemed to indicate that he regarded the weli as residing in the stone.

"At Karyaten, the last outpost for travelers making the journey to Palmyra . . . . in the vineyard, at the rear of the house of the governor of the town, known as Feiyad, is a prostrate pillar, by the side of which, about midway and close against it, is a structure of mud about the size and shape of a straw beehive; in the side of this is a small hole, where the vessel is placed in which the oil that has been vowed is burned, when a vow is paid. The shrine consisting in this pillar is called by the Moslems Abu Risha, and by the Christians Mar Risha.

[1] Private letter from Mr. Henry C. Harding, Kerak, winter of 1901.
[2] Palmer, The Desert of the Exodus, New York, 1872, p. 218.

It is in honor of a saint of the sect of the Jacobites. The pillar is thought by the Syrian priest to mark the site of an ancient church. It is surrounded by a low wall, leaving an inclosure about twenty feet square. The practices in making a vow and in payment of it among the Moslems and Christians are the same. They come to the shrine and make their request; they also tie red and blue silk around the weeds in the inclosure as a sign to the saint that they want help. Payment, as has been intimated, is made in oil, which is burned at the altar." [1]

Here, then, is a sacred stone, part of the ruin of an ancient church, which is revered by ignorant Moslems, and Christians as a weli.

At Sheik Sa'd, near el-Merkez, the capital of the Hauran, is a Moslem place of prayer; in it, just in front of the prayer niche, is the Weli Sakhret Eyyub, or Shrine of the Rock of Job, seven feet high and about four feet wide. It is a monument of Ramses II., has a representation of his head in the right hand upper corner and an inscription in hieroglyphics. It is significant that it is in front of the prayer niche. Here is undoubtedly a case of syncretism, of Moslem and ancient Semitic worship combined. Unfortunately this is a theory, which did not occur to me at the time when I visited Sheik Sa'd, and which there was no opportunity to put to the test, but I have no doubt that the natives regard it as a sacred stone. There can be no question that such a stone, in such a position, would be considered by the ignorant Moslem as the dwelling place of a weli.[2]

[1] See my article, "Ancient Shrines in Northern Syria," The Independent, Vol. L., pp. 1448, 1449.

[2] Journal V. El-Merkez, summer of 1899. Cf. Dr. Schumacher, Zeitschrift des Deutschen Palästina-Vereins, Vol. XV., p. 147: " I therefore assume that the present building over the Sachrat Ejub

THE ROCK OF JOB AT SHEIK SA'D.

THE LOCAL DIVINITIES

The most conscious example of the survival of the ancient worship of rocks or stones, as the abodes of spirits, is found in the popular belief of ignorant Moslems that a weli resides in the "Rock Chair" (*Kalat el-Kursi*) or "Chair of the Companions" (*Kursi el-Aktab*). While those who are more orthodox say that the companions of the Prophet Mohammed come on Fridays, and find their abode in a room which the servant of the shrine has never seen, the ignorant believe that they are to be found in the rock itself.[1]

There are quite a number of passages in the Old Testament, notably, though not exclusively, in the thirty-second chapter of Deuteronomy, where "rock" is as much a term for God as El or Elohim.[2] These two last terms belonged to other branches of the Semitic family as well as to the Israelites. In the same way it seems likely that the term "rock" was used by other Semitic stems for the Divine Being as well as by Israel. There are various Old Testament passages where the term "rock" is predicated of God, as fortress or stronghold would be predicated,[3] but there are others where it is as

---

originated in the Arab age before Islam. . . . . It probably served the heathen Arabs as a place of worship, according to whose tradition, as is known, Job lived in this place." The inscription has been read by Erman, ibid., pp. 210, 211.

[1] Journal X., Kursi, el-Aktab, summer of 1901. "The common people believe that the spirits dwell in the rock." "Any day you can summon them by prayer. Friday is better, and the day of sacrifice (dahhiyeh, the tenth of the pilgrim month) is the best of all. There is a room where the ten companions meet, only those to whom God has revealed it know where it is." While then the common people think that the ten leaders (Aktab, that is, poles, leaders) are in the stone, the representative Moslems give what they think is a higher idea, namely, that they meet in a room.

[2] Deut. xxxii. 4. "Ascribe ye greatness unto our God. The Rock, his work, is perfect." Cf. vs. 15, 18, 30, 31. Cf. 2 Sam. xxiii. 3; Is. xxx. 29.

[3] Ps. lxii. 2.

88 PRIMITIVE SEMITIC RELIGION TO-DAY

truly a designation of God as El, or Elohim. May it not be that this name for God among the Semites may go back to a time when the rock was looked upon as the medium of divine revelation? Indeed it seems pretty clear that while rock is used in some passages as fortress is used in others, that there are passages where rock is as spiritual a designation for God as Elohim, and where it is employed without reference to its original Semitic signification.

It seems quite clear that when Jacob took the stone which he had put under his head as a pillow, and raised it up as a pillar, poured oil upon it, and called it "House of God" (*beth Elohim*),[1] he was on the same plane as the ignorant Moslems to-day, who conceive of the weli, who is practically their God, as dwelling in a rock.

The most remarkable use of stones that I have seen is in connection with the shrine of the Prophet Job (*Nebi Eyyub*) at Busan, in the Druse Mountains. In front of this shrine are three broken pillars, three and a half feet high. They are the only examples I have seen of the pillars (*mazzeboth*), of which we read so often in the Old Testament, which seem to have been regarded as legitimate at one period of Israel's history, as at the conclusion of the covenant at Mount Sinai, when Moses set up twelve pillars in connection with the altar.[2] This use of pillars, which seems to have passed without reproof in the earlier history of worship,[3] was condemned in the Deuteronomic code[4] and the Deuteronomic history.[5]

There are conspicuous examples among modern

[1] Gen. xxviii. 18, 19, 22; xxxv. 7.
[2] Ex. xxiv. 4.
[3] Gen. xxxi. 13; xxxv. 14; Hos. iii. 4; Is. xix. 19.
[4] Deut. xii. 3; xvi. 22; cf. Ex. xxxiv. 13.
[5] 2 Kings iii. 2; xvii. 10; xviii. 4; xxiii. 14.

THE LOCAL DIVINITIES 89

Semites of the revelation of saints in the neighborhood of sacred waters. Sometimes the saint seems to be considered merely the proprietor of such a stream as at Nebk, in the Syrian desert,[1] which I shall discuss in another place. The stream is regarded as belonging to the saint, rather than as the means of revelation. But it may be a question, whether the distinction between the saint and the water spirit who inhabits the stream is clearly drawn in the minds of the people, since the defilement of the stream is regarded as equivalent to the defilement of the saint himself, as is evident from the language used.

The Sabbatic fountain in northern Syria ('Ain Fowar), is considered as belonging to St. George; and yet sacrifices are brought to the fountain rather than to the shrine itself.[2]

The hot springs at Callirrhoe (Zerka Main) are regarded as being under the control of a saint (*weli*) or spirit (*jinn*), who makes the fire and keeps it burning. The natives, who go to be healed of their rheumatism, invoke the spirit to keep up the fire, so that the water may be hot, and to this end they offer sacrifices.[3]

[1] Journal X. Damascus. Interview with Rev. J. Stewart Crawford: "One section of the village attributed the saint's displeasure to the fact that another section had performed certain religious ablutions in the courtyard of the shrine, and that the dirt had come on the saint to his disgust."

[2] The Independent (personal visit, autumn of 1898), Vol. L., p. 1447, note 3.

[3] Journal VIII. Interview with Mr. Henry C. Harding, at Kerak, summer of 1898. The same custom obtains when they visit the hot springs (Zerka Main). They believe that the furnace is in charge of a jinn who must be placated before he will make up the fire to heat the water. Mr. Harding heard a man all the time he was in the bath invoking the spirit. Cf. Journal VI., Zerka Main, summer of 1900.

"After lunch, Mr. Forder and I went to the source of two of the springs bursting out of the mountain. Over them were sticks on which the Arabs sit wrapped up in their abbas, and thus they get

At Hamath, in the court of a lunatic asylum, which is simply a place where the insane may be kept securely by putting the most violent in irons, there is a small pool, or fountain, which is called a weli, and which is visited by Moslem women.[1]

Such sacred waters, and many more which might be mentioned, are of the same sort as those described in some manuscripts of John v. 2, 3, though excluded by the Revised Version as not belonging to the original text; "Now there is in Jerusalem by the sheep gate a pool, which is called in Hebrew Bethesda, having five porches. In these lay a multitude of them that were sick, blind, halt, withered." The additional matter not included in the revised is evidently an outgrowth of the old Semitic belief in sacred waters under the control of a spirit: "Waiting for the moving of the water: for an angel went down at a certain season into the pool, and troubled the water; whosoever then first after the troubling of the water stepped in was made whole of whatsoever disease he had."

There are numerous examples of sacred trees among Syrians and Bédouin from one end of the country to the other. Some of these are at shrines, and are sacred merely as the property of the saint. They are as inviolable as anything else that belongs to him, or that has

vapor baths. Mr. Forder says they offer sheep, taking them by their legs and dipping them in." Ibid. Arab camp two hours from Zerka Main: "The Arabs say they consider the hot springs at Zerka Main a weli, so whenever anything is the matter with their flocks they offer a sacrifice."

[1] Journal XI., Hama, summer of 1901: "At the insane asylum of Hama there is a pool to which they take the robe of a troublesome child, and wash it. . . . . The reason for the virtue is that in the pool is a certain weli. . . . . He is the patron saint of all insane people. He appears at night and blesses the insane by touching them." At this so-called asylum I saw a stalwart madman with a heavy chain about his neck. The only asylum in Syria and Palestine is at Asfuriyeh, near Beirut, recently founded by Mr. Theophilus Waldmeier.

SACRED TREE HUNG WITH RAGS.

been put under his protection. At the same time they may be conceived of as sacred from the general notion that the saint reveals himself through the medium of trees. Thus Mr. Harding writes: "Trees, however, are honored apart from welis. A tree near Gaza el-Maisi is distinctly held to be indwelt by a divine spirit, and accordingly receives divine honors. Where a tree is connected with a weli it probably was the original object of honor."

There are many trees, apart from shrines, which are believed to be possessed by spirits, to whom vows and sacrifices are made. Such trees are often hung with rags or bits of cloth. It is not easy to determine the significance of the rags. Some say they are intended to be a constant reminder to the saint of the petition of the worshiper, like a string tied around the finger;[1] others that the rag taken from the ailing body of the suppliant, and tied to one of the branches, is designed to transfer the illness of the person represented by the rags to the saint, who thus takes it away from the sufferer and bears it vicariously himself.[2] Sometimes the man who is ill takes a rag from the tree, as one tears off a bit of the pall from the cenotaph of the shrine, and carries it about on his person, and so enjoys the advantage of virtue from the saint.[3] It may be that in this use of rags we have

[1] Journal I., Karyaten, Vineyard of Feiyad, with the Rev. J. Stewart Crawford, autumn of 1898: "They also tie red and blue silk around the weeds in the inclosure (of Mar Risha) as a sign to the saint that they want his help."

[2] Journal X., Beirut, William Van Dyck, M.D.: "The suppliant, who approaches a sacred tree, tears off a piece of his garment and ties it to the tree, by which he commits to the weli his sickness. He then takes a bit of the rag from the tree which he carries about with him and by which he receives healing from the tree."

[3] See The Independent, journey of 1898, loc. cit. p. 1448. The teacher at Mehardeh in northern Syria told of a sheik among the

92   PRIMITIVE SEMITIC RELIGION TO-DAY

the same idea as that found in Acts xix. 11, 12: "And God wrought special miracles by the hands of Paul; insomuch that unto the sick were carried away from his body handkerchiefs or aprons, and the diseases departed from them, and the evil spirits went out."

There is no doubt that in the minds of the people sacred trees are places where spirits reveal themselves. Near 'Ain Fijeh, one of the sources of the Barada, thought to be the ancient Abana of Scripture,[1] is a weli, called Sheik Rihan, decorated with flags. A peasant woman said that it was customary for the people to make a vow to give such flags if their petitions were fulfilled.[2]

Doughty mentions angels, or "the power of the air," who come to a sacred grove, under whose leafy canopy one who is ill lies down and finds recovery, while he who is well, who takes the same liberty, receives only a curse for his presumption. Flesh is hung upon such trees as if it were the food of the spirits residing in them.[3] There is a similar custom of hanging meat in the branches of the trees among the Tongas, though my informant was not certain what was the intent of the natives.[4]

It has been pointed out that we have two clear traces of sacred trees in the Old Testament, one is of the burning bush, upon which Moses looked, wondering that it was not consumed, and out of which God spoke,[5] an

Ismailiyeh who carried about some of the hair of the sacred virgin in his keffiyeh.

[1] 2 Kings v. 12.

[2] Journal X., Ain Fijeh: The woman "spoke as if the spirit were in the tree, and only said that she asked God when Mrs. John Crawford of Damascus, who was my interpreter, reminded her that it was wrong to pray to a tree."

[3] Op. cit. Vol. I., p. 449.

[4] Journal X. Interview with W. L. Thompson, M.D., spring of 1901.

[5] Ex. iii. 2-4.

THE LOCAL DIVINITIES 93

obvious use of ancient tree worship, though in the revelation of God to Moses clearly avoiding the superstitious notions connected with it. A similar vision was lately seen at a weli. A holy man at Nebk reported that he saw in flames a sacred walnut-tree which was by the shrine of the saint.[1]

So, too, the sound of the going in the mulberry-trees, for which David was to wait, was nothing less than the divine voice speaking to the sweet singer of Israel, in accordance with ancient conceptions.[2]

Trees under which saints rested are considered holy.[3] Here there is the same notion as with respect to sacred places among the ancient Israelites. The seat of a theophany was ever afterwards regarded as sacred, for where God had revealed himself once he was likely to reveal himself again. This is clearly indicated with respect to the Mount of Jehovah, which must have been understood to indicate the site of the temple, for we read: "And Abraham called the name of that place 'Jehovah sees,' as it is said to-day in the Mount of Jehovah, 'he is wont to be seen.'"[4] Indeed, all the ancient shrines of Israel had been consecrated by some theophany, and men went there in the expectation of its repetition.

Trees are also objects of worship. As the term weli is

---

[1] Journal X. Nebk.

[2] 2 Sam. v. 24.

[3] Journal X., Beirut. Interview with Dr. Van Dyck: "There is a wild myrtle in the valley below .... which is referred to a man known as the Lord, who is believed in by the Druses, and who passed through the country working wonders. As he journeyed he rested under trees, which from that time on assumed miraculous powers."

[4] Gen. xxii. 14. This was most likely written in the belief that Abraham received a revelation from God on the site of the Temple.

applied to them, a saint is evidently conceived of as residing in them. In a Turkish village in northern Syria, there is a large and very old oak-tree, which is regarded as sacred. People burn incense to it, and bring their offerings to it, precisely in the same way as to some shrine. There is no tomb of any saint in its neighborhood, but the people worship the tree itself.[1]

The discussion of caves, as the dwelling places of spirits, is germane, in this connection, if we consider that there is a point in Semitic thinking where there is no essential difference between deity, saint, and spirit. There is, undoubtedly, a tendency to differentiate these beings, to give God the highest place as the author of good and evil, the saints the next place, with much the same functions as God, and to distinguish between beneficial and harmful spirits. But it is quite likely that the original Semitic conception was much simpler, namely, that the primitive idea of a divine being was that of spirits, who might be friendly or hostile to men. When we remember that the sacrifices to spirits are precisely of the same sort as those to saints, and that sometimes the distinction between the spirit and the weli does not seem to be clearly drawn—as at Zerka Main, he may be considered a weli, or may be regarded as one of the jinn—it is evident that the notion of divinity is not sharply defined among the ignorant, whose minds furnish the most perfect mirror of ancient views about divine beings.

There are doubtless many caves to be found in Syria, some of which are conceived of as being under the control of a weli, and some as inhabited by jinn. One of the former class is resorted to by mothers who have an insufficient supply of milk for their children;[2] a second

[1] The Independent, loc. cit. p. 1446.
[2] Ibid. p. 1447.

THE LOCAL DIVINITIES

is a place visited by married couples who are childless and who desire offspring.[1]

Near the foot of Mount Carmel, above the sea, is an artificial cave which is said to have been tenanted by the Prophet Elijah, which is visited by all the sects, and known by the Moslems as Khuddr. I saw this cave in the summer of 1901, and had an interview with the Moslem minister, or custodian, who said, when speaking of the income which came to him through the weli, "Khuddr is my God and my father's God; he has supported us for years."[2] Thus there was put into concrete form a confession which expresses the belief of many an Arab and Fellahin, as to the being upon whom he depends in the hour of his distress, and who exerts the greatest restraint upon his life.

[1] Journal X., summer of 1891; An American physician, living in Syria, who is childless, said "he was recommended by a native to visit a cave near Juneh, where barren women go attended by their husbands. There is a pool in the cave. They first bathe together in the cave, and then expect their marriage will be fruitful."

[2] Journal XIII., Haifa, summer of 1901.

CHAPTER VIII

DEIFIED MEN

Inasmuch as the teaching of the Moslem creed insists, "there is no god but God," it is easy to see, that wherever Islam has sway, it excludes anything like the deification of men; nevertheless we have seen in the preceding chapter, that the saints, once men, are treated as divine. They are addressed directly in vows and prayers. Blasphemy against Mohammed is a state offense,[1] and ignorant Moslems sometimes offer prayers directly to him.[2]

Wherever heresy exists, and the working of the native mind is untrammeled by fear of being unorthodox, we may observe two phenomena, which are none the less significant, although they are found among a people who may be descended from a Canaanitish stock. I refer to the Nusairiyeh, in northern Syria, who are commonly reckoned among the Shiites, of whom the Ismailiyeh,[3] a closely related sect, the Druses,[4] and the Babites[5] are conspicuous examples. Indeed the Turkish government,

---

[1] Journal X., Damascus.

[2] Journal XIII., Brummana, summer of 1901.

[3] Journal XII., summer of 1901.

[4] For a brief account, see Sell's Essays on Islam, London, 1901, pp. 147-184. The classic authority on the Druses is De Sacy, Exposé de la Religion des Druses, I, II, Paris, MDCCCXXXVIII.

[5] Browne, A Traveller's Narrative, written to illustrate the Episode of the Bab, Cambridge, 1891; New History of Mirza Ali Muhammad the Bab, Cambridge, 1893; Sell, op. cit. pp. 46-98; Andreas, Die Babis in Persien, Ibre Geschichte und Lehre quellenmäsig und nach eigener Anschauung dargestellt, Leipzig, 1896. The titles of numerous books and articles on this sect may be found in Browne, op. cit.

in order to remove the Nusairiyeh from the influence of Protestant missions, classifies them as Moslems to-day, but with no good reason, as must appear to any one who has the opportunity to look into any of their sacred books.[1] They are divided into the initiated and the uninitiated. For one of the initiated to disclose the secrets of the sect means death.[2] These were made known years ago by an entire unbeliever through the medium of the famous Dr. Van Dyck, of Beirut, father of Dr. William Van Dyck. While at Beirut he wrote his treatise in the house of the Rev. Henry H. Jessup, D.D. Lulled into security by the promises, fair speeches, and abounding hospitality of his former coreligionists, he was afterwards lured to Mersina, where he was buried alive.[3]

There is every reason for believing that the book, which was published about 1863, and which was translated in part by Professor Salisbury, of Yale College, and issued with the text in the Journal of the Oriental Society, 1866, contains a true account of the ceremony of initiation, as well as of the tenets of the initiated. A sheik of the Nusairiyeh, who was very intimate with a Protestant pastor, confessed as much to him two years ago.[4] They went over the book in detail, and the sheik uttered no dissent, except with respect to prayers con-

---

[1] A good idea of these may be had from Salisbury's translation of the book by Suleiman of Adana, supplemented by Lyde, The Asian Mystery, London, 1860.

[2] It is customary to appoint twelve sponsors for each one who is to be initiated. The Imam inquires: "In case he discloses this mystery, will ye bring him to me, that we may cut him in pieces and drink his blood?" Journal of the American Oriental Society, Vol. VIII., p. 232.

[3] Journal XII.

[4] The name is not given, for obvious reasons, but I had an interview with the pastor, a most trustworthy man.

sisting in curses, in which other sects are mentioned.[1] The existence of such curses in the ritual of the Nusairiyeh he denied. But his denial did not persuade his Protestant friend. He was soon suspected by the Nusairiyeh of revealing the secrets of their religion. Nothing but the strongest affirmation that there had not been any such interview freed him from immediate death. The information contained in this chapter is not derived mainly from the book of Suleiman of Adana, or from books about the Babites. I made a journey into the mountains of the Nusairiyeh, visited Ain Kurum, a village where lawlessness is rife, where there are no marriage rites, boys of fifteen and girls of ten meeting and pairing in the romantic and dark recesses of the beautiful woods, leaving the matter of dowry to be decided in angry dispute by their parents after the consummation of a marriage. It was to this place, perched on the side of a mountain, that a neighboring village came, several hundred strong, two years before, and attacked the men of Ain Kurum, leaving ninety dead, and thus lighting the flames of blood revenge which will not be extinguished for generations.[2]

Sixty Turkish horsemen visited the same place to collect the taxes, and had such a bellicose reception that they begged for their lives. The only night we spent there was made wakeful and anxious by clamor and frequent shots.

As by reason of the blood feud with the village, an

[1] "Whoever desires salvation from the glow of infernal fires let him say . . . . 'Curse thou those who play with apes . . . . together with all Christians and Jews. . . . . Moreover, lay thou thy curse upon John Marun the patriarch . . . . and upon all those who feed upon thy bounties, while they worship thee not.'" Journal of the American Oriental Society, loc. cit. p., 273.

[2] Blood revenge is still the most binding institution of ancient Semitic life in Syria, Palestine, and Arabia.

DEIFIED MEN 99

hour and a half distant, we were unable to take the usual way into the western country of the Nusairiyeh, over their mountains to Ladikiyeh, we were compelled to make a steep and very difficult ascent under the guidance of one of their religious sheiks. We saw one of our mules roll over and over for more than a thousand feet down an incline that seemed almost perpendicular. We heard the despairing cry of the muleteer, and the appeal of our sheik to Khuddr. Wonder of wonders! thanks to our baggage, which broke the force of his fall, we saw the mule rise to his feet. Our muleteers, overcome by thirst, and their exertions over this fall, and others which followed, were, after seven hours of climbing, when they reached one of the most beautiful forests[1] is Syria, ready to lie down and die. It was then that the greed of the religious sheik came to the surface. As we sat down in one of the shadiest nooks of that beautiful forest, and our muleteers seemed in the last stages of collapse, he told of a spring of ice cold water, frequented by beasts of prey, which he would show us for a good bakshish. After he had led us to this spring, we went through fastnesses which no Turkish soldier could

[1] There are perhaps three really fine forests in Syria and Palestine, some might say four, and even more: 1. The cedars, *par excellence*, near the valley of the Kadisha. 2. Over the Nusairiyeh Mountains, on the way from Ain Kurum to Matwar, is "a primeval forest of oak, perhaps the finest in all Syria." Journal XI., 3. From Ain Jenneh to Irbid: "For the first four hours one could hardly see in any country a more delightful region. . . . . Here are old forests." Merrill, East of the Jordan, New York, p. 181. "The ride was delightful for about three hours. There is no other like it that I have seen in eastern or western Palestine. . . . . The trees are not more than twenty or twenty-five feet high, but the tops are handsome. One has the delightful experience of riding a long distance in the shade." Journal V., summer of 1899. Another forest may be seen on the way from Arak el-Emir to Wadi es-Sir. There are pine forests that have been planted and fostered at various points, but the finest natural forests are those just mentioned.

attempt, past a high place—a conical hill, towering in solitary grandeur, crowned with one of the most beautiful, awe-inspiring groves imaginable. At last we reached an entirely different kind of life among the foothills of the mountains. We sought protection from a sheik, a noble-looking man, surrounded by men of fine appearance. We caught glimpses of comely women, who were in sharpest contrast to their degraded sisters at Ain Kurum, for theirs was the happier lot of a life comparatively free from violence and mere animalism.

Accompanied by Rev. James S. Stewart of Ladikiyeh I visited a company of Christians in a village of the Nusairiyeh, and received most interesting information from them, though they were still under the dominion of ancient Semitic ideas, in spite of their Protestant training.

On our return journey we went to Behammra, where Lyde, the first English missionary labored, built mission premises, which, with one exception, are in ruins. In Lyde's own home we gathered, and heard of the indignities from which he suffered in being yoked with an ass to a plow by the barbarians to whom he was attempting to preach the gospel. It required some finesse to keep away spies who came to listen, and who might have caused the death of our informant had they heard all that was told us. They were emboldened by a governor of the Turkish government, disputing the claim of the mission of the American Reformed Presbyterian Church to the property. Through the courage and skilful diplomacy of the American consul, Mr. G. B. Ravndal, of Beirut, this property was saved to the mission, and the official who had made himself so offensive was removed.

It is not a reassuring sight in such a region to see a band of armed men watching the highway by which you are approaching, or to have them follow you, however friendly their subsequent professions may be. This, to me, at the time, was an alarming experience, though my missionary companion, accustomed from childhood to tales of murderous raids by the Bedouin, showed no sign of fear; to him it was merely an incident of travel.

We spent a night in Musyaf, a lonely, walled town of the Ismailiyeh, after we had traveled through their country with two mounted guardsmen who had been sent to overtake us from the picturesque and romantic town of Kadmus. Musyaf is the place where the chief of the Assassins once lived in Syria, Rashid ed-Din, with whom Saladin had to come to terms, though he had attempted Saladin's life repeatedly through his minions. These were so completely under his control that, at a given signal, two of them threw themselves down from a high tower to a violent death, in order to demonstrate to a visitor, Henry, count of Champagne, their implicit obedience, and to strike terror into his heart.[1] Here, three years before, I was under arrest, because I did not have a passport (*tezkereh*). We were guarded by four soldiers at night, on my second visit, by command of the governor, who marvelled at our presumption, which would have been prevented could it have been foreseen. But in the eyes of the government "might makes right," and an act questionable before its performance is condoned if it has been accomplished.

In the same way my visit to Abbas Effendi, the head of the Babites, was not effected under easy circumstances. Quarantine had shut off all regular communication of Beirut with Haifa, except by "Prince George," derisively known as the "Jolly Boat," which can furnish

[1] Porter, The Order of The Assassins, The Bibliotheca Sacra, Oberlin, Ohio, 1895, p. 129.

as great a complement of human misery as any craft afloat. The Moslem, the inmate of the harem, and the Chicago professor had the touch of nature that sometimes makes all the world kin at sea. The day after my arrival I spent nearly four hours with the head of the great Persian sect, who is really a prisoner at Acre, and who is recognized by Frenchmen, Russians, and Americans, notably by some American ladies of fortune, as an incarnation of God himself. I had the honor of dining with Abbas Effendi, and of taking afternoon tea with him. He seemed to throw off all reserve, was eager to welcome me as a possible disciple, and when I left "the master," as he is invariably called by his followers, he voiced the hope, evidently adapting a New Testament expression, that we might drink tea together in the heavenly kingdom. Besides this interview, and reading all the works that were at hand, by Abbas Effendi's permission, I had an interview with his private secretary.

While it is true that neither the Nusairiyeh, nor the Druses, whose heaven, as we have seen, is in China,[1] nor the Babites, who are a Persian sect of comparatively recent origin, and have been strongly affected by New Testament and Christian teaching, belong to the Semitic stock, as we have seen, I do not feel that I should drop them wholly out of this investigation. They furnish some good illustrations of the deification of men, though in all these Shiite sects this idea has been modified by their gnostic notions, their hospitality to Neo-Platonism, and a pantheistic philosophy, all of which elements appear in Sufiism.[2]

While the Nusairiyeh, like the Druses, assume in public the guise of Islam, which they change on occasion

[1] P. 62.
[2] Ellis, op. cit., pp. 1–45.

DEIFIED MEN

like a "garment,"[1] we have in them the contrast between the survival of ancient heathenism, in the worship of heavenly bodies,[2] which they identify with Ali, the cousin and son-in-law of Mohammed, and his deification as a spiritual being. The ancient worship of the heavenly bodies comes to the surface because the heretical sect of the Nusairiyeh does not exercise any such restraining influence as Islam, and because the uninitiated, at least among the Nusairiyeh, have never been purged by a purer faith from the popular worship of the sun and moon.

It is not difficult to trace the process by which Ali has come to receive ascriptions of praise as a divine being, such as are not found in the orthodox literature of Islam.[3] The sect of the Shiites, of which the Nusairiyeh are a subdivision, view with indignation the treatment that Ali received with respect to the succession in the caliphate. Instead of being the immediate successor of the prophet, he was not the recognized head of the Moslems until Abu Bekr, Umr, and Uthman had preceded him. As indicating how lasting is the feeling of the Shiites, the Nusairy bride, when she is washing herself preparatory to her nuptials,[4] curses the first three caliphs who succeeded Mohammed. But the most influential cause in bringing this indignation to white heat

[1] "They simulate all sects. . . . . The simulation of sects is set forth by them allegorically, as follows: We, say they, are the body, and all the other sects are clothing; but whatever sort of clothing a man may put on, it injures him not." Salisbury, Sulaiman on the Nusairian. Religion, loc. cit., p. 298.

[2] "They hold that God is the sun and moon. . . . . God is called Ali, the highest. They are divided into two sects, some believe he is in the sun, others that he is in the moon." Journal XI., Country of the Nusairiyeh. Cf. Salisbury, op. cit., pp. 300, 301.

[3] Salisbury, op. cit., p. 278.

[4] Journal XI., Behammra.

was the assassination of Ali, the supposed assassination of his elder son, Hasan, by an inmate of his harem, who, as the Aliites falsely claim, was bribed to do the deed by the caliph, and the assassination of his younger son, Hosein, by a cruel emissary. The pathos of his ending has never been forgotten. The lips that had fondly kissed those of Mohammed became cold in death. Passion plays are still annually celebrated at Kerbela, where he met his death. All its bloody details are repeated before the horrified populace, who still utter loud lamentations, as if their taking off had just occurred, and who, with pale and quivering lips, call out these names, Hasan and Hosein as of beloved first-born.[1] The fact that Hasan was a weak character, and won the title of divorcer, on account of his numerous matrimonial ventures, makes no difference in the popular esteem.

There can be no doubt that the poignant sense of the injustice done to Ali has contributed largely to his deification. On the one hand, he is regarded by the heirs of the ancient heathen worship of the heavenly bodies as being in the sun; others think of him as in the moon, while the angels are the stars, and the true believers are identified with the Milky Way.[2] There are indeed traces of such worship of the heavenly bodies among ignorant Moslems. A missionary was trying to teach the children of a Moslem woman that they were descended from Adam and Eve. "No," said the woman; "the moon is our father and the sun our mother."[3] Here, then, ignorance and heresy have joined hands to transmit the worship of the heavenly bodies, mentioned so often and with

[1] Testimony of an eye-witness, Journal XII. Cf. Muir, Annals of the Early Caliphate, London, 1883, p. 442.
[2] Nofel Effendi Nofel, History of Religion in Arabic.
[3] Miss M. T. Maxwell Ford of Safed.

so much reprobation in the Old Testament.[1] Even to-day many ruins of ancient sun temples remain. Rev. Franklin E. Hoskins, of Beirut, of the American Presbyterian Mission, has made important investigations with respect to ancient sun temples, which have never been published.[2]

Even to-day many ruins of ancient sun temples remain. The outlook is toward the east. The situation is most beautiful, whether on some mountain summit, as on Mount Hermon,[3] or on the Anti-Lebanon, opposite some notch in the mountain, where the worshiper could catch the first rays of the rising sun. Mr. Hoskins has found more than twenty-five such temples. Some of them exist in pairs, one being in the village, and the other on the mountain.

There are rites among the Nusairiyeh in other parts of the country, which indicate a worship of the heavenly bodies, such as the turning of silver coins to the moon, as a presentation of the coin, indicating the worship of that body. There can be no question that the ignorant and uninitiated among the Nusairiyeh worship the heavenly bodies, and it is likely that the initiated are not entirely free from that worship.[4]

[1] Deut. iv. 19; 2 Kings xxiii. 11; Ezek. viii. 16.

[2] It is to be hoped that Mr. Hoskins will find the time to complete his researches and to give them to the learned world.

[3] It seems to me there can be no question that, whatever may be determined as to the ruins as they exist to-day, there was a time when the sun was worshiped from the summit of Hermon. A platform can be traced which faces toward the east.

[4] Mr. Jabur of Nebk, a very intelligent Syrian, thinks the real religion of the Ismailiyeh and the Nusairiyeh is an ancient heathenism. He says that the sun, moon, and stars are worshiped in the northern portion of the country. He maintains that under the pretense of worshiping Ali, they worship the heavenly bodies. I consider this merely a conjecture which is not supported by facts. Journal XII.

106 PRIMITIVE SEMITIC RELIGION TO-DAY

Some adore the heavens and the twilight, while others adore the sun and moon. This adoration is indicated by symbolical acts. Those who adore the heavens and the twilight, when they recite a certain prayer, indicate it by the symbolical act of placing "the right hand upon the breast" and "applying the inner part of the thumb to the middle finger." "While among the worshipers of the moon," when engaged in the same prayer, "some spread out the hand with the thumb erect, so that it has the shape of the new moon, and others place both hands upon the breast, opening them wide, with the fingers of one over those of the other, and two thumbs erect, so as, in this way, to represent the shape of the moon."[1]

Lyde says that the Nusairiyeh are divided into two sects, the "Shemseeh" from "shems," the sun, and the "Kumreeh" from "kumr," the moon. He reports that his servant told him, "that his people, who are of the Kumreeh sect, are extremely 'afraid' of the sun and moon, and pray to them." He says, also, "that it is a common thing for the women and children to speak of the moon (which probably looks greater to them) as the face of Ali, and the sun, as that of Mohammed."[2]

The deification of Ali by the Nusairiyeh has become complete. It rests on the principle that "spiritual things appear in physical forms," thus "the Angel Gabriel was incarnate and came in the form of a Bedouin, and Satan may appear in human form, so, too, the jinn, and God himself. As there is no prophet higher than Ali, and after him his sons, because they are the best of the creation, God revealed himself through them, and therefore they call them gods. . . . . They apply a saying of Mohammed to Ali: 'I judge by externals, God knows

[1] Salisbury, op. cit., pp. 254, 255.
[2] Lyde, op. cit., pp. 138, 139.

DEIFIED MEN 107

the secrets.' They believe that Ali had charge of all the secrets of God. . . . . They maintain, judging from Mohammed's statement, that he considered Ali equal to Christ. Ali existed before the heavens and earth. He was on the right hand of the divine throne before his incarnation."[1] He is not only regarded as the incarnation of God, as having ascended to heaven without dying, but he is considered as God, as the first cause, as the creator of the heavens and the earth, and as the only God. When this point has been reached it is easy to see how it comes in conflict with the facts of history. Hence there are those of the Nusairiyeh who deny *a priori*, that Ali had children.[2] As they affirm that women were created from "the sins of devils," they could not well conceive of a divine being having connection with a daughter of the devil; indeed, they deny that their religious sheiks have any such connection, and claim that their children are begotten through passes which these leaders make with their hands over the bodies of their wives.[3]

Among the Druses, who are classed as a Moslem sect, but only wear the Moslem or any other faith as a cloak or defense in time of danger, and who hold an esoteric teaching, which one reveals at the peril of his life, there is the deification of a man, Hakim, whose wickedness and cruelties were the terror of his time, and are among the marvels of history.[4] And yet this monster of wicked-

[1] Unpublished MS.
[2] Journal XI. Cf. Lyde, The Asian Mystery, p. 116: "The Ansaireeh do not suppose Ali to have been flesh and blood, but rather a luminous appearance. They speak of his acts as *zahir*, apparent only. For instance, says the Ansairee lad, they say he was not really married; for how, say they, could he be, being God?" Salisbury, op. cit., p. 253.
[3] Salisbury, op. cit., p. 297.
[4] Sell, op. cit., pp. 147 ff.

ness has been deified by the Druses, and they confidently look for his second coming.[1]

In treating of the Babites, we have to deal with a sect which began in the year 1844, though its immediate parentage was from the Shaikhis, which is also an outgrowth of Shiism, and has some points of similarity with the Nusairiyeh and the Druses. Though a heretical sect of Islam, and a hybrid of the teachings of Islam and the Bible, especially of the Gospels, and with an ancestry extending back to the Sufis, it is, in its aims, its ideals, and in the men and women that it has produced, by far the noblest sect born of Islam. Its founder, those who suffered martyrdom with him, and many more who have endured a like fate, have won the sympathy, and largely the approval, of those who have studied their system and portrayed their lives.[2]

So far as Babiism is founded on the philosophical

---

[1] Ibid, p. 176.

[2] Browne, op. cit., p. 226: "Kazem-Beg says . . . . that one day, falling into an ecstasy, Mirza Ali Muhammad discovered that he was the Bab, the gate of truth." Bab is the Arabic for gate. It is interesting to note that the related sect of the Nusairiyeh use the same term of Bab. Lyde, op. cit., p. 110 writes: "The Ansaireeh believe in one God, self-existent and eternal. This God manifested himself in the world seven times in human form, from Abel to Ali son of Abu-Taleb, which last manifestation was the most perfect; that to which the others pointed, and in which the mystery of the divine appearances found their chief end and completion.

At each of these manifestations the Deity made use of two other persons; the first created out of the light of his essence, and by himself, and the second created by the first. These, with the Deity, form an inseparable trinity, called Maana, Ism, Bab.

The first, the Maana (meaning,) is the designation of the Deity as the meaning, sense, or reality of all things.

The second, the Ism (name,) is also called the *Hedjah*, or veil, because under it the Maana conceals its glory, while by it it reveals itself to men.

The third, the Bab (door,) is so called because through it is the entrance to the knowledge of the two former . . . . The third person in the trinity is the Bab . . . . who in the time of Adam was Gabriel, and in the time of Ali was Salman-il-Farisee, the Persian."

system of Sufiism, it does not belong in our discussion; but so far as it deifies certain men, and is closely connected with the sects already mentioned, it should not be passed by.

Sell, in his able essay on The Mystics of Islam, has shown how Sufiism has furnished the philosophical basis for Babiism. God is the primal element. In creation he came forth from internal to external manifestation. He is being; man and all created things are not-being. Not-being is the mirror in which being is seen. Indeed, the infinite includes all being, evil as well as good, but as evil is inconsistent with the goodness of God, as set forth in the Koran, evil is said to proceed from not-being. All that exists is God, and nothing exists apart from him.[1]

It is not difficult to see how, on the basis of such a philosophical system, the Babites hold that certain men are as truly mirrors of deity as Jesus Christ was. Indeed, Abbas Effendi pressed this illustration upon me as explaining the incarnation. Holiness of character is not necessary to the idea of such an incarnation: "To the man of God right and wrong are alike."

Sinlessness, then, is not indispensable to any of these incarnations. Indeed, it is not claimed for Ali, or Hakim, or the Bab, or Beha, or Abbas Effendi.

If we turn to the Old Testament we shall find a practical tendency of the Semitic mind to deify man. This may be a survival of a time when the distinction between gods and men was not sharply drawn, to which allusion has already been made. At any rate, men have the term god applied to them in the Old Testament. Jesus Christ himself alludes to this when he says: "If he called them gods, unto whom the word of God came."[2] This refers

[1] Sell, op. cit., pp. 3 ff.
[2] John x. 35.

to certain passages where judges and rulers are termed Elohim.[1] We find a similar usage in the Tell-el-Amarna tablets. Various kinglets, including those of Beirut, Sidon, Tyre, Hazor, Jaffa, Lachish, and others, in writing to the king of Egypt, address him as "my gods" (*ilani-ja*). Thus Abi-milki of Tyre writes: "To my lord, the king, my sun, my gods."[2]

Following the same analogy, we seem to have in the forty-fifth psalm a conspicuous example of the deification of a Messianic king. The psalm, according to modern interpreters, celebrates the nuptials of a prince and princess. There is good reason to believe that the prince was of the house of David, perhaps Joram, and the princess of the northern kingdom, Athaliah, the daughter of Ahab and Jezebel. This is a theory which was held by Delitzsch, which I rejected when he stated it to me in the first critical work that he assigned me. But now it seems to me far more probable than any other theory which has been proposed. All the historical allusions seem to me to point this way. In a single verse which, as an epitaph, sums up the achievements of Ahab's reign, only two are mentioned, "the ivory house which he built, and all the cities that he built."[3] Hence, the erection of an ivory house is made exceedingly conspicuous as it could hardly have been, if such a palace had been built before. It is also said that the Tyrians (*bath Zur*) would be there with a gift, which would well be the case when the daughter of Jezebel was to be married. Nor can there be any doubt that this is an earthly king, for not only his queen, but also, according to

[1] Ex. xxi. 6; xxii. 7–9; 1 Sam. ii. 25; Ps. lxxxii. 1.
[2] Winckler, The Tell-el-Amarna-Letters, New York, 1896, *in loc.*
[3] 1 Kings xxii. 39.

the customs of the times, his harem is mentioned. There is also the hope expressed of a numerous posterity: "Instead of thy fathers shall be thy children, whom thou shalt make princes in all the earth."[1] These are to take the place of their ancestors. When, therefore, this king is addressed, "Thy throne, Elohim, is forever and ever; a scepter of equity is the scepter of thy kingdom. Thou hast loved righteousness, and hated wickedness. Therefore, Elohim, thy Elohim, hath anointed thee with the oil of gladness above thy fellows," we have the same term applied here to the Messianic king as to the theocratic judge, who, each in his place, was regarded as a representative of God. The fact that the historical Joram fell so far below the ideal of the Messianic king who was to wage war in behalf of truth and of the lowly but righteous ones, could not affect the hopes of the psalmist, who found in the union of a prince of the southern kingdom with a princess of the northern an occasion to paint an ideal of Messianic hopes and expectations, colored by the conceptions of the time, but which the Spirit of God does not find an unworthy medium in New Testament times, setting aside the purely local features, for expressing the divine sonship of Jesus Christ.[2]

[1] Ps. xlv. 12-16.
[2] Heb. i. 8, 9.

CHAPTER IX

THE PHYSICAL RELATION OF MAN TO GOD

In the discussion of primitive Semitic religion to-day, it is necessary for us to consider the physical relation of man to God. But only rather obscure traces are to be found of the physical fatherhood of Deity among modern Semites. The subject cannot be discussed by making use of veiled expressions. I shall try not to offend against delicacy, but must use words which are unambiguous.

There is perhaps no clear proof of the existence of the notion that God is the father of a clan, tribe, or family. For this there is a sufficient reason in the fact that such an idea would be most repugnant to Islam as well as to ancient Christianity. Here, if anywhere, old Semitic ideas should have become extinct.[1] I can present only such hints as I have found in certain expressions and usages, and leave the reader to draw his own conclusions. These hints are not limited to the representations of God, since it seems quite certain, that to the ignorant mind, as I have observed, there is practically no clear distinction between the divine powers of God himself, and those of the saint, or the departed spirit; each in his own domain may exercise an authority, which to the simple peasant, or the Bedouin, is what we should term supernatural and divine.[2]

We have seen how the conceptions of God are human-

[1] For these ideas, see W. Robertson Smith, Lectures on the Religion of the Semites, New York, 1889, pp. 41-43.
[2] P. 77.

THE PHYSICAL RELATION OF MAN TO GOD   113

ized, while those of "the saints" are deified. We need, therefore, in order to make an intelligent induction, to examine every expression, or usage, which indicates that spiritual existences may have the power of fatherhood. It is certain that we cannot be sure of finding such traces at any given point, but coming to us from many points, often unexpectedly, they may be none the less significant. Were we to ask the question, "Is there evidence that God is regarded as the physical father of any clan, tribe, or people among the modern Semites?" we should be compelled, as far as my investigations have gone, to answer, "No." There is no such clear-cut statement, so far as I am aware, of a belief among the modern Semites of the physical fatherhood of Deity, such as is said to exist among the Tongas, who affirm, "God had three sons, the whites, the Zulus, and the Tongas."[1]

I found the investigation leading to data necessary in order to form a conclusion, delicate and difficult. Not because the modern Semite hesitates to discuss such themes, quite the contrary; but because the facts which have a bearing upon the subject are more likely to come to light by indirection and when least expected, than by any formal inquiries.

There seem to be pretty clear indications that ignorant Moslems and Christians conceive of God as possessed of a complete male organism, and that this is not merely popular language. Moslems at Hamath, in northern Syria, swear by God's phallus.[2] In the village of Bludan, about twenty-five miles west from Damascus, which is composed of Greek Christians of a very low type, the same oath is heard on the lips of women,

[1] Personal Interview, W. L. Thompson, M. D., missionary of the A. B. C. F. M., Mt. Silinda, East Central Africa.
[2] Journal XI., summer of 1901.

114   PRIMITIVE SEMITIC RELIGION TO-DAY

who sometimes are so shameless as to giggle when using it, thus showing that they are conscious of its meaning.[1] Another form of oath of a similar sort may be heard in Nebk, in the Syrian desert, and at Zebedani.[2]

At Kerak, whenever there is a drought, the Greek Christians dress a winnowing fork in women's clothes. This they call "the bride of God." The girls and women carry it from house to house, singing doggerel songs.[3] This expression, "bride of God," naturally reminds us of the "bride of the Nile," who, according to a tradition given by Lane, was anciently thrown into the arms of the river god, when the water began to rise.[4]

There is a further illustration, from another country, which shows how far superstition may descend in lowering the conception of God. Some ignorant members of the Greek Church in Syria speak of the Virgin Mary as the "bride of God." We do not know what they may understand by this term, but in Porto Rico a Catholic was living openly with a woman to whom he was not married. When rebuked by a Syrian, who was residing in that country, he replied that there was no wrong in what he was doing, for he was simply following the example of God, who still lived with the Virgin Mary.[5]

[1] Testimony of Rev. J. Stewart Crawford, who has his summer home at Bludan.

[2] Suleiman, teacher in the Irish Presbyterian Mission at Nebk, and Abdullah, teacher in the American Presbyterian Mission at Hamath.

[3] Letter from Mr. Henry G. Harding, formerly of Kerak, now of Gaza, of the Medical Mission of the C. M. S. of Great Britain; cf. Frazer, The Golden Bough, London, 1900, Vol. I., pp. 95, 213.

[4] Lane, An Account of the Manners and Customs of the Modern Egyptians, London, 1896, p. 500: "The Arab general was told that the Egyptians were accustomed at the period when the Nile began to rise to deck a young virgin in gay apparel, and throw her into the river as a sacrifice to obtain a plentiful inundation."

[5] Journal XI.

THE PHYSICAL RELATION OF MAN TO GOD 115

Among the Ismailiyeh there is said to be a sacred maiden, whose distinctive features, eyes, and color of hair are known from their holy books, and whose body is considered the abode of Deity. She is introduced into the sacred assemblies of the initiated, and stands exposed before them. She was once seen for a moment by a Protestant Syrian, who went to call on an intimate friend among the Ismailiyeh. Fearing for his life he fled, and emigrated to a foreign land. This sacred maiden is said to be descended from the Son of God.[1]

Procreative power is attributed by the Syrians to the spirits of the dead. It is well known that they affirm that the jinn may have sexual intercourse with men and women; of this fact Baldersperger has given some fresh examples.[2] It is said that women sometimes find that their best gowns, which they had carefully locked up in their bridal chests, have been worn and soiled by female spirits during their confinement, because they did not utter the name of God when they were locking them up.[3] But the view that the spirits of the dead may beget children is held to the extent that it is believed a widow may conceive by her husband, for nine months after his death. It is said that a woman at Nebk took the bath of ceremonial purification [4] because she dreamed she had received a visit from her deceased husband.

[1] The custom to which allusion is made has been repeatedly charged to the Nusairiyeh, and as often denied by Protestants who know them intimately. The circumstance mentioned in connection with the Ismailiyeh was detailed to me by a credible witness, who heard it from the Syrian, with whom he was well acquainted, and who was compelled to flee for his life. The point of this incident is that this young woman is alleged to be directly descended from the Son of God.

[2] Palestine Exploration Fund, Quarterly Statement for 1899, London, pp. 148, 149.

[3] Journal X., Nebk, summer of 1901.

[4] Ibid. Cf. Lev. xv. 18.

There is a man in Nebk who is currently believed to be the offspring of such a union, and no reproach was ever cast upon his mother. There is also a person in Nebk who is considered, by simple people, to be the child of a jinn.

Another form of the same belief is doubtless in a singular custom, of which I have heard of two examples. When a man had been executed for murder at the Jaffa gate in Jerusalem, more than thirty years ago, some barren woman rushed up to the corpse.[1] It may be that they felt that, inasmuch as the man had been released by death from previous nuptials, and was free, as a disembodied spirit, he was endowed with supernatural power to give them the joy of motherhood by proximity to his dead body.

We also seem to find the same idea in the connection of barren women with the spirits of sacred shrines of various sorts, or with those whom, in their ignorance, they suppose to be spirits.

It is said that they visit the hot springs at a certain place, of which the name is unknown to me, and take practically a steam bath, the weli being considered by them as the source of the vapors.

About four hours from Karyaten, on the way to Sadad (the Zedad of Scripture),[2] are the so-called baths of Solomon, where there are extensive ruins of buildings on a grand scale. Only part of the arches that supported the superstructure now remain. There are three places where the hot air comes out of the ground, many yards apart. One of these is in the floor of a room of considerable size, with walls and a roof of stone. The heat

[1] Journal VIII., summer of 1900, Rev. J. Edward Hanauer of Christ Church, Jerusalem. Cf. Lane op. cit., p. 267.
[2] Num. xxxiv. 8.

is so intense that it is not possible to endure it many minutes. The other hot air vents are in the field. One of these, called Abu Rabah, is a famous shrine for women who are barren and desire children. They really regard the weli of the shrine as the father of children born after such a visit, as appears from the rendering of an Arabic couplet, which they repeat as they go inside the small inclosure, consisting of a rude stone wall about four feet high, and allow the hot air to stream up their bodies.

> "Oh, Abu Rabah!
> To thee come the white ones,
> To thee come the fair ones;
> With thee is the generation,
> With us is the conception."

The native teacher's wife said she knew of two barren women who had recently had children after visiting this shrine. When a child is born as the result of such a visit, it is customary, after the immolation of the victim, to partake of a meal which is eaten in the shade of the vaulted ruin near by, and to which the friends of the family from the neighboring villages are invited.[1]

Almost equally significant is another curious custom in connection with some of the channels of the Orontes, used for irrigation. During a certain season of the year, the water is turned off and the channels are cleared of mud and any matter which might clog the flow of the water. The first night that the water is turned on it is said to have the power of procreation (it is called *dekr*). Barren women take their places in the channel, waiting for the embrace of the water spirit in the onrush of the stream.[2]

Naturally there are also shrines to which barren

[1] Journal I., Karyaten, autumn of 1898, Syrian teacher's wife.
[2] Journal XII., Homs and Braigh.

women go that they may have the reproach of childlessness removed. Sometimes the woman stands at a Christian shrine below one of the saint's pictures, covered with a wire netting with some projecting points, and taking her head-dress in her hand, tries to drive a sharp bargain with the saint for the gift of the desired child. Giving the cloth a fling toward the wire netting, she bids one piastre;[1] if it catches on one of the projections, she considers it a sign that the saint will give her a child, and that after its birth she is to pay the sum of one piastre. If, however, the cloth falls, she understands that her offer has been rejected, and that the saint insists on more money; so raising up the cloth, she gives it another fling, and says, "two piastres." This she does until it catches. When this takes place she goes away in the firm belief she is to have a son, and with the understanding that when he is born she is to bring to the shrine the sum last named.

There are, however, barren women of all sects, including Moslems, who go to the shrine of the most powerful saint in all Syria. There are many natives who shrug their shoulders when this shrine is mentioned in connection with women. But it is doubtless true that many do not know what seems to be its true character, and who think that the most puissant saint, as they believe, in the world can give them sons. Why should not ignorance and superstition, in the eagerness for children, in some cases be unsuspicious? If a dead husband can be the parent of a child; if Abu Rabah can give seed; if a woman can conceive by a water spirit; why should she not believe a monkish tale that St. George (*Mar Jirjis*) will be a husband to her and give her conception?

The famous shrine of St. George was once visited by

[1] Journal I., Safita, autumn of 1898.

many Moslem women who desired offspring, and who went with the full consent of their husbands. But the true character of the place is beginning to be recognized, so that many Moslems have forbidden their wives to visit it.[1]

There is a cave at Juneh in which there is a pool of water to which the same power is attributed. The natives believe that a childless couple who bathe in the waters of this cave will have children. Undoubtedly the cave is supposed by them to be inhabited by a weli, who has, as the peasants think, the power to make a barren marriage fruitful.[2]

To sum up, the idea that a weli may be a physical father is one of which there is more than one example, and the notion is currently believed, as we have seen, that disembodied spirits may still beget children from mortal women, either those who have been their own wives, or from others; while it is commonly held that a jinn may have an earthly wife, or that a man may have a spirit wife who will not tolerate his looking at any woman. These phenomena seem to point back to a time, already considered, when there was no distinction between God, the weli, the departed spirit, and the jinn. Hence the being to whom the Semite did homage was endowed with physical fatherhood. If, now, we regard the departed spirit, who is held in love and reverence, hence enjoys the title of weli, as the only deity who has any practical bearing on the life of the modern Semite, we may claim that the idea of the physical fatherhood of deity still exists.

[1] Journal XII., village near Hamath. I had one incident described to me from the lips of a man who visited the shrine, and who is one of the most trustworthy in all Syria.

[2] Journal X., Beirut, William Van Dyck, M. D.

There are various indications of a relationship between men and divine beings. The term weli, as I have shown, indicates the one who may be nearest of kin, hence the one, according to the Arabic version, to marry the childless widow of a brother, or of one closely related.

From this point of view, it is perhaps significant that the grave of the weli is often, among the graves of his tribe or clan, the most conspicuous of them all.[1]

But more than this, there are clans and families who claim to have sprung from one original ancestor, who is also a patron saint or weli. These are to be found among certain tribes of Arabs.[2] While, as we have seen, some of the Nusairiyeh make such high claims for Ali as to deny that he had children, there are others who claim that they are descended from Ali through Nusair.

The idea that God may have sons by physical generation is common among all peoples who speak of him as a man. There is one passage in the Old Testament which seems to have taken its color from such an old Semitic conception. I refer to Gen. vi. 1-4: "And it came to pass, when men began to multiply on the face of the ground, and daughters were born unto them, that the sons of God (*benai Elohim*) saw the daughters of men that they were fair; and they took them wives of all that they chose. . . . . The Nephilim were in the earth in those days, and also after that, when the sons of God

[1] Personal observation in many parts of the country.

[2] Ebers, Durch Gosen Zum Sinai, Leipzig, 1872, p. 239: "Die Sawâleha-Beduinen halten Schech Salih für ihren Anherrn und glauben, dass er ihrem Stamme den Namen gegeben." Cf. Journal XII., interview with the chief of the Rawaeein at Mehardeh: "They make their vows to patron saints, and these are mostly progenitors of tribes." . . . We inferred that the subdivisions of the Aneze and others have patron saints. As to the descent of the Nusairiyeh, Journal XI., at Behammra.

came in unto the daughters of men, and they bare children to them; the same were the mighty men which were of old, the men of renown." In the light of Semitic modes of thought, I do not think the interpretation which has been regnant in certain circles since the time of Augustine and Chrysostom, that the sons of God were the pious Sethites and the daughters of men were Canaanitish women, was at all intended by the writer. It is questionable, too, whether angelic beings, as we understand the term, were intended. So far as the meaning of the passage is concerned, were not the Sethites men? Did they not begin to multiply upon the earth? Did they not have daughters born to them? Were there not fair women among them? It seems to me that nothing but a desire to render the scriptural narrative edifying has led to this traditional interpretation, which is clearly allegorical. I am well aware that the term "son," in Semitic speech, is often not to be taken too literally, but here it certainly indicates superhuman beings, at least what we might call demigods. Out of their connection with earthly women are born men of extraordinary physical development. We are no more to go to such a passage for doctrine than to other passages in the Old Testament for teaching regarding the future state.[1] We are not, however, to suppose that any Old Testament writer thought of God as a physical father, though some appear to speak of heathen gods as if they were real existences. We have, as it seems to me, the true reading given by Wellhausen, in the Polychrome text of Ps. lviii. 1:

> "Speak ye indeed what is right ye gods?
> Do ye judge men without partiality?
> Nay, rather, on earth are your judgments confusion,
> Your hands weigh out what is wrong."

[1] Job iii. 13-18; Is. xiv. 9, 10.

It is from this point of view, in which the writer acknowledges their real existence, that Wellhausen well says: "The gods are not human rulers. They are divinities worshiped by the heathen, and placed by *Jhvh* at the head of the nations, Ps. xxix. lxxxii. They are held responsible for the conduct of their subjects. If they are righteous gods, they must maintain righteousness and justice within their domain. In point of fact, their rule is thoroughly discredited by the disorderliness and licentiousness of their subjects (v. 3-5). . . . . Seeing, then, that they fail in their duty, or are incompetent for their task, *Jhvh* himself must interpose, and execute justice against the heathen, in order that it may be seen that there is one Supreme Deity upon the earth who judges."

So the sons of God, whoever they may be, come to present themselves before the Lord, as if he held a court like an earthly king. Hence, the writer sees no impropriety in the Adversary presenting himself also, and receiving permission to lay his hand on Job.[1] It is thus that an ancient Semitic conception of divine beings, called Elohim, but not regarded as men, is alluded to in a way which would escape the reader of the ordinary English version. While the Old Testament writers never conceive of men as having physical relations to God, they do not hesitate to speak of the sons of God as having children, as we have seen, or of heathen gods as having offspring. This appears from two passages quoted by W. Robertson Smith:[2]

> " Woe to thee, Moab!
> Thou art undone, O people of Chemosh:
> He hath given his sons as fugitives,
> And his daughters into captivity,
> Unto Sihon king of the Amorites."[3]

[1] Job i. 6-12; ii. 1-6.   [2] Op. cit., pp. 42, 43.   [3] Num. xxi. 29.

THE PHYSICAL RELATION OF MAN TO GOD 123

Here, then, it is the Moabite god Chemosh who gives up his children. The phraseology of the following passage in this connection is very significant: "Judah hath profaned the holiness [sanctuary] of the Lord which he loveth, and hath married the daughter of a strange god."[1] This view of the heathen divinity, like that in the passages cited above, looks upon them as real existences, who have the power of physical fatherhood. The ancient as well as the modern Semite did not philosophize, nor see any inconsistency in acknowledging the existence of heathen deities, as subordinate to the government of God, and as having children, like the Moabites, who were sprung from their loins. In the same way, while the modern Semite does not clearly think of God as procreator, he certainly holds that a disembodied spirit, whether that of an ordinary man, or of a weli, can become a physical father.

[1] Mal. ii. 11.

CHAPTER X

MORAL RELATION OF MAN TO GOD

We have seen that to the ignorant man or woman, a spirit, a departed ancestor, or saint may stand in the place of deity.[1] It is important that we should consider the relations of the people to such a being.

Theoretically there is syncretism. The Moslem, everywhere, confesses that he believes in one God, but the Fellahin, the Arabs, and the Bedouin, not to speak of many others, including multitudes of women, believe a great deal more firmly in some weli or spirit, as the one who can help in the time of trouble. God is far away, the spirit or saint is near. God is so far away that the consciousness of him seems to be lost as a force in life. If any one doubts this, let him travel from one end of Syria, through Palestine to the Sinaitic Peninsula, and observe how the sacred shrines dominate almost every hilltop; how they are to be found in almost every village; how they are in the wilderness, apart from any human habitation, where the nomads can insure the safety of their flocks from disease, from wild beasts, and raids of hostile tribes, by timely vows. Let him interview the people and he will find that the saint is a real force in their lives.

In considering the relation of man to God, to saint, or spirit we have to deal with one word which furnishes the key. That word is known among us as sin; among the modern Semites it is often equivalent to misfortune; that is, sin and misfortune are practically correlative terms among the ignorant. Rev. W. K. Eddy, of Sidon,

[1] See pp. 77, 94.

who was born in Syria, and who knows the language and customs of the people thoroughly, says that it is a common expression among the people to-day: "O Lord, what is my sin" (*ya rubb khattîtî*)? It is to be doubted, whether there is much consciousness of sin among the ignorant, without misfortune. There are indeed two crimes that are often acknowledged as shameful, and hence as sins; these are adultery and murder.[1] But even the latter, when undertaken on a raid or in blood revenge, is, in the estimation of the modern Semite, no murder. Doubtless there are lawless men among the Bedouin, who, in their thoughts of a future life, owing to the instruction of the sheiks of Islam, may confess that they are fit candidates for the fire.[2] But the great mass of the sons of the desert, if they give any thought to the matter at all, doubtless have the spirit of bravado and assurance expressed in the language of one of them, as reported by Palgrave: " 'What will you do on coming into God's presence for judgment after so graceless a life?' said I one day to a spirited young Sherarat, whose long, matted lovelocks, and some pretensions to dandihood, for the desert has its dandies, too, amid all his ragged accoutrements, accorded very well with his conversation, which was nowise of the most edifying descrip-

[1] Palgrave, op. cit., p. 33.
[2] Some Arabs told Miss T. Maxwell Ford that they were going into the fire. Cf. Doughty, op. cit., Vol. II., pp. 381, 382: "'And tell me, what can so bind to religion this people full of ungodly levity and deceitful life?' 'I think it is *the fear of the fire* (of hell) that amazes their hearts! all the time of their lives.' Fire is the divine cruelty of the Semitic religions." But in the index Doughty qualifies this general statement, by applying it to Moslems." (Ibid., p. 580. " Fire of hell! 'the dread of — in Moslem hearts.'") It is evident that Mohammed preached physical torments, Koran, IV., 59: "Verily, those who disbelieve our signs, we will broil them with fire; whenever their skins are well done, then we will change them for other skins, that they may taste the torment." Palmer's translation. Cf. Ibid., xvii. 5-7; xxxviii. 3-9, etc.

tion. 'What will we do?' was his unhesitating answer. 'Why, we will go up to God and salute him, and if he proves hospitable (gives us meat and tobacco), we will stay with him; if otherwise, we will mount our horses and ride off.' This is a fair specimen of Bedouin ideas touching another world, and were I not afraid of an indictment for profaneness, I might relate fifty similar anecdotes at least. Nor did I ever meet, among the genuine nomad tribes, with any individual who took a more spiritual view, whether of Deity, of the soul of man, or of any other disembodied being soever. God is for them a chief, residing mainly, it would seem, in the sun, with which, indeed, they in a manner identify him . . . . somewhat more powerful than their own head man . . . . but in other respects of much the same style and character. The spirits of their frequent ghost stories . . . . are, for all their diabolical propensities, very corporeal beings, and can even intermarry with the human race. . . . . The souls of the dead, for their part, are little better; they are pleased with, nay require, sacrifices at their tombs, and the blood thus shed nourishes and satiates them."[1]

The Bedouin and ignorant Syrian has every reason to believe that his relations with the being he regards as most powerful are good until some misfortune comes; in his misfortune is the evidence of his sin, and he seeks at once to put himself on good terms with the being he has offended by means of some gift.

The fact that sin and misfortune are regarded as essentially synonymous terms came out in a very impressive way in an interview with some Nusairiyeh who were Protestants. When visiting Jendairiyeh, with Rev. James S. Stewart, missionary of the Reformed Presby-

[1] Palgrave, op. cit., Vol. I., pp. 33, 33.

terian Church in northern Syria, I had a long interview with some of these people. To get their idea of the reason for misfortune, I asked Mr. Stewart to tell them, in outline, the story of the afflictions which befell Job,[1] and to ask them what they thought about them. They said at once, "That man must have been a great sinner." When they heard of the man that was born blind,[2] they said, "Either that man sinned in a previous state, or his parents must have sinned."[3]

In another part of Syria I heard of a Moslem whose wife, a virtuous woman, had borne him four children, but whom he adjudged as guilty of some secret sin because the children had died. He therefore proceeded to put her away.[4]

The governor of a certain town in Syria was considered by the people as a tyrant. He lost two sons; it was at once said that he had been punished for his unrighteous deeds. The Syrian who related the incident, a man of wide observation and rare intelligence, in commenting on the incident, said that when misfortune comes people begin to think about their sins, but do not recognize them otherwise.

Whenever, then, any member of a family falls ill, or a misfortune of any kind seems to impend, the conclusion is at once reached by those interested, that the saint is offended, and that his favor must be secured through the medium of some gift. Oftentimes the one who is afflicted, or some near friend or relative, promises to give something to the saint if the affliction is removed; or such a

[1] Job i. 13-19.
[2] John ix. 1.
[3] Journal XI. The Nusairiyeh as well as the Druses believe in the transmigration of souls.
[4] Journal XIII.

128   PRIMITIVE SEMITIC RELIGION TO-DAY

gift may be paid unconditionally. Where the orthodox view is maintained, that the saint is an intercessor with God, the vow is made as payment for his intercession. There is no such thing as a recognition of dependence upon the saints, so far as I am aware, among the Bedouin and ignorant peasants, except when things go wrong.

In these respects the modern Semite has the same conception of misfortune as equivalent to sin that the ancient Semite had. Of this we have a conspicuous example in the case of Job's friends,[1] and even in the time of Christ, for he felt called upon to correct the view of the populace, who held that the eighteen upon whom the tower of Siloam fell were offenders above all who dwelt in Jerusalem.[2]

The same idea appears in the Moabite inscription of King Mesha. "Omri was king over Israel, and he afflicted Moab for many days, because Chemosh was angry with his land."[3] No reason is assigned for this anger; it is something with which the king has to reckon. Because the king has suffered misfortune he argues that the god must be angry with him. The same King Mesha, when the battle goes against him, offers up his first-born son to his god. He would not have done this had he not believed, because of his defeat, that Chemosh was angry at him for some sin, and that the only way to appease his anger was by the sacrifice of his son.

Aside from the annual festivals, which are found only in connection with a small number of shrines, there would be no gifts at the great majority, if men and women did not fear some misfortune, or were not in actual danger

---

[1] Job iv. 7; viii. 6; xxii. 5-10.
[2] Luke xiii. 1-5.
[3] The Inscription of Mesha, vs. 4-6. Driver, Notes on the Hebrew Text of the Book of Samuel, Oxford, 1890, p. lxxxvii.

of it. In other words, there would be no sense of dependence on these welis; their cult would end. The modern Semite feels as dependent on their favor as the ancient Semite did upon the favor of the Baalim for good harvests. The motive for vows, gifts, sacrifices is in both cases the same.

The consciousness of sin as actual guilt is not ordinarily very strong among the Arabs and the Fellahin. They fear to swear falsely by their saints, but it is not because of the sin of false swearing. They swear falsely by God without the slightest compunctions, because they think that he is forgiving, and will not notice this misappropriation of his name. They fear to swear falsely by the saints, because they are afraid of their anger, and so of their punishment. If they have promised anything to the saint they are afraid to break their word for the same reason.

It is notorious that the mouths of many Arabs and Syrians are full of foulness. This is not merely the frankness which pertains to all the relations of life, in a way that is sometimes exceedingly embarrassing to English and American missionary ladies, but it arises from corrupt minds. They do not fear to use such language, although offensive to God, but it is related of the Nusairiyeh, that when they visit a certain shrine, they refrain from all obscene language, because offensive to the weli; yet when they have paid their vows, and are returning to their homes, they give free rein to their tongues.

The relation of the modern Semites to the saints is entirely different from that to God. The people are in fear of them, and seek to secure their favor through gifts, and to avert misfortune by a timely and satisfactory bakshish.

It will thus be seen that sin, as identified with misfortune, comes to be without ethical character. The conception of a powerful being, as such, is much like that of an earthly ruler, who makes right and wrong by edict. That which is pleasing to the ruler is right, that which is displeasing to him is wrong. It is in this way that Judah proposes that he shall be regarded by his father, if he does not return his brother Benjamin, when he says: "I will be surety for him; at my hand thou shalt demand him; if I do not bring him unto thee and set him before thee, then I shall have sinned against thee all the days."[1]

Thus, by the law of solidarity, all Israel is held responsible for Achan's disobedience in taking the devoted thing.[2] To the ancient Semite, as well as to the modern, spoil captured in battle would be legitimate. There would be no moral wrong in Achan taking from the spoil of the enemy, but the command of God made that wrong which would have been right under other circumstances. So there could ordinarily have been no wrong on the part of Saul and the people of Israel in appropriating the spoil of the Amalekites, but as God had decreed otherwise, it became a sin.[3] Later, when they fought against the Philistines and defeated them, after the slaughter of Goliath, and spoiled their camp, not a word is said by way of reproach.[4]

So long, then, as misfortune is regarded as equivalent to sin; so long as good and evil may come from God; so long as right is not right in itself, or wrong, wrong by its own nature; but right and wrong are made by God's decree, just as by any earthly potentate, the consciousness of sin, as guilt, is dulled, and men's minds are con-

[1] Gen. xliii. 9 (Hebrew).
[2] Josh. vii. 1-12.
[3] 1 Sam. xv. 2-24.
[4] 1 Sam. xvii. 53.

MORAL RELATION OF MAN TO GOD 131

fused. The forbidden thing becomes a means of wrongdoing, simply because it is forbidden, and not with respect to its ethical character, and the relation of men to spiritual beings becomes a matter of barter. If bakshish will avail to cover over almost any offense which an Oriental may commit against his government, it must avail in dealing with the only supernatural powers that he knows. Their favor may be secured and their anger turned aside, if a satisfactory gift is promptly made. Freed, then, from all dread in this sphere, what need the Arab or Fellahin, who has not come under the dominion of the teaching of Islam, fear for the future?

On the other hand, we find a marked advance in the conception of sin in the best of the Babylonian penitential psalms;[1] for in these at the first blush we seem to have reached a consciousness of guilt as profound as in the Old Testament. But a closer examination discloses the fact that sin is still revealed through misfortune, through the manifestation of the anger of some god or goddess. It is sin, too, concerning whose character the victim is unconscious, so that he has no idea how his misfortune has come upon him.

In his trouble he seeks the help of each known or unknown god or goddess. In true Oriental fashion, after he has called in vain without any hand being outstretched, he lies on the ground sobbing and kissing the feet of each god and goddess in turn. But there is no relief, and again he makes piteous appeal for mercy. What can he think in the midst of such misfortunes and such expressions of anger but that he is a great sinner?

As a result of this conclusion, he first makes a general confession of men's lack of insight, so that they cannot

[1] Zimmern, Babylonische Busspsalmen, Leipzig, 1885. pp. 61-66.

distinguish between good and evil, or between those things which are pleasing to the divinity and those which are not, and then he makes that pathetic confession of sin which we find at the end of the psalm, which may not be divorced from the Semitic idea of misfortune as sin:

"My god, my sins are seven times seven, forgive my sins.
"My goddess, my sins are seven times seven, forgive my sins.
"Known and unknown god, my sins are seven times seven, forgive my sins.
"Known and unknown goddess, my sins are seven times seven, forgive my sins.
"Forgive my sins and I will bow myself before thee in humility.
"May thy heart be glad as the heart of a mother who has brought forth.
"Be glad as of a mother who has brought forth, as of a father who has begotten a child.

It is clear from the above confessions that the Babylonian had made great progress beyond the primitive Semite in his consciousness of sin, and if he could have had the teaching of an Isaiah, he might easily have passed on to such a discovery of the true nature of sin as is indicated by the Old Testament saints.

CHAPTER XI

HIGH PLACES AND SACRED SHRINES

All readers of the Old Testament, whether scholars or not, are familiar with the passages which refer to high places, and the worship of the Baalim. Modern critics claim that according to the most ancient documents the patriarchs and some of the most devoted servants of God worshiped at these high places, and often under sacred trees. Thus Abraham builds his first altar and receives the first revelation which God makes to him under the terebinth of Moreh,[1] which, according to Baudissin, signifies the terebinth of the prophet;[2] that is, a place to which the people of the country came for information about those affairs which were beyond their ken.

The next altar which he builds is under the terebinths of Mamre in Hebron.[3] Here he pitched his tent, and here, in a place recognized as sacred, God revealed himself to him again.[4] In Beersheba he plants a tamarisk and calls on the name of Jehovah.[5] Later Isaac builds an altar there, and likewise calls on the name of Jehovah.[6] It is at this same place, and probably on the same altar, under the same tamarisk, that Jacob offers sacrifice.[7] It was under an oak that the angel of Jehovah appeared to

[1] Gen. xii. 6 and 7.
[2] Studien Zur Semitischen Religionsgeschichte, Leipzig, 1878, Vol. II., p. 224. I have derived valuable help from the work of Baudissin in the preparation of this chapter. Cf. especially Höhendienst der Hebräer in Realencyclopädie für Protestantische Theologie und Kirche, Leipzig, 1900, Vol. VIII., pp. 177–195.
[3] Gen. xiv. 13.   [4] Gen. xviii. 1.   [5] Gen. xxi. 33.
[6] Gen. xxvi. 25.   [7] Gen. xlvi. 1.

Gideon, and it was under the same oak that he built an altar.[1] It is at the oak in Shechem that the men of the city go to make Abimelech king.[2] It is not stated that these sacred trees were on high places, but this seems altogether probable.

The use of mountains and high places for worship among the early Hebrews provokes no reproof. Indeed that ancient, anonymous prophet, who is embodied by both Isaiah[3] and Micah,[4] says: "And it shall come to pass in the latter days, that the mountain of Jehovah's house shall be established in the top of the mountains, and shall be exalted above the hills, and all nations shall flow unto it."

It is on Carmel, a sacred mountain, that the Prophet Elijah repairs the altar of Jehovah that was thrown down.[5] It is upon a mountain that Abraham is directed to offer up his son.[6] It was on a mountain that Jacob offered up a sacrifice before parting from Laban.[7] It was on Mizpah, signifying lookout hill or mountain, whither Jephthah went to speak all his words before the Lord.[8] It is Mount Sinai or Horeb, which is called repeatedly the Mount of God,[9] upon whose summit God revealed himself to Moses,[10] and long afterwards to Elijah. The Mount of Olives was a place where David or his contemporaries were wont to worship God.[11] With reference to the use of high places for legitimate sacrifice, there are conspicuous examples. When Saul goes to get

---

[1] Judg. vi. 11, 21, 24.
[2] Judg. ix. 6.
[3] Is. ii. 2.
[4] Micah iv. 1.
[5] 1 Kings xviii. 30.
[6] Gen. xxii. 2.
[7] Gen. xxxi. 54.
[8] Judg. xi. 11.
[9] Ex. iii. 1; iv. 27; xxiv. 13; 1 Kings xix. 8.
[10] Ex. iii. 5; xxiv. 12.
[11] 2 Sam. xv. 30, 32. The imperfect indicates customary action.

HIGH PLACES AND SACRED SHRINES 135

information about his father's asses, he finds that the people have a sacrifice that day on a high place, which is followed by a meal, of which the invited guests do not partake until Samuel first blesses the sacrifice.[1] It was to Gibeon that Solomon went, after he had been made king, to offer a thousand burnt-offerings, because, as the writer says, "that was the great high place," and there Jehovah appeared unto him.[2]

This worship upon mountains, hills, high places, and under trees, was nothing new. It is found among other nations, and is of great antiquity. When the centralization of worship in Israel is emphasized under Josiah, the effort is made to do away with the worship on the high places, and to give effect to the command contained in Deuteronomy: "Ye shall surely destroy all the places, wherein the nations which ye shall possess serve their gods, upon the high mountains, and upon the hills, and under every green tree."[3] Hosea is the first ancient prophet who sets forth the true nature of this worship, which he regards as whoredom. He says of it: "My people ask counsel at their stock, and their staff declareth unto them: for the spirit of whoredom hath caused them to err, and they have gone a whoring from under their God. They sacrifice upon the tops of the mountains, and burn incense upon the hills, under oaks and poplars, and terebinths, because the shadow thereof is good: therefore your daughters commit whoredom, and your brides commit adultery."[4]

Jeremiah and Ezekiel characterize these places of worship more than once in similar terms: "For of old time I have broken thy yoke, and burst thy bands; and thou saidst, I will not serve; for upon every high hill and

[1] 1 Sam. ix. 12, 13.
[2] 1 Kings iii. 4, 5.
[3] Deut. xii. 2.
[4] Hos. iv. 12, 13.

under every green tree thou didst bow thyself playing the harlot."[1] "For when I had brought them into the land, which I lifted up my hand to give unto them, then they saw every high hill, and every thick tree, and they offered there their sacrifices, and there they presented the provocation of their offering, there also they made their sweet savor, and they poured out their drink offerings. Then I said unto them, what meaneth the high place whereunto ye go? So the name thereof is called Bamah unto this day."[2]

It is difficult, perhaps impossible, to determine whether any of the *bamoth* were artificial elevations—so Baudissin holds,[3] but on insufficient grounds, as it seems to me, because his argument is sustained by that which may be a doubtful reading in Ezekiel, namely, *ramah* for *bamah*. While there are a few passages where the term "houses of high places" occurs, and the parallelism sometimes indicates a sanctuary, it is evident from a few other passages that the word *bamah* not only indicates the high place, but also the sanctuary that was often erected upon it. In common usage it is applied to a building even in a valley. The terms employed indicate that the popular reference was to a building, in many passages where the word *bamah* is used. Thus we read that Solomon built "an high place for Chemosh the abomination of Moab, in the mount that is before Jerusalem, and for Molech, the abomination of the children of Ammon";[4] "that the children of Israel did secretly things that were not right against Jehovah, their God, and they built them high

[1] Jer. ii. 20.
[2] Ezek. xx. 28, 29.
[3] Op. cit., Vol. II., pp. 258, 259. Neither the LXX. nor Jerome understood that we have to do with an elevation. Cf. G. F. Moore, High Place, Ency. Bib., New York, 1901, Vol. II., col. 2,067.
[4] 1 Kings xi. 7.

HIGH PLACES AND SACRED SHRINES 137

places in all their cities";[1] and that Manasseh, "built again the high places, which Hezekiah, his father, had destroyed."[2] The verb *asah* (to make) is also used as a synonym of *banah* (to build). Sanctuaries, or houses, are also indicated by the words used for their destruction, as *nathatz* (to tear down),[3] and *saraph* (to burn).[4] The term *hishmîd* (to destroy) is less definite, but is probably to be understood with respect to the destruction of a building.

We have every reason to suppose that the Baalim were worshipped on the high places, where there were buildings as well as where there were none, under the shadow of trees,[5] or on the bare heights.[6] We have the term Bamoth Baal, used as the name of the place in Moab, whence Balaam could see Israel, where he erected seven altars for sacrifice, and where God met him.[7] This name also occurs in Joshua,[8] and is mentioned in the twenty-seventh line of the inscription of King Mesha. Not only the context of several passages indicates that the Baalim were worshiped on the high places, but the Baalim are directly mentioned in connection with the *bamoth*.[9]

We have no details in respect to the rites used in connection with the worship of the Baalim. Hosea indicates that the Israelites consider them the givers of their prosperity, whose favor they are to seek.[10] The worship is of a joyful character. There are feasts, new moons, and sabbaths.[11] At such times the people are decked with their jewels and are dressed in their best attire.[12]

[1] 2 Kings xvii. 9.
[2] 2 Kings xxi. 3.
[3] 2 Kings xxiii. 8.
[4] 2 Kings xxiii. 15.
[5] Hos. iv. 13.
[6] Jer. iii. 2.
[7] Num. xxii. 41—xxiii. 4.
[8] Josh. xiii. 17.
[9] Jer. xix. 5; xxxii. 35.
[10] Hos. ii. 7.
[11] Ver. 13.
[12] Ver. 15.

All is hilarity. In this there is syncretism, for the prophet represents the people as calling God Baali (my baal), as if the worship were intended for him, while the thought is somewhere else; as if a woman should call her husband John, by the name of her paramour Charles.

In the visit of Saul to Samuel, and in the account of his participation in the feast which follows the sacrifice, we have a glimpse of a meal which seems to have been conducted with piety and dignity. Doubtless most of the sacrifices were followed by such a meal. It was to such a yearly sacrifice that Jonathan reported that David had gone when Saul missed him from the royal table. There can be no question that this feast would follow the sacrifice at the high place of Bethlehem if there were only one. This is a legitimate inference from 1 Kings, iii. 2: "The people sacrificed in the high places, because there was no house built for the name of Jehovah until those days," interpreted in the light of the present usage of the people. The passages which describe the worship of the *bamoth* in a general way, affirm that the people "sacrificed and burned incense on high places."[1]

In the discussion which follows, on high places in Syria, Palestine and the Sinaitic Peninsula, I have drawn on my own observations throughout the countries named, supplemented by quotations from the works of Burckhardt, Conder, Ganneau, Tischendorf, and Palmer, which will be found in Appendix E.

My researches began in the autumn of 1898, during a tour in northern Syria, when I had the company of two missionaries of the American Presbyterian Board, Rev. F. W. March and Rev. W. S. Nelson, D.D., both of Tripoli, whom I have already named in other connections. My first observation of a sacred grove was at a

[1] 1 Kings xxii. 43; 2 Kings xii. 3; xiv. 4.

missionary station at Beinu. On making inquiry regarding a grove that I saw on a neighboring height, I was told that it was sacred. The following is the record in my journal: "One of the most beautiful and characteristic places in the vicinity of Beinu is what must anciently have been a high place, known in Hebrew as *bamah*. On the top of it are oaks, called sacred trees. There is also a Greek church among the trees, without a roof." I afterwards visited the grove. I found that there was a cave in connection with it, which doubtless has a sacred character, although I did not think of investigating the subject at the time. Inside the ruin were various places where incense had been burned. I was told that on the 7th of October, at the feast of Mar Sarkis, the people are in the habit of coming from all around to this high place and of bringing food for a feast. I was informed that they now celebrate a mass, as this is a Greek shrine, but twenty years ago they made their vows and brought bread or a sheep and gave to the poor.

I need not say that when I first recognized this as a high place and a sacred grove, it had for me the charm of a new discovery. From this time on every energy was spent in securing information regarding this characteristic of northern Syria; for while high places and sacred trees are to be found in almost every village and settlement from Syria to the Sinaitic Peninsula inclusive, not to speak of Asia Minor, Egypt, Abyssinia, and other countries, there is no part of the East where sacred groves and high places are so abundant and form such a conspicuous part of the landscape as in northern Syria. I saw more than fifty such in my journey from Beinu to Safita—a portion of the country which is rarely traversed by travelers. By interviewing peasants in the neighborhood of these high places, as well as congregations of

Protestant Christians, who had once been slaves of these superstitions, I was able to get a mass of testimony mostly consentient, which to my mind sheds at least some light on the history of Israelitish religion.

The next shrine that I investigated was at Musulleh, a settlement of the Nusairiyeh. Here we found a sacred grove around the tomb of Sheik Ahmed. The tomb was in the form of a large mound, about eight feet long, three feet wide at the base, but narrower at the top, and about three feet high, covered with white plaster. It was in an inclosure about a rod square, and surrounded by a rude stone wall about three or four feet high, with an entrance two feet wide on one side, with a long stone across the top, probably to exclude any one who might try to ride in. This was the general character of all these tombs, which were open to the sky. In one place the stone laid across the entrance was carved in the shape of an immense phallus. It was impossible to get an interview with the sheik of the village, who was reported, in the language of some society ladies, as "not at home." We were therefore compelled to question one of his servants. From him we gained the following information: "The spirit of the saint resides in the tomb. He would visit any desecration of the grove, such as the cutting or mutilation of the trees, with death."

We heard this latter statement repeated over and over again. On the tomb is a green cloth. If any one is ill he tears off a piece of the cloth and ties it around his neck or wrist, thus vicariously transferring the healing properties of the weli to himself. Those who are ill or in trouble come to the tomb and make their vow to the saint, promising him, in case of recovery, grain or sheep. In the event of a favorable issue, they make payment of what they have promised and use it as a meal at the tomb

HIGH PLACES AND SACRED SHRINES 141

of the saint. Any one who chooses may come and partake. I found it was also a universal custom that a feast was always instituted after the payment of vows, although often more than one sheep or goat is slaughtered, and sometimes even bullocks. Guests are often invited to partake of the meal which follows the sacrifice.

Another shrine, which we visited the same morning, is especially good for the eyes. The saint is an oculist. A man who has trouble with his eyes takes a cock, cuts off its head, puts a drop of its blood in each eye, gives the cock to some poor person, and his eyes get well. Another place belongs to Moslems and Christians. There are other examples where high places are held sacred by Moslems and Christians, by Nusairiyeh and Christians, by Greeks and Maronites, or by all the leading sects, of which I shall give examples later. At a caravansary we sought to get information as to whether the spirit of St. John (*Mar Yehanna*), which I have mentioned in another connection, was in the stone, before which we found incense. We got different replies. One said the spirit of the saint must be in the ground. But we said, "When the saint was buried, did not his soul go to heaven; what is there here?" The answer was, "We do not know anything about heaven, so that the place where his body was is the place where you are to worship him." In regard to another shrine, a man said, "If you are ill, you must go and lay your hand on his tomb and make your vow."[1]

---

[1] The account of these shrines is substantially as I recorded it about three years ago. Those which I have seen since are often in small rectangular buildings, with a dome, like the whited sepulchres of which Christ speaks (Matt. xxiii. 27).

A description of many of these shrines is to be found in other connections in this book, as it is impossible to disassociate them altogether from the discussion of local divinities, ministers, "holy men," etc.

Those who desire to see something of what has been already

We are now prepared to make an induction from the passages cited in the Old Testament, from my own personal observations and studies in northern Syria, from those things which came to my notice in Palestine and the Sinaitic Peninsula, as well as from the statements of eminent travelers quoted in Appendix E.

The sacred character of mountain tops is evident to any one who travels widely in the parts named. On Mount Hermon, near the highest summit, are the remains of more than one temple, as well as of small bones and ashes which lie on a bed of gravel around the ruins on the east side for more than one hundred feet, and in some places, for a depth of more than a foot and a half.[1] On Mount Gerizim there are not only ruins indicating that from ancient times it was a place of worship, but the Samaritans annually celebrate their passover there.[2] Sacrifices are also still offered, according to the testimony of travelers, on Mount Sinai and Mount Serbal.[3] It is doubtless true that from time immemorial these mountains, not to speak especially of Tabor, Carmel, and others, have been favored seats of worship.

made known on this subject by others will find some valuable excerpts in Appendix E. There has been much more published on this subject by travelers and scholars than in connection with any other part of my investigation.

[1] I know of no other way to account for the presence of this deposit, which has the appearance of ashes, and is intermixed with small bones.

[2] Appendix F.

[3] When Rüppel visited the top of Mount Serbal, in 1831, he found a circular inclosure of rough hewn stones, reached by rude steps of stone, placed against the shelving precipice leading up to it. His guide removed his sandals from his feet when he entered into the midst of it to pray, and afterwards told him that he himself had twice offered a sheep as a thank-offering, the first time after the birth of a son, and the second after his own recovery from illness. (Cf. Lepsius. Letters from Egypt, Ethiopia, and the Peninsula of Sinai. London, MDCCCLIII., p. 310. Note.)

SHRINE AND SACRED TREES OF NUSAIRIYEH AT DER MARIA.
AFTER REV. W. S. NELSON, D. D.

HIGH PLACES AND SACRED SHRINES 143

Nor can there be any question that the *bamoth* of the Canaanites and the Hebrews were sometimes the same as the *makams*, now observed from northern Syria throughout Palestine and in the Sinaitic Peninsula. We have seen that the *bamah* was not always a high place, that it often indicates a sanctuary, which may be in a city or valley, and which is evidently a building. In this respect the usage corresponds precisely to what we find to-day. The makam is the place of the saint. It is preferably on a hilltop, but may simply be a tomb of a saint in a rude inclosure under the open heavens, or the tomb may be in a little building, usually with a dome, called a *kubbeh*. Such a tomb may be in town or village, or even on low ground, like the makam of Abu Zenimeh, of the Sinaitic Peninsula, which is a frail hut by the shore of the Red Sea.

There can be no doubt that the sacred groves and sacred trees are essentially of the same character as those mentioned in the Old Testament, and that they exist in much the same places as of old, wherever trees can grow; at least one is often found near a makam. There is such a tree at Tell el-Kadi over the grave of a weli. There is also a sacred grove not far away. The only tree I saw in a ride of nine hours between Beersheba and Gaza was a sacred tree. The trees themselves, as we have observed, are sometimes the objects of worship. Though the name of the Baalim has perished in connection with these places, their cult is still observed.

CHAPTER XII

PRIESTS AND "HOLY MEN"

One of the surprises in the investigation of primitive Semitic religion to-day was to find that there is virtually a priesthood in existence at the shrines. They do not have the designation of priests; they are known rather as sheiks[1] of certain shrines, or as servants of certain saints. But their duties and emoluments correspond in some degree to those about which we read in the Old Testament.

In 1898 I heard that there was a priestly family connected with the shrine known as the "Mother of Pieces" (*Umm Shakakif*),[2] but could learn nothing further about it at that time.

Three years later, after discovering the "Chair" (*Kursi*), above the valley of ez-Zebedani, I had the great joy of having my first interview with the servant of the shrine, which consists, as we have seen, of a monumental rock, over thirty feet high, underneath which is a little cave known as a weli. Before making our visit, Rev. J. Stewart Crawford, whose summer home is in Bludan, had arranged to have the minister of the kursi ready to meet us on our arrival.

After climbing the steep mountain-side above the Moslem village of Madaya, where the servant of the kursi resides, we found him and a companion reclining under one of the sacred oaks, the largest of the group which are near the weli. He and his friend at once

[1] This is a common designation.
[2] See pp. 44, 45.

PRIESTS AND "HOLY MEN" 145

joined us on a flat rock behind the kursi, from which, however, the view of the source of the Barada was unobstructed. I have seen Moslems frequently at prayer, once in a police court in Damascus; once on a housetop, where I was spending the night; once under a sacred terebinth at Gadara (Mukes), where fifteen men, including our mounted horseman, went through their prayers; often by the roadside; and once on the way to Engedi (*Ain Jidi*). I saw the sheik of our Bedouin escort stop by a grave, where many of the clan seemed to be buried. While standing he engaged in an act of prayer. Moslems always prostrate themselves when engaged in their devotions. Our surprise was, therefore, very great when the minister of the kursi and his companion, standing side by side, and turning their faces toward the source of the Barada, which was west by south, engaged in prayer. Not once did they bend the knee. When they had finished the first petition they paused for a few moments, took a step forward, and resumed their prayer, then paused again, took another step forward, and then uttered the third and last petition. When we asked them afterwards why they did not look toward the south, toward Mecca, the Moslem Kibla,[1] they said, that, as their prayer was to the "God of the place," it was a matter of indifference which point of the compass they faced. It is needless to say that an interview which began in such a way was most instructive and most inspiring. Here was the priest, or "servant of the kursi," a shrine which they claimed was next in importance after

---

[1] Cf. Muir, The Life of Mahomet. London, 1894, p. 117: "Jerusalem had been long regarded by the prophet with the utmost veneration; and indeed, until his breach with the Jews at Medina, the temple remained his Kibla, or place toward which, at each stated genuflection, he turned to pray." He afterwards changed the Kibla to Mecca. P. 183.

Mecca, or rather on a par with it, consisting of a great monolithic rock, in which the common people believed that the ten companions of the Prophet Mohammed reside, with a cavern so small that five people could not sit upright in it. This servant lived in the village below as a good orthodox Moslem, but in the presence of this sacred stone, hallowed for millenniums, the ancient heathenism was too much for him, as it had been for the priestly family from which he was descended through many generations.

The following day the minister of the "Mother of Pieces" came, at our invitation, from the village of Zebedani, where he resides, to Mr. Crawford's house. We learned that in the spring there was an annual festival, when the people of the villages in the vicinage marched in procession to the shrine following a banner borne by thirty or forty who were called his disciples.

In the course of our travels we found many men whose business it is to care for the shrines, and to lead the worship at them, but none so interesting as the servant of the kursi.

Usually only one priestly family is connected with a shrine, though there may be a father and sons, as in the case of Hophni and Phineas.[1] Boys are sometimes dedicated to the service of a shrine, like the lad Samuel. But there are also cases of several priestly families living at one shrine, as at Nob.[2] Such are found at Nebi Daud, on the traditional Mount Zion, at the northwest corner of Jerusalem, outside the wall. There are said to be at least ten priestly families dwelling in the houses surrounding the court of the traditional tomb of David.

[1] I Sam. i. 3.
[2] Such was the testimony of several belonging to different priestly families.

PRIEST OR MINISTER OF THE MEZAR AT JAFAR.
NOTICE THE SEMN AND HENNA PLASTERED ON THE LINTEL AND LEFT DOORPOST.

PRIESTS AND "HOLY MEN" 147

It seems to be the case that such a priesthood is hereditary. It is transmitted from father to son, or to some scion of the family, and so on throughout the generations.[1]

They are supported, in part at least, by the sacrifices which are brought to the makam. The dues of these priests, who are commonly known as ministers, or caretakers, are much the same as among ancient Israel. Ordinarily they receive the hide of the animal offered and one of the quarters, sometimes other parts. For example, the servant of the "Chair" receives the hide or leg of the sacrifice, and whatever money is left in the little cavern, also the offerings of olive oil. The servant at Berza is presented with the hide, the right hind quarter, and the bowels; so the Moslem caretaker at Nebi Safa gets a quarter of the animal, and usually the hide. The dues of the priests in ancient Israel were not essentially different. According to the Deuteronomist, the one bringing a sacrifice was to "give unto the priest the shoulder, the two cheeks, and the maw."[2] According to the Priests' Code "the priest that offereth any man's burnt-offering, even the priest shall have to himself the skin of the burnt-offering which he hath offered";[3] "And the right thigh shall ye give unto the priest for an heave offering out of the sacrifices of your peace offerings. He among the sons of Aaron that offereth the blood of the peace offerings, and the fat, shall have the right thigh for a portion."[4]

The vows which are made by modern Semites yield an important part of the income of the minister of the

[1] Journal XIII., Rasheya, summer of 1901.
[2] Deut. xviii. 3.
[3] Lev. vii. 8.
[4] Lev. vii. 32, 33.

shrine. During the year, at a popular makam, many sheep and goats, and sometimes larger animals, are killed in payment of vows. Besides there are vows of grain, which are promised on condition of good harvests. These vows are collected by a servant of a shrine. Such collections are so customary that Rev. W. K. Eddy, of the American Presbyterian Mission, Sidon, has had the collector of vows come to his house, asking if there were any vows for the shrine. Large revenues come to the monastery of St. George in northern Syria from this source. The income is so great that the abbot is able to buy himself a bishopric. The servant of a shrine, if it occupies a building, keeps it in order. Sometimes such a building is quite alone by itself, as the shrine of Aaron on Mount Hor; or it may be one of several buildings gathered around a court, like Nebi Daud, where there are homes for one or more priestly families, who live in great comfort. He may slay the victim, if for any reason the one bringing the sacrifice, does not choose to do so. Sometimes it is stipulated that the minister of the shrine is to slaughter it. "The special *dahhiyeh* sacrifice is slain by the person bringing it, but if he is afraid, or his hand trembles, he can say to any proper person, 'I appoint thee my representative in offering this sacrifice; dost thou accept?' But when they appoint a representative they put their hand on the back of the animal slaughtered. The hand may be put on any part. The same ceremony is observed in the case of a woman, who may choose a representative, or may slaughter with her own hand if she prefers."[1] According to the same authority, any one may kill the sacrifice for vows. The minister of the "Chair" said: "If the sheik, that is, the minister of the shrine, is present, he kills the victim, otherwise any one

[1] So the Derwish Hatib of Der 'Atiyeh, summer of 1901.

PRIESTS AND "HOLY MEN" 149

who can read the first sura of the Koran. He uses the formula, 'This is from thee and for thee.' The *dahhiyeh* sacrifice is slaughtered by the one who brings it. If, however, it is brought by a woman, she puts her hand on that of the man who kills it.'' The butcher often kills it. So, according to the various codes, the one bringing a private victim usually slays it himself.[1] It is quite significant among the modern Semites, that while they do not lay their hands upon the head of the sacrifice, they do lay their hands upon it, if they ask some one else to kill it.

In addition to the care that the minister takes of the shrine,[2] he is the repository of such legends as may exist with respect to the origin of the shrine, and the life of the saint whose name and deeds are celebrated.

Besides the ministers there are "holy men." This term must be understood in the old Semitic sense of those set apart to the service of Deity. Thus we read of "holy men" who were Sodomites, and of "holy women," or priestesses, of Astarte, the Syrian Venus, who were temple prostitutes.[3] It is the Old Testament

[1] Cf. Bissell, Biblical Antiquities, Philadelphia, 1888, p. 388. Of course it is understood that the one slaying a sacrifice must be a Moslem, in order that it may be legal. Cf. Hedaya, Vol. IV., p. 63. Or, at least, if slain by a Christian, it must be by the command of a Moslem. P. 83.

[2] The duties of the ancient Bedouin in the care of their shrines seem to have been essentially the same as to-day. Cf. Benzinger, Hebräische Archäologie, Leipzig, 1894, pp. 409, 410: " In ausserordentlich interessanter Weise wird das alles bestätigt durch die aufallenden Parallelen bei den alten Arabern. Das Amt des Priesters ist bei ihnen die Bewachung des Gotteshauses . . . . für Darbringung des Opfers auf einem einfachen Stein ist er entbehrlich . . . . Das Amt ist in erblichem Besitz gewisser Familien."

[3] The Hebrew term for Sodomites is *kadesh*, and for temple prostitute *kedeshah*, from *kdsh*, to be set apart. Deut. xxiii. 17. (Rev. Ver.) Cf. Hos. iv. 14. According to what seems to be unimpeachable testimony, sodomy is extensively practised in certain cities of Syria, and according to Hugronje, as quoted by Zwemer (Arabia: The Cradle of Islam), p. 41, in the sacred mosque of

which gives this ancient Semitic term an ethical meaning. The word, as connected with the God of Israel, has the signification which is always assigned to it in theological and devotional literature. The "holy man" of the modern Semites may be anything but a moral man, as we shall see.

There are said to be seven holy men in the world, so that all who resemble them are given the benefit of the doubt. So far as they are not imposters, they are men whom we would call insane, known among the Syrians as *mejnûn*, possessed by a *jinn*, or spirit. They often go in filthy garments, or without clothing. Since they are regarded as intoxicated by deity, the most dignified men, and of the highest standing among the Moslems, submit to utter indecent language at their bidding without rebuke, and ignorant Moslem women do not shrink from their approach, because in their superstitious belief they attribute to them, as men possessed by God, a divine authority which they dare not resist.[1] Such an attitude

Mecca itself. Likewise, the priest of the shrine of Ali at Kerbela asked an Armenian, now resident in New York, if he wanted a wife during his stay at the annual festival. These temporary wives are kept veiled in the sacred inclosure.

[1] In a certain family in Nebk the wife, a perfectly respectable woman, apparently with the consent of her husband, considers it wrong to refuse a "holy man." Her name is well known in the community where she lives. Such cases are probably rare, and occur among the very superstitious. A Moslem said they should not be blamed or struck for such approaches, and added that the "holy man" when he comes near a woman begins to shiver and retires. Another Moslem explained such reports by affirming that some "holy men" had been led astray by immoral women. Casting aside the specific testimony of Christians, even the admissions of Moslems and the case cited seem to indicate that these mendicants have their way with the ignorant in everything. Cf. Frazer, The Golden Bough, London, 1900, p. 147: "Women are taught to believe that the highest bliss for themselves and their families is to be attained by yielding themselves to the embraces of those beings in whom the divine nature mysteriously coexists with the form and appetites of true humanity."

PRIESTS AND "HOLY MEN" 151

of compliance may be exceptional, but there are more than rumors of its existence. These "holy men" differ from the ordinary derwishes whom travelers so often see in Cairo,[1] and from the ordinary madmen who are kept in fetters, so that they may not do injury to themselves and others. But their appearance, and the expressions regarding them, afford some illustrations of the popular estimate of ancient seers, or prophets, in the time of Hosea: "The prophet is a fool, the man that hath the spirit is mad;"[2] and in the time of Jeremiah, the man who made himself a prophet was considered as good as a madman.[3] We are reminded, too, of one of the signs by which Saul was considered a prophet, when he stripped off his clothes, and lay down naked all that day and all that night, so that the people in view of these demonstrations, with which they were so familiar, said, "Is Saul also among the prophets?"[4]

The sinlessness of "holy men" is considered as of the same sort as that of little children; that is, like little children they are innocent, because they have had no experience of sin.[5]

---

[1] See Lane, Manners and Customs of the Modern Egyptians, London, 1886, pp. 439ff., 461ff., and Baedeker, Egypt, Leipsic, 1898, pp. lxxxvii-lxxxviii: "A considerable number of them [of the derwishes] are insane, in which case they are highly revered by the people, and are regarded as especially favored by God, who has taken their spirits to heaven, while he has left their earthly tabernacle behind." Essentially the same view is held in the Syrian desert: "They think the spirit of the 'holy man' is shut up in heaven."

[2] Hos. ix. 7. Cf. George Adam Smith, The Book of the Twelve Prophets, New York, 1896, p. 28 n.

[3] Gen. xxix. 26.

[4] 1 Sam. xix. 21-24.

[5] A simple Moslem was explaining to Suleiman of Nebk how a "holy man" is sinless. He said, "your child is pure and innocent because she cannot distinguish between good and evil; the same is true of the 'holy man.'"

They are also believed to be possessed of prophetic power, so that they are able to foretell the future, and warn the people among whom they live of impending danger.[1]

The "holy men" and the religious sheiks cast out evil spirits, which resemble closely those about whom we read in the time of our Lord. They exorcise evil spirits from those who are ill. They think such persons are possessed by the jinn, who seem to be the same as the demons in the time of Christ. The religious sheiks, who fulfil a different function from the holy men, and who are religious teachers,[2] all exorcise. The following account of a young woman possessed by an evil spirit, which was exorcised, was given to Suleiman, a Protestant teacher in Nebk, by his wife, who knows the girl: "The holy man commanded the spirit to come out of her. He replied, 'I will come out of her head.' 'But if you do,' said the holy man, 'you will break her head.' 'Then,' said the spirit, 'I will come out from her eye.' 'No,' said the holy man, 'you will destroy it.' At last he proposed to come out of her toe, and this was permitted."[3]

---

[1] A "holy man" foretold a conflagration. Journal of 1901.

[2] The religious sheiks visit the Bedouin two or three days each year to give them religious instruction.

[3] Baldensperger relates a similar case in Palestine, Quarterly Statement, London, 1893, pp. 214, 215: "On the 31st of December, 1891, a woman living next field to ours, in Jaffa was seized by a man wrapped in white. . . . . She was struck dumb with terror, and ran into the house, but could show only by signs that something extraordinary had happened. Immediately a sheik from Saknet Abu Darwish, near by, was fetched, who brought his sacred books—ghost books—and to begin with, administered a severe flogging to the patient. Then burning incense all the time he began questioning:

Sheik.—Who art thou?
Ghost.—(Out of the woman.) A Jew.
Sh.—How camest thou hither?
Gh.—I was killed on the spot.
Sh.—Where art thou come from?

PRIESTS AND "HOLY MEN" 153

A boy had epileptic fits. The boy felt the spirit coming up through him. The sheik gave the boy such a heavy blow on the shoulder as to make a wound; through this wound the spirit came out of him.[1]

In this connection we may speak of those who correspond somewhat to the ancient Nazirites, who are vowed to God by some doting mother, as Samuel by Hannah. The hair remains uncut until they arrive at a certain age, is weighed when cut, and money is paid in proportion to its weight. One thus consecrated becomes a derwish if a Moslem, and a monk if a Christian.[2]

There are no "holy women," or temple priestesses, among the Syrians, who prostitute themselves in the service of some shrine, as was customary among the ancient Israelites,[3] and among their heathen neighbors, as we see from the worship of Baal Peor, or from that of Afka, where, in the most romantic place in Lebanon, at the source of the ancient River Adonis, which leaps fullborn from a cavern in a perpendicular rock, more than a

    Gh.—I am from Nablus.
    Sh.—When wast thou killed?
    Gh.—Twelve years ago.
    Sh.—Come forth from this woman.
    Gh.—I will not.
    Sh.—I have fire here and will burn thee.
    Gh.—Where shall I go out?
    Sh.—From the little toe.
    Gh.—I would like to come out by the eye, by the nose, etc.

After long disputing, the ghost, after a terrible shake of the body and of the leg, fled by the toe; the exhausted woman lay down and recovered her language."

[1] Journal X., summer of 1901.

[2] The late Rev. John Zeller, for more than forty years resident in Palestine, said: "Women sometimes vow to give a son to God. He is regarded as a sort of Nazirite and his hair is not cut until he comes of age. Then a great feast is made. Such a boy, if a Christian, may become a monk, if a Moslem a derwish." Journal VIII., summer of 1898.

[3] Deut. xxiii. 17; Hos. iv. 14.

thousand feet in height, was situated the temple of Venus, at which her priestesses practised licentious rites, until it was torn down, by the command of Constantine. It is an interesting illustration of the permanence of the memory of such a site that a sacred fig-tree, which has grown out of the ruins of this temple, is known by the natives as "Our Lady Venus." The designation "Our Lady," is here combined with the heathen goddess. Otherwise it is used only in connection with the Virgin Mary.[1]

Nor are there those in Syria who vow themselves once, as Herodotus says was the custom among Babylonian women in their service of Venus,[2] known as Istar. It is said that a Syrian woman vowed, in case the saint granted her request, she would serve as a prostitute three days. And a Syrian is authority for the statement that Egyptian women, in connection with the *molid* service,[3] at a shrine in Tanta, follow the ancient custom of Babylonia.

[1] Dr. William Van Dyck gave the following account: "At Afka, a wild fig-tree, besides one or two terebinths, grows out of the east wall of the ruined temple, which is considered sacred, and is credited by all the inhabitants, Maronites as well as Metawileh, with healing virtues. It is called *Sayyidat-az-Zahra* (Our Lady Venus, literally Lady Venus). The word *sayyideh* designates the Virgin." Journal X., summer of 1901.

[2] Book I. Cic: "The most hateful custom among the Babylonians is the following: Every native woman must once in her life sit in the Temple of Aphrodite and give herself up to some stranger." The price of her prostitution is considered sacred to the goddess. Cf. Deut. xxiii. 18. Is there a hint here of the terrible crime mentioned in Lev. xviii. 23? Such customs, doubtless dating from the time when the land vomited out its inhabitants (Lev. xviii. 28, Rev. Ver.) are attested as existing in Baalbek by a missionary who has resided long in the vicinity. Cf. Doughty, Arabia Deserta, Cambridge, 1888, Vol. I., pp. 265, 266. I have heard of such a practice among a tribe of the Bedouin, from what seems to be a trustworthy source. This may be a survival of ancient totemism. Cf. Barton, Semitic Origins, Religious and Social, New York, 1902, p. 37.

[3] Hanna Khizani of Hamath visited Tanta, Egypt, and saw the great annual festival of Seiyid Ahmed el-Bedawi, " probably the most popular saint in Egypt," when there were "upwards of

Such sporadic rites, if they exist to-day, have come from the same sentiment as underlay human sacrifice—that the worshiper would devote his, or her, most precious possession to God. This, rather than any desire for license, must be the explanation of religious vows and rites on which, in ancient as well as in modern times, the devotee must have looked with the deepest mortification and loathing.

half a million persons" present, including singers, dancers, jugglers and showmen of every kind. It is at this festival that "some of the honorable women vow the use of their bodies to the first one who happens to approach them," following precisely the custom described by Herodotus.

CHAPTER XIII

VOWS AND ANNUAL FESTIVALS

According to the strict tenets of Islam, vows are contrary to its fatalistic philosophy.[1] But the natural religion of the people finds expression in vows; indeed, there could be no shrines if the ordinary people did not believe in saints and the efficacy of vows and prayers. Whether the saint is regarded simply as an intercessor, as among orthodox Moslems, or as having power in himself, the worshiper at the shrine believes that evils can be averted, and misfortunes changed into blessings.

There can hardly be said to be any definite view as to the attitude of the saints with respect to men. It is the etiquette of the country not to approach any powerful person without a gift, and it is a belief, deeply ingrained, that no great favors are to be expected from any one for nothing. Besides, there is the feeling, as has already been remarked, that some of the saints are to be feared rather than loved, and there is the dread of spirits that injure men. A vow may be given in advance like a retaining fee to a lawyer, or it may be a promise that if certain benefits are received the thing vowed will be given. Vows are of various sorts, and will be more particularly considered in connection with sacrifice.

There are vows having respect to the personal con-

[1] Mishcat ul-Masabih; or, A Collection of the Most Authentic Traditions Regarding the Actions and Sayings of Muhammed, Vol. II., p. 155: "Do not make a vow with the dependence of its opposing fate, because a vow does not do away fate and predestination, but all it does is extracting something from the wealth of the miser."

SHRINE OF NEBI DAUD, JERUSALEM.

dition of the one making the vow, or of some near relative. As barrenness is considered almost the greatest disgrace that can befall an Oriental woman, and girls are not reckoned in the enumeration of a family, a barren woman often seeks a son from a local saint, or weli; thus the story of Hannah[1] is not unfrequently repeated. One of the most conspicuous cases was related to me by Rev. E. A. Hanauer, of Jerusalem, who was an eye-witness of part of the incident. There was a Syrian woman who was barren, and who, in the bitterness of her soul, went to Neby Daud, on the traditional site of Mount Zion, and vowed that if the saint would give her a son she would give him a fat sheep. In due time a boy was born. The father and mother, on their way to the shrine, stopped to rest at a house, where the missionary heard the story from the lips of the glad mother.[2] Sometimes a man vows that if the saint will grant him a son he will pay for his weight in silver coins. The teacher of a Greek school in Safita was present at the payment of such a vow. When the silver placed in the balances nearly tipped the scale, the father threw in two or three gold pieces.[3]

Sometimes a woman, in her ardent desire for a son, will vow that if the saint will grant her request she will sacrifice a sheep each year. Such was the vow of a woman at the cave where Abraham is reputed to have been born at Berza near Damascus. At the last report she had already sacrificed three sheep. There can be no question that barren women, as the result of such vows, sometimes receive the power to bear children. Perhaps this is an indication of the domination of the mind over

[1] 1 Samuel i. 9-11.

[2] The same incident is given by Lees, Village Life in Palestine, London, 1897, pp. 24, 25.

[3] This was given by Mr. Yazzi. Cf. Ancient Shrines in Northern Syria in The Independent for 1898, p. 1448.

the body; or, as a native physician suggests, the very exertion consequent on visiting a shrine may bring the body into a normal condition.[1]

When the little ones fall ill the mothers have recourse to the saints. The following is an incident told by a Moslem woman with respect to her daughter, at the shrine of Nebi Safa, about two hours and a half from Rasheya. Her daughter had lost one son and another little boy of nine months lay gasping in her lap. She shrieked, "To whom shall I vow, mother?" Her mother replied, "They are all God's prophets, vow to whom you please." So she vowed to Mar Elias (St. Elijah) that if her boy got well she would take him to the church and have him baptized, though she was a Moslem. As soon as she had made the vow the child gave a long quivering sigh and recovered. She afterwards carried out her promise. Vows of this kind are quite common, and not a few Moslem boys thus receive Christian baptism.

The formula of a vow, as given by the same woman, is: "O prophet of God! O Safa! leave me this boy and I will bring you a sacrifice." The vow is addressed directly to the prophet. Another form is, "I need so and so, and if you will do so and so for me I will bring you a sacrifice."

The forms of vows here are not different from those of the ancient Israelites. It was Hannah who vowed a vow and said, "O Lord of hosts, if thou wilt indeed look on the affliction of thy handmaid, and . . . . wilt give unto thy handmaid a man child, then I will give him unto the Lord all the days of his life."[2] It was Jacob who "vowed a vow," saying: "If God will be with me, and will keep me in this way that I go, and will give me bread

---

[1] This is the view of Dr. A. A. Antounyan of Aleppo, as expressed to me in an interview at Brummana, Aug. 16, 1901.

[2] 1 Samuel i. 11.

to eat and raiment to put on, so that I come again to my father's house in peace, then shall the Lord be my God . . . . and of all that thou shalt give unto me I will surely give the tenth unto thee."[1] So Absalom asked permission to go to Hebron to pay a vow: "For thy servant vowed a vow while I abode at Geshur in Syria, saying: 'If the Lord shall indeed bring me to Jerusalem, then I will serve the Lord.'"[2]

Vows are restricted to actual cases of need. If any member of a family falls ill, it is customary to offer a sacrifice. Mr. Hanauer of Jerusalem relates that a young woman belonging to a Moslem family living next door fell ill. A sheep was killed at the door, the flesh was cooked, and it was given to the poor. This is the most meritorious use which could be made of vows. There is an allusion to such a use of vows in feeding the poor in Ps. xxii. 25, 26: "I will fully pay my vows before them that fear him; the miserable shall eat and be satisfied." This language is perfectly clear in the light of customs in the disposition of vows to-day; the miserably poor often eat of the sacrificial meals, served in connection with vows, and are satisfied. Doughty relates how dependent he was in the summer, in Arabia, on such sacrificial feasts to keep up his physical strength.[3]

[1] Gen. xxviii. 20–22.

[2] 2 Sam. xv. 8.

[3] Travels in Arabia Deserta, Cambridge, 1888, Vol. I., p. 442: "Sorry were the Aarab to mark my wasted plight. . . . . As the sun's vast flaming eye rose each day upon us . . . . the remembrance revives in our fainting breasts of our want, with the hollow thought, 'What shall be for this day's life?' And the summer I passed thus fasting. . . . . Yet in this low state there was hardly a week when some householder had not a sacrifice, whether . . . . for the birth of a son, for his recovery from sickness, or for the health of his camels. Then a man's friends assembled for the distribution of boiled flesh; they look also for the thaif-Ullah [guest of God, or stranger] and I went, lest any should forget me."

Delitzsch, in giving the passage from the psalm a literal and ritualistic interpretation, has seen the true meaning, which some other modern interpreters have missed.[1]

There are certain saints that have almost the powers of physicians assigned to them. Some of them would seem to be specialists. They perform cures for rheumatism, for bad eyes, and other ailments. One shrine, near Solomon's hot-air baths, about four hours from Karyaten, in the Syrian desert, is good, as we have seen, for barren women.

Vows are also offered by people setting out on journeys, though I have heard of only one shrine where this is done, at Mahin, in the Syrian desert. Such a vow is natural, and is probably not uncommon.

A large number of vows are made for flocks and herds. These, among the nomads, are liable to various mishaps, to disease, and from marauding bands. Frequently villages in the Syrian desert are despoiled of several thousand sheep and goats. Hence it is customary for those who have flocks and herds to make vows to the weli; that is, they promise him a gift if he will see that these possessions are kept in safety.

[1] A Commentary on the Book of Psalms, New York, Vol. I., p. 397: "There is no need to assume in our passage that in the mind of David the paying of vows is a purely ethical and not a ritual act. Having been delivered he will bring the . . . . thank-offerings, which he vowed to God when in mortal danger. After sprinkling of the blood . . . . and the laying of the fat pieces upon the altar . . . . the remaining flesh of the shelamim was appropriated by the offerer for joyous feasts. . . . . The invitation to the poor to participate in these feasts . . . . is suggested by these legal enactments. . . . . To this verse 27 refers: He will invite the spiritually and outwardly poor to this 'eating before Jahve.'" But Baethgen, Handkommentar zum Alten Testament says of verse 27: "Schwerlich ist das Essen materiell zu verstehn," and Duhm, Die Psalmen, Freiburg, 1899, remarks: "Essen und satt werden" ist sprichwörtlich für "ganz glücklich werden." All of which goes to show how important the study of archæology is for the Old Testament interpreter.

VOWS AND ANNUAL FESTIVALS

It is more difficult to determine how far the saints are regarded as patrons of the land like the ancient Baalim. Hosea indicates a custom in ancient Israel, where the agriculturist, believing that his piece of ground belonged to a particular Baal, and that he could not expect a good harvest without the favor of the Baal, was accustomed to seek it by a gift. This did not imply that he might not theoretically recognize Jehovah as the God of the country. He did, for Hosea represents God as the legitimate husband, and the various Baalim as paramours. The modern Syrian, whatever he may say of God's power, considers the saint as supreme in his own district.

It is well known that anything placed in the saint's shrine is safe. I have seen plows and other agricultural implements piled up on the grave of a weli, exposed to the sky; and timbers leaning against the walls of a mezar in the land of the children of Ammon; and grain inside of a ruined church in the Druse Mountains, once sacred to St. George, now known as Khuddr. No thief would dare to touch any of these. No Arab, though he might seek to rob a threshing-floor in the immediate vicinity, would ever dream of invading the sacred precincts of the makam. He would expect the weli to visit dire vengeance upon him. It is for this reason that the boldest spirits do not ordinarily venture to molest sacred trees, because they are considered as the property of the saint. On his premises he has a power which the people would never think of assigning to God.

Some of the saints are regarded as well nigh omnipresent; others have power, according to Conder, extending fifteen or twenty miles.[1] It is true that some of the

[1] Tent Work in Palestine, London, 1895, p. 305: "This Mukam represents the real religion of the peasant. It is sacred as the place where some saint is supposed once to have 'stood' (the name signifying 'standing-place'), or else it is consecrated by

Fellahin promise a certain proportion of grain to the weli, with the understanding that he will give them good harvests. At the same time, it is a survival of that worship described by Hosea in allegorical language, where it is said that Israel considered the Baalim the givers of her corn, her wine, her wool, and her flax,[1] although she was directly indebted to God for these things. So the Arab and the Fellahin to-day, whatever views they may profess in regard to God, ask the saint to give them children, to heal their diseases, to redeem their lives from destruction, and sometimes to give them bountiful harvests.[2] They even present the first-fruits to the saint, or reserve certain trees or vines for him,[3] as we were treated at Nebi Safa to some of the fruit from the saint's mulberry-trees.[4] This resembles old Semitic usage, as we see from certain passages in the Old Testament.[5] The

some other connection with his history. It is the central point from which the influence of the saint is supposed to radiate, extending in the case of a powerful sheik to a distance of perhaps twenty miles all around."

[1] Cf. Hos. ii. 5, 8, 12.

[2] It is the testimony of Mr. Theophilus Waldmeier of Asfuriyeh that "Syria is full of churches and convents dedicated to various saints. In the district to which a given church belongs, the people ask the saint to grant a blessing on their land." Journal IX., summer of 1900.

[3] Hanna Demishky of Kerak, who was in Lydda for thirty-seven years, has seen a woman bring the first-fruits of her vines to a saint. They were eaten by the people who were present. Afterwards she was permitted to enjoy the fruit. Journal VIII., summer of 1900.

[4] "We took lunch under one of the mulberry trees that is said to belong to the Nebi. There are four trees of which he is the owner. When they brought us a large plate of mulberries, they said that the fruit was from the Nebi." Journal XIII., summer of 1901.

[5] The minister of the kursi said: "When a peasant is planting he says, 'I will give half a *midd* (about two gallons) of wheat or barley to the saint if I have a good harvest.' When he fulfills

priests of the shrines and the monks of the monasteries go about to collect the cereal vows.[1] I know of two such cases. The minister of the shrine near Hamath, called *Zeyn el-'Abadeyn*, was collecting such tithes in villages near Hamath, and it was said that he was likely to be gone several days; so, too, the minister of the shrine of Nebi Safa came, while we were waiting for him, with a large sack of grain which he had received in payment of a vow.

The vows are either paid when the benefit has been received, or at the annual festivals. There are no shrines which are not the recipients of vows, but there are many which do not have an annual festival. Even such an important shrine as Nebi Daud at Jerusalem, has no yearly festival. There are others, like Nebi Musa, near the Dead Sea; Nebi Rubin, south of Jaffa; and Nebi Salah, in the Sinaitic Peninsula, which are sometimes attended by thousands of people.

With respect to Nebi Musa, the festival occurs on the Friday before the Greek Good Friday, old style. The attendance is estimated at fifteen thousand, from all parts of the country. It lasts for seven days. The people bring their vows, which they have vowed during the preceding year, to offer them at the festival. Besides,

his vow he presents the grain to the poor. It is very common that two of the vines in a vineyard should be dedicated to Khuddr. When a man sold a field he said, 'I must clear my conscience, by telling you that there are two vines in it that belong to the saint.'" Journal X., summer of 1901. Cf. Ex. xxiii. 11; Lev. xix. 9, 10.

[1] In connection with such a great shrine as that of St. George in northern Syria they have agents appointed in every town by the monastery who are empowered to receive the vows of the people. Such vows consist of flocks, of grain, etc. Thus the income of this shrine, which is the most popular in all Syria, is very large. Journal XII., summer of 1901.

the priestly family provides about twelve lambs a day, with rice, bread, and Arab butter.[1]

At Nebi Rubin the people spend a month. From the 10th to the 20th of September they flock together in greater numbers than at other times, and the poor save provisions for this festival throughout the year. The shrine is exclusively for Moslems, though during the past ten years, adherents of the Greek Church have attended the festival. They kill many sheep and goats in fulfilment of vows. To these feasts they invite the sheiks, the derwishes, and the poor people. The nights are spent in dancing, singing, and rejoicing; besides, there is a special dance, called *zikr*, in which from thirty to fifty people unite, including derwishes. They have a leader who tries to excite them.[2] During the day the Bedouin give exhibitions of horse racing.

From Burckhardt and Tischendorf we may gather interesting pictures of the ceremonies and festivities attending the performance of vows at the shrine of Sheik Salah: "The coffin of the sheik is deposited in a small rude stone building; and is surrounded by a thin partition of wood hung with green cloth, upon which several prayers are embroidered. On the walls are suspended silk tassels, handkerchiefs, ostrich eggs, camel halters, bridles, etc., the offerings of the Bedouin who visit this tomb . . . . [in] the most revered spot in the peninsula, next to the Mountain of Moses; they make frequent vows to kill a sheep in honor of the sheik should a wished-for event take place; and if this happens, the votary repairs to the tomb with his family and friends, and there passes

---

[1] Information communicated by one of the priests of the shrine, through Mr. C. Hornstein of the Society for Promoting Christianity Among the Jews. Journal VIII., summer of 1900.

[2] Hanna Demishky, ibid.

a day of conviviality. Once in every year all the tribes of the Towara repair hither in pilgrimage, and remain encamped in the valley round the tomb for three days. Many sheep are then killed, camel races are run, and the whole night is passed in dancing and singing. The men and women are dressed in their best attire. The festival, which is the greatest among these people, usually takes place in the latter part of June, when the Nile begins to rise in Egypt, and the plague subsides."[1]

Tischendorf's account of what he saw as a witness of the same festival may serve as an interesting conclusion:

"After a brief hour there was a solemn procession around the tomb of the prophet. The women went in advance most modestly dressed. . . . . The procession moved up the hill around the tomb, and finally entered it, where the women appeared to pray for some minutes. In connection with the procession youths led the sacrificial lambs to the hill. A few hairs were cut from their foreheads, and they were scratched until they bled. Then followed the slaughter of all these fifty or sixty lambs. . . . . They were hung up on the tents, their skins were removed, and with great knives, which served as short swords, they were cut into several pieces.

"While the meal was being prepared on the fire there was a race between the dromedaries. . . . . Next in order was the feast. All the meat was cooked. . . . . All [the people] reclined in groups; in each case, from four to six were grouped in a small circle around the skin of the lamb. The meat was brought in great wooden bowls, and was put on each skin. Of this all partook, as well as of Arab bread and cold water."[2]

This account should have been followed by the descrip-

[1] Travels in Syria and the Holy Land, London, 1822, p. 490.
[2] Reise in den Orient, Leipzig, 1846, pp. 212, 213.

tion of a dance, which was prevented by a storm. It is described, however, by Schimper, who witnessed it.[1] The dance was participated in by men and women, and was accompanied by singing and clapping of hands. It was of a very graceful and solemn character, and I fancy was much like a dance I saw at a wedding feast in northern Syria, where men and women danced in a line, comprising perhaps twenty people, whose hands were joined, five women being at the end of the line. Such a dance would be very different from that already mentioned at Nebi Rubin, in which the derwishes had a part, and of which there was a leader who sought to excite them. Such a dance I saw at Tell el-Safi, in which an archæologist joined. He tried to stimulate them by shots from his revolver.

The features so graphically sketched are to be found at other shrines. Multitudes gather dressed in their best. There is one particular day, the great day of the feast, but the rest of the time is spent in races, dances, and other amusements.

Looking back from the modern Semites we find the same customs among the ancient Semites. At the Sinai of the time of Moses were the same observances as in the time of Tischendorf. It was nothing new, or different from present-day usages, when Aaron, after he had finished the calf, and built an altar, "made proclamation and said, To-morrow shall be a feast to the Lord. And they rose up early on the morrow, and offered burnt-offerings, and brought peace offerings, and the people sat down to eat and drink, and rose up to play." As Moses drew near he heard singing, and saw the dancing.[2] As an adjunct of legitimate worship, such dancing is not

[1] Ebers, Durch Gosen Zum Sinai, Leipzig, 1872, pp. 246, 247.
[2] Ex. xxxii. 5, 6, 19.

open to criticism. At the annual feast of the Lord at Shiloh the maidens of Shiloh were accustomed to engage in dances.[1]

When, at Nebi Rubin and the other shrines, the man who brings the vows eats them with poor people, derwishes and others, he is on the basis of old Deuteronomic usage, which has been observed at the shrines for thousands of years.[2] The feasts described in Amos were not radically different in form from those observed at many shrines, where the people, to quote the expression of a Syrian physician who had studied in America, "have a regular picnic."[3]

We have seen that at the annual festival animals are often provided which have no connection with the payment of vows. They are the contribution of the congregation, or of the sheik in their behalf.

If vows are not brought at the annual festival, they are taken to the shrines at other times. The villagers, or the immediate friends of the person who has made a vow, if it be of the herd or flock, are summoned to partake of it, unless the man should give it to the poor.

Vows are of various sorts. A man may vow his son or daughter to the saint. In that case the child is not slain, as may once have been the case, but is redeemed. Of such cases there are various examples. Walpole mentions one. He says: "A poor girl had been given me; being rather at a loss how to dispose of such a present, I gave her to the mazar. This is a common custom among fathers; they dedicate before or after birth their children to particular saints; these, when of age, are made to labor for the benefit of the deceased.

[1] Judg. xxi. 19, 21.
[2] Deut. xii. 11, 12, 17, 18.
[3] Cf. Amos v. 21-23.

168   PRIMITIVE SEMITIC RELIGION TO-DAY

Girls thus vowed have a hard life of it, and it is a controverted question whether they may marry or not; but if they do, they must remain on the spot and labor."[1]

Such a vow may be a remnant of the kind which Jephthah used, when he "vowed a vow unto the Lord, and said, If thou wilt indeed deliver the children of Ammon into my hand, then it shall be, that whatsoever cometh forth of the doors of my house to meet me, when I return in peace from the children of Ammon, it shall be the Lord's, and I will offer it up for a burnt-offering," and found he had vowed his daughter. As the modern Semite insists on the literal fulfilment of his vow in every particular,[2] it seems altogether probable that when he "did with her according to his vow, which he had vowed," he offered her up as a burnt-offering.[3]

It is said to be customary among Christians, where there is only one child in the family, to make a vow to slay a goat or sheep at the annual festival. The origin of the custom is supposed to be that they vow the child to the saint; thus every year they offer an animal to the saint, as long as the child lives.

[1] The Ansayrii, London, 1851, Vol. III., p. 377.

[2] Ahmed Ghazaleh, a peasant of Nebk, said: "One must always follow the wording of a vow. For example, his uncle coming from Tripoli with a load of rice got into trouble at the ford, and vowed a *rotl* of rice to a holy man who was in his house at the time. The mule came out of the ford safely, but his uncle did not mention it to the holy man. God, however, revealed it to him, and he took the uncle to task, and required him to pay his vow." Journal XI.

A woman agreed to make her husband divorce her in order to marry a man who was in love with her. She made her lover swear by Saint Abbas that he would marry her when she was divorced. Later, when she had carried out her portion of the agreement, he declined to fulfil his. So she went to the shrine, shook the pall over the tomb of the saint, and appealed to him to make the man fulfil his promise. The man fell ill at once, and was brought to the shrine, where the marriage ceremony was concluded. Journal XII.

[3] Judg. xi. 30, 31, 34-36.

A woman, as we have seen in the previous chapter, may vow her own body. Such a vow, according to Moslem law, is void,[1] but the practice survives in spite of the prohibition.

While the life of animals is most commonly vowed, I must reserve the discussion of the significance of this until I come to treat of sacrifice. Vows are often made of oil, of bread to prisoners, or to the unfortunate, or of money. Even dances are vowed at certain shrines. There is probably no festival without dancing. These are simply the joyful accessories of a sacred feast, and the people do not regard the exercise of the terpsichorean art as in any sense a sacred rite. But there are well-attested, exceptional cases where it is so regarded, and where the sheika leads the dance in honor of the saint, as Miriam led the dances in honor of Jehovah in the days of old. Long investigation developed the fact that dancing before the saint may be as truly a religious rite as when "David danced before the Lord with all his might."[2]

From all our consideration of vows, it is clear that they are designed to dispose the saint favorably to the suppliant, so that he may receive the petition that he seeks.

[1] Cf. Hedaya, Vol. I., p. 502: "If a man bind himself by a vow, to the commission of a sin . . . . it is incumbent on him to violate his vow and perform an expiation."

[2] 2 Sam. vi. 14.

CHAPTER XIV

THE INSTITUTION OF SACRIFICE

While the institution of sacrifice exists as a part of the ritual of Islam,[1] and in connection with the pilgrimage to Mecca,[2] it is evident that the custom of sacrificing at shrines and in other places has not been derived from the Moslem ritual, but that it has existed as usage through the millenniums. Indeed sacrifice, as practised among the Moslems, and at the shrines, may be traced back to the ancient Semites. The custom of offering sacrifices on the tenth day of the pilgrim month was directly derived from the "times of ignorance."[3] "The idolatrous Arabs had been in the habit of making an annual pilgrimage to Mecca. . . . . The offering of animals in sacrifice formed a part of the concluding ceremony of that pilgrimage. That portion, the sacrifice of animals, Muhammad adopted from the pagan Arabs in the feast which now, at Madina, he substituted for the Jewish fast."[4] The sacrifices at the shrines represent

[1] Cf. Hamilton, The Hedaya, or Guide; a Commentary on the Mussulman Laws, London, 1791, Vol. IV., p. 76: "It is the duty of every free Mussulman arrived at the age of maturity to offer sacrifice on the *Eed Kirban*, or festival of the sacrifice." This is on the tenth of the month of the pilgrimage to Mecca.

[2] Cf. Sale, The Koran, London, 1734, p. 120: "The tenth of *Dhu'l-hajja*, the pilgrims slay their victims in the said valley of *Mina*, of which they and their friends eat part, and the rest is given to the poor."

[3] See Sell, The Faith of Islam, London, 1896, p. 321.

[4] This is evident from the customs of the ancient Arabs, as indicated in the Koran (VI. 135). See Palmer's note, The Qur'an, Part I., p. 132: "The pagan Arabs used to set apart certain of the produce of their fields to Allah the chief God, and other portions

170

THE INSTITUTION OF SACRIFICE 171

a usage inconsistent with the principles of Islam, and with the latest form of the Israelitish ritual,[1] but present striking points of contact with the worship of the Baalim, as practised among the ancient Semites.[2]

There is no place, so far as I can learn, where any portion of the sacrifice comes upon the altar. Indeed there is no altar unless the threshold or the stone used by Arabs in the immolation of victims be regarded as such. The part of the animal which is left, after the minister or the saint has received his due, is used for a feast. If this is the oldest mode of sacrifice, as the critics claim,[3] it is of interest to remember, that aside from the celebration of the Samaritan Passover,[4] on Mount Gerizim, it is the only form which has been retained by the modern Semites.

Such sacrifices, aside from those ordained in the Moslem ritual, are made by the mass of the people to the weli, either at his shrine, or at the home of the one offering them.[5] An orthodox Moslem may give a differ-

to minor deities of their pantheon. . . . . This custom survives to a certain extent in the desert to the present day."

[1] As seen in the priestly portions of the Pentateuch.
[2] Hos. ii. 5-8, 11-13 (R. V.).
[3] See W. Robertson Smith, Ency. Brit., ninth ed., Vol. XXI. p. 133.
[4] Appendix F.
[5] According to the servant of the kursi, a man may slay his offering in the village where he resides, especially if it is far away. In case of necessity he may even sell it and bring the money received to be expended for the shrine (cf. Deut. xiv. 24-26). But the ministers of some shrines are inclined to frown upon the custom of preparing the sacrificial meal away from the shrine. Thus the sheik at Berza said that a man who brought a meal already prepared found, to his great mortification, that the meat was sour when he came to set it before his guests. If the minister does not live at the shrine, and it is difficult of access, like that of Mount Hor, or the kursi on Mount Zebedani, it is quite common to slay and eat the victims at the home of the one presenting the sacrifice.

ent account of them, but the views of the people who offer them must be determinative. It is certain that they seek help of the weli, and that their vows are made directly to him, and are paid to him.

While the ordinary word for sacrifice and slaughtering is the same, as in Hebrew,[1] there is never any doubt in the mind of the modern Semite that what he has killed has a sacrificial character. There are abundant facts from which to make an induction. I never found any question as to the use intended in the offerings made at the shrines.

We must remember that the great majority of sacrifices are made in payment of vows furnished to some saint. As soon as the animal is killed, it ceases to belong to the one who offered it, and becomes the property of the weli. This fact is sometimes clearly recognized in the sacrificial feast, when the man who brings the offering says, in inviting the people to the meal following the sacrifice: "This feast does not belong to us, it belongs to the saint. . . . . This feast is given at his expense."[2]

The ritual observed among Mohammedan Semites in slaying the animal has been modified to some extent. The victim, if a sheep or a goat, is thrown down upon its

---

[1] The word *dhabh* (Egyptian pronunciation *zabh*, Heb. *zabah*), signifies the act of slaughtering, sacrificing. It is an interesting fact that *madhbah* may be rendered either altar or slaughter-house. The other Arabic terms for sacrifice may be found in Hughes' Dictionary of Islam, London, 1896, pp. 551ff.

[2] Journal XII., summer of 1901: "If they fulfil all the regulations exactly in respect to slaughtering and eating, the saint is well pleased with them. The most important thing is the expression of joy in the presence of the saint (Deut. xii. 12). The saint is present, but he does not eat with them. He is the host, they are all his guests. The men who present the sacrifice say, 'This is not ours, come and eat.'" There were several times when the ministers of shrines spoke of the sacrificial meal as being at the expense of the saint ("on his purse," *kis*).

THE INSTITUTION OF SACRIFICE 173

left side, and its throat is cut, as has been customary, doubtless, from time immemorial. But in accordance with the usage of Islam, the butcher or the one killing the animal, says: "In the name of God, God is great,"[1] and the minister of the shrine, known as the religious sheik, sometimes reads the first sura of the Koran.[2] After the minister has received his quarter, the rest of the animal is boiled, and may be served as in any other feast, with boiled rice, or wheat, or with loaves of Arab bread. Such seems to have been the mode of preparing the sacrifice in the time of Eli, when the priest, Hophni, or Phineas, sent around his servant to demand his portion before the fat was burned, and failing in this, plunged his fork into the pot to take what belonged to his master.[3]

I do not know that the modern priest of the shrine makes so strong a demand; he sometimes yields that which belongs to him. When there are many guests, and the one who offers the sacrifice fears there is not enough flesh to provide for all, he may ask the minister to give up his share. Such a request is sometimes granted.[4]

In some localities only males are used. This is true

[1] *"Bismillah! Allahu akbar."* Burton, Personal Narrative of a Pilgrimage to Al-Madinah and Mecca, London, 1893, Vol. II., p. 217, also frequent notices in my Journals.

[2] This is customary in the payment of vows, according to the testimony of many natives. In offering the annual *dahhiyeh* sacrifice, whether on the pilgrimage to Mecca or at home, it is usual to deliver a stereotyped sermon before the sacrifice. See Sell, The Faith of Islam, London, 1896, pp. 323ff.

[3] 1 Sam. ii. 12–16.

[4] We were told by the minister of Nebi Safa (Journal XIII, 1901): "If their three-quarters are not enough for the company [after the priest has had his quarter] they make the priest give up his quarter or pay him for it."

174   PRIMITIVE SEMITIC RELIGION TO-DAY

among the Nusairiyeh[1] and Ismailiyeh,[2] who consider females unfit for food or for sacrifice. It is possible that the rejection of females is due to the very low view which, as we have seen, the Nusairiyeh have of women, who they say were "created from the sins of satans.[3] Be this as it may, they use only males in sacrifice. These must be at least six months old, but are usually older.[4] Camels are also rejected by these Shiite sects, although specified by the prophet as fit for sacrifice.[5]

The offerings are in general to be without blemish, and in this respect, the regulation may have been influenced by Islam, or that of Islam may have been derived from ancient Semitic usage. They may be of the herd or of the flock, or even of fowls. A cock may be offered if the one paying his vow is too poor to bring a more expensive offering.[6] A bullock or camel is considered a sufficient offering for seven persons. This, too, is according to the ritual of Islam.[7]

[1] Journal XI., pp. 57-58 (June 29, 1901): "They are exceedingly particular never to eat the flesh of the female, though they drink the milk. It is customary for the butchers to afford ocular demonstration that the carcass is that of a male. The aunt of our informant, when a bullock was killed, called one of the Nusairiyeh to see that it was a male, so that he need not afterwards scruple to eat it."

[2] Ibid., p. 46: "The sacrifice must be a perfect male of the flock, at least a year old. They sacrifice it to the weli.

[3] "They do not teach women prayer, because they believe they were created from the sins of the satans, so that it is known from their belief that the souls of women are to perish like animals." Nofel Effendi Nofel, History of Religion (Arabic).

[4] Journal XI.: "Sacrifices should be perfect. A female may be used if not with young. A sheep must be more than a year old, a goat or bullock more than two years old."

[5] The Koran, xxii. 35.

[6] Journal XII.: "St. Rih once revealed to his minister in a vision, that when the suppliant could not bring a complete sacrifice he would accept a perfect cock, a perfect *rotl* of bread (5 lbs. 10 oz.), and a perfect *piastre* (four cents).

[7] Hedaya, Vol. IV., p. 77.

THE INSTITUTION OF SACRIFICE 175

There is a great difference, as has been intimated, between the orthodox sacrifices of the Moslems and those offered by the people at the various shrines.

The sacrifices offered by orthodox Moslems are in connection with the pilgrimage to Mecca, on the tenth of the pilgrim month, about three miles from the sacred city, at Muna.¹ These sacrifices are called *dahhiyeh*.² The meaning of the term is not clear. It comes from a root which signifies "early in the morning," so it is supposed to indicate those sacrifices which are offered about ten o'clock in the morning. These sacrifices are in commemoration of the sacrifice of Ishmael,³ by Abraham his father. They are not used at all for feasting by those who are most pious, but are buried, or are appropriated by Bedouin.⁴

Besides the *dahhiyeh* at Muna, the faithful all over the Moslem world are required to offer sacrifices in commemoration of Abraham's sacrifice on the tenth of the pilgrim month. Hence the strange scene may be witnessed of sheep and goats slaughtered in the streets of Damascus, on this day; though otherwise it is contrary to law to slay animals outside the slaughter-houses.⁵

¹ Sell, The Faith of Islam, p. 297.
² There are other forms and transliterations used, e.g., Hughes op. cit., *Uzhiyah*, Sell, op. cit., *Idu'z-Zuha*, "the feast of sacrifice."
³ This is the Arab form of the tradition.
⁴ Journal VIII.: "Ahmed Hindi of Damascus, who had been on a pilgrimage three times, said, 'They do not eat the sheep, but put it in a hole in the ground.'" Cf. Burton, op. cit., p. 218. "It is considered a meritorious act to give away the victim without eating any portion of the flesh. Parties of Takruri might be seen sitting vulture-like, contemplating the sheep and goats, and no sooner was the signal given than they fell upon the bodies and cut them up without removing them." Cf. Burckhardt, Travels in Arabia, London, 1829, p. 276.
⁵ Mrs. John Crawford of Damascus saw thousands of sheep and goats on the tenth of the pilgrim month, waiting in the streets of Damascus to have their throats cut.

They are also put to death in cemeteries and in the courts of private houses.

Through the influence of ancient Semitic custom this great sacrifice has come to be diverted from its original use. It is employed for the dead, though the people make the distinction between the ordinary sacrifice for the dead and the *dahhiyeh* by saying that the blood of the latter is holy and that it is of use on the judgment day.

There are other sacrifices which are offered by Moslems on their pilgrimage, because of their shortcomings in the rites required, either through inability or indisposition to endure the hardships which are imposed on pilgrims.[1]

The traditional sacrifices offered at the shrines, by the various sects of Islam, as well as by Christians, are entirely distinct from the sacrifices just described, and have evidently been transmitted from ancient times.

The spirit of all sacrifices made at the shrines, as has been observed, is contrary to Islam. Through them worship is rendered to the saints, to whom divine powers are assigned. As in ancient Israel, there is syncretism. Just as the Israelite claimed that Jehovah was his national God, while he engaged in Baal worship, so there are many Moslems who confess no God but God, and Mohammed as the prophet of God, who yet recognize the saints as their real deities; not only Bedouin, Arabs, and Fellahin, who are simply Moslems by profession, but also multitudes who sincerely confess the Moslem faith. Shrines are found everywhere, as we have seen. They exist because the people make vows to the saints, and in payment of these vows, sacrifices are being

---

[1] Cf. Burton, op. cit., Vol. II., p. 140. He adds in a note, "The victim is sacrificed as a confession that the offender deems himself worthy of death."

THE INSTITUTION OF SACRIFICE 177

continually offered in addition to those made at the annual festivals, or in connection with the annual *dahhiyeh* sacrifice.

Besides the vows there are various kinds of sacrifices which are not included in the Moslem ritual.

There is "the sacrifice between the feet." This is made in behalf of a pilgrim on his return from Jerusalem or from Mecca, or in behalf of some one who has been long away from home, as a soldier, or a prisoner. The ceremony consists in a sheep or goat being slaughtered for the one who returns. Just before he enters the door of the house he stands with his legs spread out so that there is room for the victim to be placed between them. It is then thrown on its left side, with its head toward the south, or Mecca, if he is a Moslem, and toward the east, or Jerusalem, if he is a Christian. Its throat is then cut, sometimes just before the threshold, sometimes upon it.[1] Some of the blood is placed upon his forehead, if he is a Christian in the sign of a cross. He then steps over the victim and the blood into the house, though it is not considered good usage to step over the blood among strict Moslems. If he is a Christian, he then takes the bundle of clothes which he is to wear to the church. These are blessed by the priest. After he returns home he puts them on. Sometimes the priest comes to the house and blesses them.

There are also sacrifices for houses, which we shall discuss in another chapter.

Sacrifices are quite commonly offered for children, especially if there is fear that a son may not live. In Nebk one victim is brought for a girl and two for a boy; in other parts of the country, and perhaps usually, no

[1] Cf. Trumbull, The Threshold Covenant, New York, 1896, pp. 3, 4.

sacrifices are brought for girls. For a boy, when he is seven days old, they offer a sacrifice without breaking a bone, because they fear that if a bone of the sacrifice should be broken, the child's bones would be broken, too.

It is also customary to offer sacrifices in connection with the circumcision of boys. This may not take place until they are five or six years of age, or even later, when they are often brought to such shrines as Nebi Musa or Nebi Rubin, at the great annual festivals, and sacrifices of sheep are offered before the door of the makam, the blood of the victim being placed on the threshold.

In all parts of Syria, Palestine, and Arabia, there are sacrifices for the dead. The evidence of this is derived from many personal interviews, as well as from the testimony of Doughty. I reproduce some of the testimonies received on my travels. The following is from the minister of the kursi: "They kill animals for the dead in behalf of his spirit. They call them *fedou*. They go before him as light, serve him in the next life as he approaches God. They become a *keffareh* for his sins. Some people have all this done before they die, in order to cover their sins."

Ahmed Ghazaleh, a peasant at Nebk, said when questioned with respect to sacrifices for the dead: "When a man comes to die he appoints some one as executor to sacrifice some animal. It is preferable for a man to offer the sacrifice during his life. . . . . He rides the animal across the narrow way on the day of judgment. Because of his obedience to God in offering the sacrifice, the victim serves him in the day of judgment as Abraham was saved by obedience [in offering up Ishmael]."

The minister of a Moslem shrine in Homs, who became very friendly when he was told that I was a

GRAVE OF HOLY MAN NEAR MEDERA.

THE INSTITUTION OF SACRIFICE

teacher of the Torah and a friend of Abraham, affirmed that, "Only the Arabs offer sacrifice for the dead." This does not seem to be correct, as it is spoken of as a universal custom. Another testifies: "The relatives of the dead man make some one executor who is to see to the sacrifice. He must not partake of it, but it must be given to the poor." The particular time of such sacrifices undoubtedly varies. Among a tribe of Arabs in northern Syria they sacrifice three days after the death a goat or sheep, which must be a perfect animal and may be male or female. They are ashamed not to sacrifice for the dead.

Of such sacrifices among the Arabs Doughty gives interesting examples: "There is a sacrifice for the dead, which I have seen continued to the third generation. I have seen a sheik come with devout remembrance, to slaughter his sacrifice and to pray at the heap where his father or his father's father lies buried, and I have seen such to kiss his hand in passing any time by the place where the sire is sleeping, and breathe out, with almost womanly tenderness, words of blessing and prayer."[1]

Whether there are sacrifices *to* the dead as well as *for* the dead is a question which cannot be easily determined, if an immediate ancestor is intended. The sacrifices offered to the saints are, of course, really made to those who were once mortals. It is true of the Nusairiyeh that they "sacrifice not to God, but to the weli. They pray to the weli who did good deeds, and when he died was saved without any punishment."

According to Doughty, some of the Arabs among whom he traveled sacrificed to the angels. They cooked part of the flesh, which they distributed among their friends, and part of it they hung upon the branches of

[1] Travels in Arabia Deserta, Vol. I., pp. 240, 241.

sacred trees, which are the places where angels are thought to reveal themselves.[1]

It will be seen from the foregoing that no part of the animal is consumed upon the altar; but rather it is eaten by the one offering and his friends, or is given to the poor, or is buried. But I shall reserve the discussion of that in which the sacrifice really consists until a later chapter.

[1] Id., p. 449.

CHAPTER XV

THE USE OF BLOOD

In the investigation regarding the primitive religion of the Semites, the facts with respect to the use of blood among modern Semites have proved to be the most surprising of all.

On my way from Beirut to Jerusalem in the summer of 1900, I fell in with a young Englishwoman, who, moved by love of adventure, had acquired a use of colloquial Arabic, and had made a journey in the Druse Mountains.

In reply to my inquiries as to the most remarkable thing she had seen in connection with the customs of the people, she mentioned that she had been present at a festival, celebrated at a shrine, and had seen the blood of the victim put on the door-posts and lintel of the makam.

On reaching Jerusalem I sought information in regard to this custom from missionaries who had been longest in the country. One of them, Rev. J. E. Hanauer, of the London Society for Promoting Christianity Among the Jews,[1] had heard rumors of such a usage, though he had never seen it. Later its existence was questioned

[1] In Jaffa, where Mr. Hanauer was a missionary for many years, he was told by one of the Baldensperger brothers that the people are accustomed to sprinkle blood on the lintel and door-posts of their houses.

Hanna Demishky, now of Kerak, in the employ of the Church Missionary Society, who was stationed in Lydda for thirty-seven years, has seen Moslems in villages near Jerusalem kill sheep and sprinkle their blood on the lintels and door-posts of their houses in connection with the great pilgrim festival (*id dahhiyeh*).

with skeptical sarcasm by a famous authority on the geography of the country, and was denied by learned Moslem friends of Percy D'Erf Wheeler, M.D., as having any connection with Moslem makams. It became perfectly clear that it is never safe to decide *a priori* what any custom must be, because we know what it should be. The scientific method of investigation always asks: "What are the facts?" The facts with respect to the use of blood are more numerous than in regard to any other religious usage among the modern Semites. As far as possible, I shall give some account of the way in which they came into view.

A few days later, on the way from Beersheba[1] to Gadis,[2] I came to Ruheibeh, thought by Professor Palmer and others to be the same place as ancient Rehoboth.[3] There we were made most welcome at the tent of one of the Arabs. Soon a company of about fifteen men were gathered in a circle around the young man of the family, who was to prepare refreshment for us. Yielding to our encouragement, three women, one with flashing black eyes which could not be concealed by the veil made of coins hanging down over her cheeks, joined themselves to our company.

Meanwhile the young man who had roasted the coffee over the fire, began with a rhythmic measure to beat it fine in a mortar. When it was ready he brewed it

[1] The Arabs evidently connect Bir es-Seba with the thought of seven wells. On my first visit to this place, in the summer of 1899, June 11, they were opening a fourth well; on the second visit, June 21, 1900, there were five wells, and the Arabs pointed out the sites of two others. Cf. p. 36; for details, see Appendix C.

[2] Cf. p. 34. When we asked the Arabs of the South Country for Ain Kadis, not one of them understood us. Various travelers have identified Gadis with Kadesh Barnea. See Trumbull, Kadesh Barnea, New York, 1884. Cf. Williams, The Holy City, Vol. I., pp. 466, 467; Palmer, op. cit.

[3] Cf. Palmer, op. cit., p. 236, and *passim*.

THE USE OF BLOOD 183

with care, then cleaned the cups, and filling one, poured it into the middle of the fire, a libation to Sheik Shadli.[1]

After the coffee was served in the minute cups of the country, and he had struck with his whip at the belle of the harem, as she had become immodest in speech, he began to sharpen his crescent-shaped knife. A young goat was then brought near the camp, was thrown on its left side with its head toward Mecca, and its throat was cut. One of the women rushed to the victim before the blood had ceased gurgling, and caught the crimson flow in a *tannur*.[2] When I asked her what the blood was for, she replied, "For a blessing." One of our muleteers dipped his finger into the blood and put it on one of the tent cords. A little later the Arabs called my attention to a light-colored camel, on whose neck they had made a stripe of blood, about two and a half feet long and about three inches wide. Here, then, was an interesting example of an ancient custom among the Arabs, in a country once frequented by the patriarchs.

On the next journey, which was to Petra,[3] further examples were observed. In addition, the following valuable accounts were given by Mr. Henry C. Harding, of the Church Missionary Society, then of Kerak, on the east side of the Dead Sea, now of Gaza: "There is an interesting relic of pagan times at Kerak. When the

[1] This curious legend about Shekh Shadli, or Shazli, as the originator of coffee, is heard from one end of the country to the other, as at Kerak, Nebk, and Hamath. At the last place mentioned we heard that when a pilgrim returns, the coffee-maker meets him and pours the whole pot between his feet as a libation.

[2] A *tannûr* is a convex and concave piece of iron, on the outer surface of which the thin Arab loaves are baked by the nomads, who have no oven, when they do not bake in the ashes.

[3] July 11-13, 1900.

people go into the country to cultivate the soil, they often live in caves near the harvest-field. Before taking up their abode in a cave they offer a sacrifice to the spirit of the cave [1] by cutting the animal's throat at the entrance. They use some form of invocation when they do so . . . . and pour the blood of the sacrifice upon the ground."

"When a newly married couple take up their residence in an old house, or any one makes his home in a new one, it is customary to take a goat or sheep upon the flat roof, and cut its throat so that the blood runs down over the lintel." When Mr. Harding entered a new house the landlord gave him a goat for this purpose. The people affirm that it is the custom of their forefathers, both Moslems and Christians observe it.

"When the foundations of the new government school were laid at Kerak, along with other religious services, two sheep were brought, their throats were cut, and the blood ran down into the trench, excavated for the purpose."

Instances of the same custom in all parts of the country, on laying foundations of public buildings, or the beginning of public works, are too numerous to give in detail.

The following incident was witnessed by Rev. George E. Post, M.D., of the Syrian Protestant College, Beirut. When the ground was broken for the railroad from Beirut to Damascus, ten sheep were placed in a row, their throats were cut, their blood flowed down upon the ground, and the flesh was given to the poor.

At shrines on the way from Kerak to Petra, which are called *mezars*, signifying visiting places, there is a cus-

[1] Selim Semain of Kerak says the people think there are evil spirits in some of the caves.

SHRINE OF HAMED EL HADEFI.

tom which undoubtedly has the same significance as the use of blood. On reaching Jafar[1] I visited the tomb of the sheik. There was Arab butter (*semn*), colored with henna,[2] daubed over the lintel and on the door-posts. When I asked the minister of the shrine what it was for, he said: "It is for a blessing," thus using the same expression that the woman at Ruheibeh employed in respect to the blood. I think that, as wine is used as a sacramental symbol for blood, so this mixture is especially acceptable to Moslems in this part of the country as a substitute for blood.

Between Et-Tafileh[3] and Shobek we visited the weli of Hamed el-Hudefi. There was no minister in attendance, but many beams for buildings were piled up by the side of the mezar. Being thus under the protection of the weli, there was no fear of their being stolen. While henna and semn had been daubed over the lintel, leaving the imprint of hands, it seemed as if a sheep or goat had been killed on the flat roof, so that the blood would run down on the lintel. I scraped off the substance and submitted it to a surgeon in Jerusalem, who declined to analyze it for the reason stated.[4]

It was my good fortune to inspect the tomb of Aaron, on the top of Mount Hôr. On account of the fanaticism and greed of the Arabs at Petra, such a visit is not easily

[1] According to Mr. Harding, his tomb is honored not only by Moslems but also by Christians. It is supposed that among many of the same name this is Jafar-ibn-Abu Talib, the brother of Ali who was son-in-law of the Prophet.

[2] Semn is Arab butter, henna is somewhat lighter in color than blood, and the mixture is thicker.

[3] Et-Tafileh is the ancient Tophel (Deut. i. 1).

[4] Because, as we have seen, Moslems assured Dr. Wheeler that such a use of blood was impossible.

accomplished.[1] Inside the shrine I saw the prints of many hands in semn and henna.

My next journey was to Palmyra. While I did not make any new observations of blood-sprinkling, I received some fresh illustrations through interviews and books. Mr. Richards, the British consul in Damascus, who had spent more than twenty years in Oriental countries, including three years at Jiddah, the seaport of Mecca, said that on entering a certain Moslem village an address of welcome was given by the representative of the village, and at a given signal a sheep was brought forward in front of his horse and its throat was cut.[2]

My last tour for the summer of 1900 was to the Druse Mountains. This is a section of country not easily penetrated by travelers, described by Rev. J. L. Porter, in his Giant Cities of Bashan, in terms which seem to be grossly exaggerated. Dr. Merrill has given a sober account.[3] We were received with such hospitality as to be at times almost burdensome, and had a good opportunity to observe the life of the people, as we were welcomed at their places of public entertainment in a way that often warmed the heart.[4]

At the shrines we found various examples of the use

[1] It was visited by Palmer, op. cit., pp. 364-366, also by several recent travelers.

[2] This seems to be a common custom. Layard speaks of it as occurring among the Yezidis: "Before we reached Guzelder, the procession had swollen to many hundreds. The men had assembled at some distance from the village, the women and children dressed in their holiday attire, and carrying boughs of trees, congregated on the housetops. As I approached, sheep were brought into the road and slain before my horses' feet, and . . . . the women and men joined in the loud and piercing 'tahel.'" Discoveries in the Ruins of Nineveh and Babylon, London, 1853, p. 43. Cf. Trumbull, The Threshold Covenant, New York, 1896, pp. 189, 190.

[3] East of the Jordan, New York, 1881.

[4] Every village in the Druse Mountains has a place of entertainment for strangers, called a *medayfeh*.

SHRINE OF ST. GEORGE.

THE USE OF BLOOD 187

of blood. At Smed is the Weli of St. George, an old Greek church with three Greek inscriptions on it. The people take the blood of the sacrifices and put it over the lintel; on the door-posts and on the door itself one can easily trace the marks of bloody hands.

At Ayun, a ruined town not far from Salkhad, is a weli called Abu Hur. It is near a large sacred mulberry-tree, consisting of five trunks which grow up separately from the root. Near the tree is an old oblong building with a stone door after the ancient custom of the country.[1] There were stains on the door where blood had run down, as well as on the lintel. At one end of the building was something of stone, about four feet high, which looked like a baptismal font. It was covered with cloths. Our cameleer removed his shoes on entering the weli, and reverently kissed the cloths on the stone.

Tell Sh'af, near Busan, is an eminence of considerable height, crowned with a weli, called Nebi Khuddr, or the Prophet George. The building, like the temples of the sun,[2] and so many ancient buildings, fronts the east. The cenotaph of the saint is at the western end. The original door on the north side, which was ornamented with a pretty design, has been taken away. On the front step, leading to the front door, and on the front door-step was abundance of blood. The victim had evidently

[1] Ancient roofs, doors, and windows were once all of stone, on account of the scarcity of wood; now wooden boxes in which petroleum is shipped from Russia are used in the construction of doors.

[2] Rev. Franklin E. Hoskins, of Beirut, has made some very interesting studies with respect to ancient temples of the sun and has found at least twenty-five in Syria. He says they are built in a notch of the mountain (Lebanon and Anti-Lebanon) where the sunrise is finest. They face toward the east; the altar is by the west wall.

188   PRIMITIVE SEMITIC RELIGION TO-DAY

been killed not many days before. There were some faint traces of blood on the door-posts.

In Busan was a remarkable use of blood. At the entrance to a court was a double door. On one leaf of it were stripes of blood, crossing another stripe at a slant, as indicated by the accompanying figure. We could get no explanation of it except that the people had been killing a sheep some days before and had put some of the blood on the door.

In the same village is a makam known as Nebi Eyyub, a name which occurs often as the designation of a shrine. It is a little building with a dome, which was plentifully smeared with blood; there was also blood on the threshold, the door-posts, and the lintel. In front of it were three pillars about three and a half feet high; on the top of one of them was a peculiar-shaped stone, of which I saw many examples in the country.[1] The broken pillars were also smeared with blood.

Although examples of the use of blood in worship are so numerous, as will be seen from the preceding account, as well as from that which is to follow, some of those who are most familiar with the customs of the country have not had occasion to make any investigations in respect to this important custom. Rev. Henry H. Jessup, D.D., has been a distinguished missionary in Syria since 1856; he is most familiar with the language and institutions of the people, and is a keen observer,

---

[1] The stone may perhaps be connected with ancient phallic worship. On the flat roof of one of the makams I saw a row of such stones near the outer wall. At a shrine on a high place in northern Syria under the open heavens and a sacred grove I saw, as I have already remarked, a shrine in the form of a long grave, surrounded by a wall about three feet high, with the usual entrance at one end, and an immense phallus laid across the two walls so that no one could ride in.

THE USE OF BLOOD 189

but aside from the slaughter of sheep when ground was broken for the railroad at Beirut, when foundations were laid for the clock-tower in the same city, and when sheep were sacrificed by the governor of the city after the blowing up of a torpedo-boat, which was used for an excursion, he could speak of only one instance of bloodsprinkling at a shrine. This was at Tell Abu en-Neda, a volcanic hill from which there is a charming view, and on which there is a makam, near Kunetra. Here, in 1893, he and Rev. W. K. Eddy, of Sidon, saw blood on the lintel, the door-posts, and the threshold, which had been put there by the Bedouin. An old man, Abu Ibrahim, an elder of the Protestant church at Ain Kanya, near Bainiyas, thought the blood was to seal a vow. The feet of the animals had been cut off and had been stuck into the interstices of the wall.

Similar uses of blood are doubtless found among the aboriginal inhabitants of almost every country. Mr. Theophilus Waldmeier, for ten years missionary in Abyssinia, and for thirty years missionary in Syria, now superintendent of the first insane asylum in Syria at Asfuriyeh,[1] said that he had seen the blood of black fowls on the lintels and thresholds of the houses of Abyssinians.

It was in connection with this second journey that interesting parallels were found in the volumes of Lyde[2] and Doughty.[3] The former, in speaking of the feast of St. Barbara, mentions a significant rite. "Before sunset they prepare wheat by beating it in a mortar to remove the husk. They then kill a fowl, which they strike on

[1] Previous to the opening of this asylum the insane were confined in caves, bound in fetters, in the hope that the weli to whom the cave belonged would grant them restoration.

[2] The Asian Mystery, London, 1860.

[3] Travels in Arabia Deserta, Vols. I. and II., Cambridge, 1888.

the door, and the wall on each side of it, and sometimes on the lintel and side posts."[1]

The examples of Doughty will be found illuminating for our investigation. They serve to illustrate the closeness of his observations, as well as the peculiarity of his English, which sometimes needs retranslation to make his meaning apparent.

The first quotation is used to show how blood-sprinkling is supposed to propitiate the jinn: "The fatness of the Hejr loam is well known in the country; many have sown here, and awhile, the Arabs told me, they fared well, but always in the reaping-time there has died some one of them. A hidden mischief they think to be in all this soil once subverted by divine judgments, that it may never be tilled again or inhabited. Malignity of the soil is otherwise ascribed by the people of Arabia, to the ground demons, *jan, ahl el-ard* or earth-folk. Therefore husbandmen in these parts use to sprinkle new break land with the blood of a peace-offering: the like, when they build, they sprinkle upon the stones, lest by any evil accident the workmen's lives should be endangered."[2]

Another account of an Arab named Mishwat shows that the same custom that was noticed in the South Country is also to be found in Arabia: "At evening, he offered a young sheep for the health of his camels,—*mesquin!* unwitting of the Will above and the event determined against him! A month later they were in the power of the enemy.[3] The ewe he had cast silent and struggling to [the] ground (the head of every sacrifice is turned towards Mecca); then Mishwat, kneeling upon it, in the name of God, drew his sword across the throat. Some

[1] Op. cit., p. 176.
[2] Op. cit., Vol. I., p. 136.
[3] He refers here to a marauding band of Bedouin.

THE USE OF BLOOD

of the spouting blood he caught in the bowl, and with this he passed devoutly through the troop; and putting in with his fingers he bedaubed with a blood-streak the neck and flank of every one of his couching great cattle."[1]

In another passage Doughty speaks of the custom of sprinkling new buildings with blood, which differs a little in detail from that at Kerak, although the reason for it is very likely the same: "I asked wherefore the corner of his new building had been sprinkled with gore? They wondered to hear me question them thus (and felt in their hearts that I was an alien)! They thought I should have known that it was the blood of a goat which had been sacrificed [to the jan] for the safety of the workmen, lest, as they said, any one should be wounded."[2]

Convincing as the examples cited are with reference to the use of blood and blood-sprinkling, the facts gathered during the summer of 1901 are numerous and decisive. The following incident is given on the authority of Mr. Faris el-Khuri, a graduate of the Syrian Protestant College: "In the neighborhood of Nablus it is customary, when a reconciliation has been made between the murderer and the avenger of blood, for the murderer to kill a goat or a sheep. He then kneels before the avenger with a red handkerchief tied about his neck. Some of the blood of the animal slain is put on the palms of his hands. The avenger draws his sword and intimates that he could take his life from him, but that he gives it back to him."

The use of blood at Moslem shrines has already been alluded to. The following instance was given by an eyewitness, Selim, a teacher of the Irish Presbyterian Mission

[1] Op. cit., Vol. I., p. 499. "Couching great cattle" are, of course, camels.
[2] Op. cit., Vol. II., p. 100.

at Nebk: "There was an Arab who had two sons who were to be circumcised at a Moslem shrine at Der Atiyeh. As preparatory to the rite, he begged from various shepherds a flock of about one hundred and twenty sheep and goats. When all was ready, he invited the villagers of Der Atiyeh, Moslems and Christians, to the sacrifice, which took place in the morning. A butcher uttered the customary formula, "In the name of God"; each animal was placed between the legs of the boys who were to be circumcised, the throat of each was cut, and its blood was sprinkled on the door-posts and on the lintel. Later the younger boy fell ill, and in about three hours died. Then his elder brother also became ill, hence they concluded that the saint was angry because blood had been sprinkled on his shrine, so they tried in every way to efface the blood. As the elder boy recovered, they came to the conclusion that the saint had been displeased because of this use of blood. The animals slain were cooked with wheat and Arab butter, and were eaten by those present. A Derwish from the same village confirmed the story, and as an orthodox Moslem, said: "We do not think well of such a use of blood."

A few hours northwest of Hamath is a shrine used exclusively by Moslems, known as Abu Obeida, one of the companions of the Prophet Mohammed, and a famous general.[1] It was my good fortune to visit this makam. There is a small building, with a court in front of it, and graves behind it. Here were blood marks, such as I had never seen or heard of before, in the shape of a capital T, or possibly designed to represent a cross. These marks were visible on the outer door of the court. In front of it the place could clearly be seen where the

[1] Muir, Annals of the Early Caliphate, London, 1883, p. 3, and *passim*.

BLOOD MARKS OF ARABS ON THE MOSLEM SHRINE OF
ABU OBEIDA.

animal was slaughtered, and at a little distance from the steps leading to the entrance was a small hole in the ground, into which they had evidently attempted to pour the blood they had not used. On the door of the shrine itself was a large T, also on the corners of the lintel, as in the accompanying diagram, and underneath it. There were twelve blood marks of the same character on the inside walls and two in the prayer niche, as may be seen from the photograph. The tomb is railed off from the rest of the makam, but over it is an inscription in Arabic, of which the following is a translation: "This is the makam, of the honorable Abu Obeida Ibn Gerar, may God have mercy upon him."

These examples must suffice to show how general is the use of blood, or a substitute for it, at shrines. Other uses of it and expressions with respect to it will be considered in the discussion as to the significance of sacrifice in a subsequent chapter.

CHAPTER XVI

REDEMPTION AND THE "BURSTING FORTH OF BLOOD"

Hughes, in his Dictionary of Islam, affirms: "Muhammedanism, true to its anti-Christian character, ignores the doctrine that 'without the shedding of blood there is no remission' (Lev. xvii. 11; Heb. ix. 22)."[1]

It will be interesting to test this statement by examining the terms used with respect to sacrifice among the people, for the traditional saying of Mohammed, as reported by Ayeshah, and the usage current among many Moslems to-day, represents a different spirit from that which is assumed by Hughes, and one which is characteristic of primitive beliefs among the Semites.

Ayeshah reported the prophet as saying: "Man hath not done anything, on the day of sacrifice, more pleasing to God than spilling blood: I mean sacrifice: for verily the animal sacrificed will come, on the day of resurrection, with its horns, its hair, its hoofs, and will make the scales of his actions heavy: and verily its blood reacheth the acceptance of God, before it falleth upon the ground: therefore be joyful in it."[2]

Another statement of Hughes, which we shall put to the test with reference to the usage of the people at the present day, is: "The doctrine of expiation or atonement

[1] A Dictionary of Islam, London, 1896, p. 554.

[2] Mischcat-ul-Masabih, Calcutta, 1809, Vol. I., p. 321.

It is interesting to know that Hughes makes use of this and other passages, which were translated by Capt. A. N. Matthews without giving any credit to the source from which he derived the translation.

REDEMPTION 195

for neglected duties, sins of omission and commission, is distinguished in the Muslim religion from the doctrine of sacrifice; sacrifices being strictly confined to the *Idu 'l-Azha*, or Feast of Sacrifice in the month of pilgrimage."[1]

It will be seen from the quotations which follow that Hughes is in a serious error with regard to the usage of the Moslems. This will be evident from considering a class of sacrifices called *fedou*. But before examining them in detail, we will cite the definitions of the term given by Lane, who defines *fada* as follows: "He gave his ransom; he gave a thing . . . . or a captive for him and so liberated him; that is, he ransomed him . . . . from captivity . . . . or he loosed him, or set him free and took his ransom: or *mufādātûn*, which signifies the giving a man and taking a man in exchange; and *fidaāûn* the purchasing him from captivity or the like; or preserving a man from misfortune by what one gives by way of compensation for him: as . . . . I purchased; that is, ransomed him with my property, and with myself (*benefsi*)."

Lane renders the Koran xxxvii. 107: "And we made an animal prepared for sacrifice to be a ransom for him and freed him from slaughter."[2]

We pass now to the definition of *fedou*, given by Derwish Hatib, of Der Atiyeh, in the Syrian Desert, who is a lecturer, and leads the service in the mosque of that village: "*Fedou* means that it redeems the other, in place of the other, substitute for the other. Something is going to happen to a man, and the sacrifice is a substitute for him. It prevents disease, sufferings, robbery,

[1] Op. cit., p. 113.
[2] Lane, An Arabic-English Lexicon, London, 1877, Book I. Part VI., *sub voce*.

and enmity. . . . . Repent of your sins and hope that God may cover your sins. Both repentance and the *fedou* cover. The essential matter is the heart."[1]

One of the most remarkable interviews that I had with any of the Syrians, was with the minister of the "Chair" on the mountain-side of Zebedani, who surprised me by the statements which he made with respect to sacrifice. He said: "They go through the opening sura of the Koran, address the spirits (*el-Aktab*), and say, 'this is from thee and unto thee (God) and, O God, receive it from such an one, the son of such a mother, as a redemption (*fedou*) in behalf of him.' This sacrifice is a sacrifice of thanksgiving looking backward."[2] *Fedou* is used for houses, for a child, at marriage, for the sick, and for the dead.

"When a man finishes a house, he makes a sacrifice on the doorstep. It is redemption for the building. Every house must have its death, a man, woman, child, or animal. God has appointed a *fedou* for every building through sacrifice. If God has accepted the sacrifice he has redeemed the house."[3]

As was stated in the sixth chapter, the servant of the "Chair," who is an orthodox Moslem, said, in commenting upon this usage, which is contrary to the fatalism of Islam, "This is according to the simplicity of our minds. Of course every man dies when his time comes."[4]

A simple Moslem at Nebk in the Syrian Desert, said: "The *fedou* is commonly for the future to ward off evil. When they lay the foundation of a house, they slaughter

[1] Journal XI.
[2] Journal X.
[3] Ibid. The primitive institution of sacrifice for houses is found among the ancient Babylonians. Cf. Zimmern, Beiträge zur Kenntniss der Babylonischen Religion, Leipzig, 1901, pp. 92, 147.
[4] See p. 65.

with the idea that (*Khuddr*) St. George, will preserve the workmen. Every house must be redeemed. If not redeemed by the sacrifice of some animal, it must be redeemed by a human life."[1]

The next quotation is made from a personal interview with Joseph Atiyeh, a Protestant pastor, most learned in Arabic literature, some of whose treatises have been translated by Sir William Muir: "He has known a custom of beginning an important building by placing the blood of a victim in the foundation. At Tripoli, when they had excavated for the foundations of a government building, they killed animals and poured the blood into the excavation. In Homs, when the carriage-road was begun, the officials took pickaxes, dug up the soil, killed animals, read the first sura of the Koran, and shed blood on the place. It is actually a proverb among the people, who are about to construct a house, 'it will not do to begin this building without shedding blood.' He does not know of any significance except that it is pleasing to God, and insures a blessing."[2]

As we have already seen, there are very many instances of the same custom in the opening of railroads, and the construction of government buildings.

It was the testimony of an orthodox Moslem, who was servant of a shrine at Homs, that he was familiar with a *fedou*. "In moving from house to house, or in occupying a new building; the first night he sleeps in the house he kills the *fedou* . . . . the object is the bursting forth of blood unto the face of God. . . . . It is for himself and family, a redemption. It keeps off disease and the jinn."[3]

We were told by members of the Protestant congregation in Hamath that "when there was cholera in Hamath,

[1] Journal X. [2] Journal XI. [3] Ibid.

in the year 1875, the Christians sent to the slaughter-house, procured blood, and placed it in the sign of the cross on the door of every room in the house. They also use red paint for the same purpose whenever any serious calamity is feared in the house."[1]

Another curious custom which was mentioned as occurring in the same place is the following: "The largest water-wheel in Hamath, which is used for irrigating purposes, and which belongs to a system which especially impresses and interests every traveler who penetrates to this antique city, has to be mended every year. When they finish repairing it, before they set it going again, they slaughter a ram to the Afrit who is supposed to inhabit the sluice through which the wheel moves, in order to propitiate him, otherwise some one is sure to be killed by the wheel in the sluice-way. No prayer is offered, but later there is a feast, as in connection with every other sacrifice."[2]

The Bedouin are in the habit of visiting hot springs in various parts of Syria and Palestine at certain seasons of the year, as a remedy for rheumatism. They believe that at Zerka Main there is a jinn, who is also called a weli, who lives below the ground and keeps the fire going, which heats the water. They are so much afraid the fire will go out that they are in the habit of killing animals in sacrifice to the jinn.[3] Dr. F. Johnson, of Kerak, says that they kill the animals so that the blood runs down into the water.[4]

One of the most remarkable incidents of which I have heard occurred at Nebk, where Rev. J. Stewart Craw-

[1] Ibid.
[2] Ibid.
[3] Journal VIII., Kerak, summer of 1900. Mr. W. G. Harding.
[4] Journal XIII., Brummana.

GREAT WATER-WHEEL AT HAMATH.
AFTER REV. W. S. NELSON.

REDEMPTION 199

ford resides. All the circumstances came under his observation. The town, like five others in the Syrian Desert, where water is usually found at a depth of twelve or fifteen feet, derives its water supply from a series of wells connected with one another. This method has been in vogue in the Syrian Desert as well as in Damascus and Palmyra for centuries, if not for millenniums, and is as follows: The wells are situated on an incline. The first well, which is sunk at the highest point, gathers water from all the ground surrounding it. At a distance of perhaps twelve feet below, another well is excavated which gathers its supply of water. This lower well is connected with the first and a third with the second. In this way a series of wells is excavated consisting of fifty or one hundred. As the water descends from the first well to the hundredth, its volume naturally increases until it comes out in a large stream at the end, sufficient to supply a town of five or six thousand people with water for all purposes including irrigation.[1] After a long residence Mr. Crawford discovered, in the spring of 1901, that the stream of water was under the protection of a saint (weli). Whether the saint was considered as equivalent to a water spirit cannot easily be determined; however, his shrine, which consists of a small building with a cupola, is near the mouth of the stream and has sacred trees in connection with it.

At the time mentioned there came a succession of three floods, owing to excessive rains which washed away the series of wells, which had been repaired after each catastrophe. The inhabitants of Nebk, reasoning according to the custom of the country, that if there is misfortune there must have been some sin, came to the conclusion that the saint had been offended. They at once began

[1] Journal I., 1898, X., 1901, Syrian Desert.

to inquire what was the reason of this offense. They discovered that the sacrifices which had been offered to the saint at a festival each year had been intermitted, that people had been accustomed to perform their ablutions in that part of the stream which was inside of the courtyard of the makam, thus defiling it, and that a dead body had been carried across the stream.[1] All this had angered the saint. The village at once arranged to propitiate the saint by offering sacrifices. A certain number of sheep, perhaps ten, were stationed over the stream, and their throats were cut so that the blood would run into the water. In this way the saint's anger was removed.[2]

A similar custom obtains with reference to children, either for fear that some misfortune will befall them, and as a protection, or because they have fallen ill, and that the father or mother may secure the favor of some particular saint. The examples which follow abundantly illustrate this usage. The servant of the "Chair" at Zebedani related the following: "The mother of a boy, when she slaughters a sacrifice vowed in his behalf, takes some of the blood and puts it on his skin. They call the sacrifice *fedou*. Taking the blood from the place where the sacrifice is slaughtered is equivalent to taking the blessing of the place and putting it on the child. People who are particular about observing all the requirements of the ritual cover up the blood."[3]

A man who has not had a child promises a fedou that he may receive the gift of one from a certain saint. If

---

[1] The contiguity of a corpse to water is regarded as defiling it. Abdu Khahil, Syrian Protestant teacher at Damascus told me that, "if a corpse passes by a house, the common people pour the water out from the jars." Journal XIII., Bludan.

[2] Journal X., Damascus and Nebk.

[3] Ibid., Zebedani.

it should be born, when it is several days old, they put the blood of the sacrifice offered in payment of the vow on its forehead.[1]

One of the most interesting men that we met in our travels was Surur, of Bagdad, who had once been a slave, but was very intelligent. He gave us many remarkable incidents which I shall relate in another connection. He said: "A man oftentimes vows, that if he has a son he will give gold ear-rings or a necklace to the mosque. A man may vow his son to the mosque, in which case he has to redeem him with money. They call the redemption *fidee*."[2]

I had the great advantage of visiting an emir of the Mawali Arabs, near Mehardeh, who is hired by the people to protect the town from the incursions of surrounding tribes of Arabs. The emir was greatly astonished at the questions that I asked him while reclining under his tent. He asked what was the object, and said, "I have never had any such questions asked me before." He was assured by the Protestant pastor who accompanied us, who was a great friend of his, that he had nothing to fear. It is a curious thing that the Arabs are afraid that Americans and Europeans will in some way exercise the "black art" upon them.

Speaking of some of the ceremonies in connection with the birth of a child, he related the following: "I give you the good news that a son has been born to you. . . . . The child must be taken on a pilgrimage to the shrine to which the sheik of the tribe belongs. The minister of the shrine sacrifices for them near the threshold. The child is anointed on his forehead, or on his nose, with a mark of the blood of the victim. They afterwards cook the meat and have a feast. The rela-

[1] Journal XI., Nebk. [2] Journal XII., Hamath.

tives and all who are present partake. The important thing is that the child should be present. If the shrine is too far away, they can sacrifice at their tents. The blood is important. They slaughter at any point of the tent, but facing toward the south. Anywhere to the front of the tent. The east is always considered the front. From the day God created the Arabs, the east has been the front of the tent."[1]

The presentation of an Arab boy at the shrine of the tribal saint reminds us of the custom which we find among the Hebrews, illustrated in the presentation of Samuel at the house of the Lord in Shiloh,[2] and of the child Jesus in the temple[3] at Jerusalem.

Another notable interview which we had was with one of the Ismailiyeh in northern Syria. He belonged to the initiated class, so that while he had the assurance of bakshish, or a gift, he submitted to the interview with no little fear, because, if his coreligionists had been aware of it, the consequences might have been serious. He said during the interview, "I do not feel happy." Speaking of the customs among the Ismailiyeh when sacrificing for children, he affirmed: "When they make a sacrifice for a child they slaughter the victim in the courtyard where he lives, and put a few drops of blood on his forehead and on his nose, to indicate that the sacrifice is in his behalf. The breaking forth of blood is fedou. It redeems the child. They vow to the saint that blood shall flow for the child if he redeems it."[4]

The sacrifice offered for a son is usually a goat or a sheep. It becomes necessary that there should be provision within the means of the poor. In one of the villages of the Syrian Desert, it is customary "when a

[1] Journal XI., Mehardeh.
[2] 1 Sam. i. 24, 25.
[3] Luke ii. 22-28.
[4] Journal XI.

Moslem woman brings forth a son to sacrifice a cock, when she bears a daughter they sacrifice a hen."[1]

We read in connection with the birth of Isaac that when he was weaned his father made a birthday feast for him. The same custom has been preserved through the millenniums to the present time, and was related by the emir whom I have already quoted. "They have a feast when the child is a year old. They sacrifice a victim, read the first sura of the Koran, and anoint the child with blood."[2]

The last interview that I had with a Syrian with respect to the customs of the country was with Abd Musa, who is the minister of the shrine of Khuddr, near the base of Mount Carmel. I had Cook's agent at Haifa as interpreter, who expressed some fear lest this ignorant Moslem should not be communicative, but I found him exceedingly friendly. He made the following statement: "All the sects visit the shrine—Moslems, Christians, Druses, Persians (Babites), and Jews."

The shrine consists of a cave excavated out of the rock where, according to monkish tradition, the Prophet Elijah found a home. "If the victim is for a child or man, they dip a finger in the blood and put it on the forehead of the boy or man for whom the sacrifice is made. All the sects do this . . . . the Jews put flowers on the horns of the ram used as a sacrifice, and the women carry it."[3]

It is interesting to observe how universal the customs are with which we are dealing, extending not only through Syria, Palestine, and Egypt, but through other parts of the world as well. This fact finds abundant illustration

[1] Ibid.
[2] Gen. xxi. 8.
[3] Journal XIII., Mount Carmel.

in such books as Dr. Trumbull's Threshold Covenant, and various works on comparative religion, as Mr. Frazer's Golden Bough.

The following account was given of the marriage customs at Mehardeh, which are common among the Greeks and Protestants. In that town they have all the weddings on a given day in the year after harvest is over. In connection with the marriage ceremony: "They slaughter a sheep outside the door of the house; while the blood is still flowing, the bride steps over the blood of the animal . . . . the pastor thinks there is much the same idea underlying this custom as in building a new house; that unless they sacrifice an animal there will be some misfortune."[1]

In almost identical language Burckhardt describes the use of blood among the Copts in Egypt. He says, "they kill a sheep as soon as the bride enters the bridegroom's house, and she is obliged to step over the blood flowing upon the threshold."[2] We have already seen that a pilgrim on his return home cannot cross the threshold of his house until a victim has been slain and he has stepped over the blood.

There is doubtless a similar, though a different, meaning in another custom which Burckhardt relates in connection with a marriage among the Ænezes, a Bedouin tribe: "The marriage day being appointed . . . . the bridegroom comes with a lamb in his arms to the tent of the girl's father, and there cuts the lamb's throat before witnesses. As soon as the blood falls upon the ground, the marriage ceremony is regarded as complete." It is also interesting to note that among the Beni Harb, in Hedjaz, it is deemed necessary to the completion of a

[1] Journal XI., Mehardeh.
[2] Notes on the Bedouin and Wahadys, London, 1830, p. 151.

marriage that the blood of a sheep should flow upon the ground.[1] Palmer mentions another significant use of blood at a marriage among the Bedouin of the Sinaitic Peninsula. After all the preliminaries have taken place, and her future husband's abba has been thrown over the prospective bride, who with shrieks and cries has attempted to escape, the women take her in charge: "A tent is next erected for her in front of her father's habitation, to which she is conducted, and then sprinkled with the blood of a sheep sacrificed for the occasion."[2]

It is quite common to slay a victim in behalf of one who is ill. A peasant at Nebk said: "A fedou is given to the face of God. It is vowed for various purposes, for one who is ill, or for one who is traveling."[3]

The same custom was in vogue among the Babylonians, as sacrifices for those who were ill were also offered by them.[4]

There is a shrine at Mahin, in the Syrian Desert, where travelers seek a blessing before setting out on a journey.[5]

Surur of Bagdad gave the following account of the shrine of Abdu Khadir, which is the largest mosque in Bagdad, and of sacrifices offered by Indian Moslems who come to it on a pilgrimage: "They vow that if a man who is ill begins to recover he shall go to the shrine. He is stripped to the waist. Then two men lift a lamb or a kid above his head, and bathe his face, shoulders, and the upper part of his body with the blood. While the butcher kills the animal the sheik repeats the first

[1] Ibid., pp. 61, 151.
[2] Palmer, The Desert of the Exodus, New York, 1872, p. 83.
[3] Journal XI.
[4] Zimmern, Beiträge zur Kenntniss der Babylonischen Religion, Leipzig, 1901, p. 92.
[5] Journal VI., Mahin, summer of 1900.

sura of the Koran. They also wrap him in the skin of the animal."[1]

I have already mentioned, in another connection, that it is customary to offer sacrifices for the dead. This is universal among the Syrians and Arabs. Sheik Yusef el-hagg Ahmed testifies that "They have a fedou for the dead. A person often leaves a sum in his will to be expended in the sacrifice of a victim in his behalf. They summon a reader to read the prayers over the animals which are slaughtered in the courtyard, and of which the flesh is afterwards eaten."[2]

The earliest testimony that I had with respect to this custom was from Mr. W. G. Harding of the Church Missionary Society, who was stationed at Kerak, which he gave in the summer of 1900: "They have the custom, also, of slaying to benefit the souls of the departed. When any one dies his relatives are supposed to kill one or more animals within a few days. They call this *fedou*, or redemption, although they do not seem to have any conception of the meaning of this term. They consider that in some way it benefits the dead, but it is rather the public feast to the poor that follows which is reckoned a good deed on the deceased's account. Even the most intelligent, however, believe that if they omit the ceremony some harm will befall them, apparently owing to the wrath of the departed spirit."[3]

The Arabs and Syrians are very sensitive on this point. They consider it necessary that a man should not neglect to perform his obligations to the departed, and they have many stories to tell of the way in which such neglected

[1] Journal XII., Hamath.
[2] Journal X., Nebk.
[3] Journal VIII., Kerak. It is very questionable whether the benefit which the dead receive is from feeding the poor by the flesh of the sacrifice.

ones have appeared to them in dreams at night, reproaching them for not performing their duty in this regard. They also relate how the saint has often taken vengeance on some worshiper for not paying a vow. It is said that the ministers of certain shrines are sometimes at pains to act for the saint in executing vengeance upon any one who may fail to fulfil a vow.

One of the words for ransom is *fidyeh*, a synonym for fedou, which, according to Lane, signifies "a ransom, a thing, or a captive that is given for a man who is therewith liberated . . . . or property given as a substitute or a ransom for a captive: and property, by the giving of which one preserves himself from evil in the case of a religious act in which he has fallen short of what was incumbent, like the expiation for the breaking of an oath and of a fast."[1]

On our way from Ladikiyeh over the Nusairiyeh Mountains to Hamath, we stopped at a little village called Dibbash, which is inhabited by Greeks, and received the following information: "At the feast of St. George they sacrifice, and the priest prays over the sacrifice. The only church is about an hour away. The sacrifices are killed several feet from the door. The heads of the victims are turned towards the east . . . . any man of good character may kill them . . . . the blood goes on the ground, they make no marks with it. The suppliant vows it to such and such a saint for the sick. It is called a *fidee*, which means *head* for *head*. It must be slaughtered, and the poor must eat it. The slaughtering of it is more important than the eating of it."[2]

On the same journey we stopped among Nusairiyeh, at Behammra, once the home of the missionary Lyde,

[1] Lane, op. cit., *sub voce*.   [2] Journal XI.

where we had a remarkable interview with one of the Protestants as to the religious customs of the people. From him we received the following information as to sacrifices offered for the dead: "They sacrifice for the dead before they put him in the grave. On the evening of the sixth day after the funeral there is a feast, and the next morning they have a sacrifice in the house of the dead. . . . . They say, 'In the name of the saint,' and pray that God may forgive him his sins." After the sacrifices have been presented, the soul may pass out of an opening over the door of the house into the body of a male child that is to be born, for the Nusairiyeh, as well as the Druses, believe in the transmigration of souls. A female soul never enters the body of a male. The soul of a good man goes into the body of a good man, the soul of a bad man enters into the form of an animal. The sacrifices cause the forgiveness of certain sins committed by the deceased. The more food is furnished, the greater the efficacy of the sacrifice. A parent may say, 'redeem soul by soul'; that is, redeem the soul of the man who is dead by the soul of the animal who is to be killed as the victim. "The animal is a spirit and the sick person is a spirit. The saint accepts one in the place of the other"; that is, the soul of the animal in the place of the soul of the man.[1] It will be seen from that which precedes that redemption is accomplished through death.

It is a common custom if a man loses a son to say to the afflicted father, "Do not mourn for him, his death may have saved your life." When a death is announced, the usual formula is: "Abdullah is dead, may God give you his life"; that is, may God ransom you through his death. The Emir of the Mawali at Mehardeh said: "If a man

[1] Journal XII.

loses a valuable horse by death, they say to the owner, do not fret about it, it has redeemed you"; that is, the death of the horse has saved your life.[1]

Joseph Atiyeh, whom I have already cited, gives the following interesting example of the redemption of Abdullah, Mohammed's grandfather, through death. "They say that Abdullah, when he was digging a well, vowed if the water came he would give one of his ten sons in death. He prepared to slaughter Abdullah, whom he had chosen by lot, but his mother's brothers forbade it. He accordingly redeemed him by slaughtering one hundred camels."[2]

The following are still further illustrations of the use of the term *fidee*. According to the testimony of Surur of Bagdad, already quoted: "There is a *fidee* by means of money, but sacrifice is in connection with a vow, not even the *dahhiyeh* sacrifice is called *fidee*, it is called alms. A man may take out a *keffareh* for an oath if he has sworn falsely. If he is a very poor man he may fast for three days, or he may feed ten poor men. This is laid down for them in the Koran. Or he may redeem a slave; this is the highest form and is called *keffareh* in the Koran itself. It is not used for any other sin but a false oath."

Another term for sacrifice which is considered as a synonym of *fedou*, and the other words named, is *keffareh*, which is defined as follows by Lane: "An expiation for a sin, or a crime, or a violated oath; an action, or a quality which has the effect of effacing a wrong action or sin or crime; that which covers or conceals sins or crimes"; from the second form of the verb, *kaffara:* "It . . . . covered, or concealed, the crime or sin . . . . or expiated it, or annulled it . . . . the saying in the Koran (v. 70) means, 'we would cover, or con-

[1] Journal XI.   [2] Ibid.

ceal their sins, so that they should become as though they had not been'; or it may mean, 'we would do away with their sins'; as indicated by another saying in the Koran (xi. 116): 'good actions do away with sin.'" Lane gives another quotation, which signifies, "God effaced his sin."[1]

In the same connection the minister of the "Chair" said: "They kill animals for the dead in behalf of his spirit. They call such a sacrifice fedou. This goes before him as light, serves him in the next life as he approaches God. It becomes a *keffareh* for his sins."[2]

Sheik Yusef el-hagg Ahmed affirms, with reference to this same subject: "The Shiites do not use the term fedou, they employ the term *keffareh* instead." Question. "Does it cover sin?" Answer. "Who knows whether it covers sin or how many sacrifices can cover sin? God only can cover it, but they offer it in the hope it will be covered."[3]

Another Moslem testified: "On the day of judgment God weighs carefully in his scales the good and bad

---

[1] Lane, op. cit., *sub voce*. Haupt: Babylonian Elements in the Levitical Ritual, Journal of Biblical Literature, 1900, p. 61, remarks in regard to *kipper:* "The original meaning seems to be 'to wipe off' not 'to cover,' as Albrecht Ritschl supposed in his famous work on The Christian Doctrine of Justification and Atonement. Ritschl's knowledge of Semitic was, according to Lagarde's Mittheilungen, somewhat inadequate. The mere fact that the government appointed Ritschl official examiner in Hebrew proves that he did not know much about it." A like criticism might apply to Lane in his Lexicon, and to Palmer in his translation of the Koran. The word *kaffara* occurs in many passages which Palmer translates "to cover," e.g, iii., 191, " Lord forgive us our sins and cover our offences." Cf. iii. 194; v. 70; xxxix. 36 and often. This seems tc be the primary meaning of *kafara*, as, to give translations: "He covered the sown seed with earth;" "the clouds covered the sky;" "he covered his coat of mail with a garment;" and very often.
[2] Journal X.
[3] Journal XI., Mehardeh.

deeds of each one, and sets up a narrow bridge like a hair over the infernal regions. They then cross the bridge on the animals they have sacrificed. Nevertheless, they call the blood keffareh and consider that it helps in atoning for their sins." A devout Moslem, of good sense but unlettered, told Suleiman of Nebk, "that sacrifice would cover sin."

Some of the above expressions with regard to the use of blood seem rather startling, and may perhaps afford a commentary on a quotation by Muir in The Life of Mahomet. "Wathic said of a Moslem saint, 'leave me alone, while thus in his blood I expiate my sins.'"[1]

I never visited any shrine in the country without finding something that was curious and helpful in my investigation. At Braigh, on the way from Homs to Nebk, I stopped at a shrine of a Persian saint, by the side of the road. We had a conversation with the sheik of the village, who said in regard to one of the channels of water from which the village derived its supply: "When the channels are cleared out once a year, and the water is afterwards turned on, they make a sacrifice for the weli, by means of the bursting forth of blood. A sheep is slaughtered in front of the weli, its head is turned toward the south, and its blood is made to run in the same direction."[2]

I have already alluded to our interview with an initiated member of the Ismailiyeh, which shows how universally the same phraseology "bursting forth of blood" is found among different sects, and in parts of the country which are remote from each other: "The *dahhiyeh* may be for a man's father or mother who is dead. It is a vow to God. It is a universal custom, long prevailing. It is for the breaking forth of blood to the face of God, on behalf of the dead. Usually before a man dies, he

[1] Vol. I., London, 1861, p. 517. [2] Journal XII.

requires his relatives to take a solemn oath, that they will make annual sacrifices in his behalf. They are afraid of God if they are unfaithful. They never neglect such sacrifices . . . . no use is made of the blood. The bursting forth of blood is absolutely indispensable."[1]

A Moslem, speaking with reference to the *dahhiyeh* sacrifices, observed: "The bursting forth of the blood is the most important thing." The Mawali Arabs hold the same view: "The vow is presented to the face of God. Any one who is washed and is ceremonially clean may kill the victim. They take its blood and make a stripe on the back of the animal. It is a mark of the good one; that is, of the weli. It indicates that the sacrifice has been presented to him. They cook the victim and eat it, and share its flesh with the poor. The sacrifice is not complete without the shedding of blood. It would not do to get a certain quantity of meat and eat it in their houses; without the bursting forth of blood, there is no fulfilment of the vow. . . . . They never use the term fedou . . . . but they employ the verb from which fedou comes." It is in this connection that the emir said: "If a man loses a valuable horse by death, they say 'it has redeemed you.' "[2]

At Snobar, a village of the Nusairiyeh, there is a shrine of the Persian saint, Ajami, where they have an annual festival. Like the Ismailiyeh they make use only of males for sacrifices. A poor man can offer a fowl, "as far as his hand reaches."[3] The shrine called among

[1] Journal XI.

[2] Ibid.

[3] The phrase here is almost the same as in the Priests' Code. Cf. Lev. v. 7: "But if his hand does not reach the sufficiency of a lamb then he shall bring for his guilt-offering, which he hath sinned, two turtle doves, or two young pigeons to Jehovah." Cf. vs. 11; xiv. 32.

the Nusairiyeh and in Asia Minor *zeyareh*, is under the open heavens, surrounded by a rude wall. Inside of this wall is a sacred tree, a wild mulberry, on which rags are tied in performance of a vow. Those who are ill tie them about their necks. Inside of this wall, which surrounds the *zeyareh*, are three swarms of bees. They are owned by the weli, and the honey is given to the poor.

With respect to the sacrifices offered in performance of vows, a man said that they vowed the bursting forth of blood to the face of God. Our informant said the sacrifices were offered to the weli. In connection with vows in case of illness, blood may be smeared on the part affected, as the stomach or the bowels.[1]

As showing how prevalent the expression quoted is, we were told by the Protestant teacher at Mehardeh: "It is St. George (*Khuddr*) who causes the Sabbatic fountain in northern Syria to work intermittently as it does. All sects sacrifice there; that is, at the fountain. It is through the power of the saint that the water flows. On April 23d is the feast of St. George, which is called the Feast of the Convent . . . . the Christians come first, the Nusairiyeh second, the Moslems third. Moslems are ceasing to go because of the unsavory reputation of the monastery. They are now, therefore, sacrificing the victims promised in their vows in their own villages, with their heads turned toward the monastery. He was in a Moslem village where a man had a calf to offer to St. George. He asked the sheik what he should do, and was advised either to sacrifice it, or bring it to the village to the agent of the shrine, who was collecting vows for the monastery, and redeem it. The agent said, what you vowed 'was the outbursting of blood to the saint.' The

[1] Journal XI.

meat is eaten on behalf of the spirit of the saint; that is, of St. George, as from his bounty."[1]

While at Rasheyeh I had an interview with a Druse woman, in which a teacher from the Girls' School at Damascus served as my interpreter. This Druse had traveled widely with her husband; had visited Urfa, the scene of the Armenian massacres, and had lived ten years in Bagdad. In Urfa there is a shrine of Nimrod. She said: "If a man is ill, or in prison, or if the flocks are diseased, his relatives go to the makam and say, 'we have come to your house, we are under the protection (*dakhiel*) of a given prophet. We have fallen on your threshold'; that is, have kissed the threshold of your shrine. They vow a sheep, either male or female, and generally have the animal selected quite young. . . . . Some of the company sleep at the shrine that night. Usually a Moslem sheik kills the animal. The head of the victim is turned toward the south. If there is no Moslem priest, a Druse slaughters. . . . . They put blood marks on the outer door of the shrine. . . . . The important thing is the shedding of the blood, the bursting forth of the blood."[2]

One of the most significant events in the Old Testament which is found in one of the oldest documents is the conclusion of the Covenant between God and Israel, where, after the reading of the book of the Covenant, the blood is sprinkled on the altar and the people.[3] We may be certain that this represents ancient usage among the Semites. Singularly enough we find a parallel custom among the Ismailiyeh, which, notwithstanding the peculiarities of their faith, has been transmitted through the millenniums. I quote from the same interview with one of the Ismailiyeh from which I have already made

[1] Ibid.   [2] Journal XII.   [3] Ex. xxiv. 6–8.

several citations: "There is an annual festival at the shrine. They vow vows. All who desire go. They wash and put on clean clothes. They dance and sing. Their own leaders do not permit men and women to dance together, unless they belong to the same family. They dance in honor of the weli. The sacrifice must be a male and a sheep, must be perfect, nothing broken, nothing wanting, must be at least a year old. They sacrifice it to the weli. They slaughter it outside of the door of the shrine, very near the threshold, at the expense of the weli (on account of his purse). A religious sheik slaughters it, and reads the first sura of the Koran over it. They believe that by the permission of God the saint is there. The head points to the east, that the throat may be toward the south. They sprinkle the stones outside the weli in the wall, and the sick person who has made the vow, with the blood of the sacrifice. They sprinkle the blood on the stones above the door and on the two sides, so that the sacrifice may be acceptable. They cook the animal and give it to the people who are there. The man who sacrifices eats with them. . . . . They must slaughter, the eating is not so necessary."[1]

In another chapter I have already cited many examples of blood-sprinkling in connection with houses, on the door, the door-posts, and the lintel. I give one other example as bearing on this discussion. Dr. Assadoun Aram Attonnyan of Aleppo related the following: "In Urfa there is a well which has healing property. It is especially good for leprosy. The well is inside the house. They kill a lamb, goat, or pigeons, then put their hands in the blood and mark the inside of the wall of the building." Such marks of the bloody hand or of a hand

[1] Journal XI.

traced in red paint are very common in Syria and Palestine—they are supposed to be efficacious in protecting a house from the jinn.[1]

Not only these sacrifices, which have been characteristic of Semitic religion throughout the ages, but also the chief sacrifice in the Moslem ritual at Muna is distinguished by the same characteristics. It was the testimony of a Moslem: "The important part of the sacrifice is the pouring out of blood. As soon as the blood of the victims has flowed at Muna, they bury the bodies in the ground. Any *dahhiyeh* sacrifice is much more acceptable to God if offered on the mountain. No use is made of the blood whatever. It is said that in Irak they take the blood of the sacrifice and put it over each door inside the court, so that there is the sign of the bloody hand."[2]

I must reserve the discussion of the significance of sacrifice for the next chapter. But it is possible that an incident related to me by the Rev. F. B. Meyer of London may have some bearing on this investigation. While he was in Calcutta, at the Temple of the Goddess Kali, he was present at a ceremony which filled him with such disgust that he rebuked the worshipers for it. Nevertheless, it seems significant. Until the English interfered, it was customary at the annual festival of this goddess to bring a human sacrifice, but since this practice has been stopped by the enforcement of an English statute forbidding it, it has been customary for the one offering the sacrifice to hold a little boy in his arms, while another brought a kid in his arms, as the substitute for the son whom his ancestors would have offered. When the throats of the kids have been cut, and the blood has flowed, it is customary for the holy men to catch the

[1] Journal XIII.   [2] Journal XI.

blood in their hands, smear it on their faces, and dance about in it. It was this ceremony that shocked Mr. Meyer, and which he rebuked, but which is undoubtedly an essential part of such an offering.[1]

[1] Journal XIII., On the train from Damascus to Beirut.
Sir William Wilson Hunter gives the following account of human sacrifices among the Kandhs in his Brief History of the Indian Peoples, Oxford, 1897, p. 49, which presents another aspect of human sacrifice as once practised in India. "The Kandhs, like the Santals, have many deities, race-gods, tribe-gods, family-gods, and a multitude of malignant spirits and demons. But their great divinity is the earth-god, who represents the productive energy of nature. Twice each year, at sowing-time and at harvest, and in all seasons of special calamity, the earth-god required a human sacrifice. The duty of kidnapping victims from the plains rested with the lower race attached to the Kandh village. . . . . The victim, on being brought to the hamlet, was welcomed at every threshold, daintily fed and kindly treated till the fatal day arrived. He was then solemnly sacrificed to the earth-god, the Kandhs shouting in his dying ear, 'We bought you with a price: no sin rests with us!'"

CHAPTER XVII

THE SIGNIFICANCE OF SACRIFICE

I went to Palestine in the early summer of 1898 with the full persuasion that the sacrificial meal was the oldest form of sacrifice, as Professor W. Robertson Smith and others maintain.[1] Indeed, my observations of the shrines and high places during the autumn of the same year seemed abundantly to confirm this view. I learned that every vow of animals that was paid was prepared as a feast, either for the one offering the sacrifice and his friends, including any that might be present, or for the poor.

Again, all the characteristics of such offerings as are described in Deuteronomy seemed to be preserved in these modern sacrifices. According to the legislation contained in that code, except in one passage,[2] fire-offerings are not mentioned. There was feasting, and every expression of joy before the Lord. So now, when vows are paid, men and women eat, sing, and dance. What could be more natural, from the study of such customs, than to see in them a confirmation of a theory which has been presented with such learning and ability?

---

[1] Encyclopædia Britannica, New York, 1886, pp. 133, 134: "A sacrifice, therefore, is primarily a meal offered to the deity .... The sacrificial meal with the general features that have been described may be regarded as common to all the so-called native religions of the civilized races of antiquity—religions which have a predominantly joyous character, and in which the relations of man to the gods were not troubled by any habitual and oppressive sense of human guilt." Cf. Smith, Lectures on the Religion of the Semites, New York, 1889, pp. 237, 327.

[2] Deut. xviii. 1. It is not improbable that the reference to fire-offerings is no more original in this text than in that of Josh. xiii. 14, where it does not occur in the LXX.

THE SIGNIFICANCE OF SACRIFICE 219

I was led, however, a year ago last summer, after my researches with respect to the use of blood, to distrust the regnant hypothesis as to the primitive form of sacrifice. And that distrust was greatly deepened by the researches made last summer, which have been set forth in the three preceding chapters. Indeed, I was amazed when I heard certain terms employed with such persistency in different parts of the country, remote from each other, as for example, the necessity of the "bursting forth of blood" before the face of the Lord, or the weli.

If this teaching were found in Islam as a necessary condition of acceptable sacrifice, we might well say that Bedouin, Arabs, Fellahin, and more enlightened Syrians, coming under the influence of positive religion, had abandoned their ancient customs in bringing their sacrifices as they are wont to do to-day. This is possible, though highly improbable. But when we find that blood is regarded among orthodox Moslems as defiling, so that they will not step over the blood of a sacrifice, and consider it *a priori* impossible that it should be placed on their shrines, or if so placed it is considered as bringing down the rightful wrath of the weli, we must conclude that we are dealing with a primitive custom, going back of the time of Ezekiel, of the oldest document in the Pentateuch, and of usages which are found in ancient Babylonia.[1]

There are three considerations which need to be emphasized in the discussion of the significance of sacrifice. The first is the persistence of custom among the Orientals, to which allusion has already been made.[2] That which is customary now in all parts of the country among all sects and classes of people, as Bedouin, Arabs, and

[1] Zimmern, op. cit. See introduction and texts.
[2] Cf. p. 52.

Fellahin, may be considered as customary from time immemorial. Custom among the Orientals is as binding as morality and religion among us; indeed, custom is morality and religion to the Oriental.[1] The second consideration, of like importance, is the ordinary conception of sin among ancient and modern Semites. There are indeed exceptions, but only enough to prove the rule. We have seen that sin is not ordinarily conceived of as guilt, but rather as misfortune.[2] There are, to be sure, traces of a nobler idea; but the dominant notion is that misfortune comes, not because a man or woman is guilty of some sin, but because God is arbitrarily angry. Hence his favor must be sought. A third consideration is in the view which obtains of divine beings among the ignorant, whose belief represents original usage. We have seen that they do not clearly distinguish in their thinking between a jinn, an ancestor, a saint (weli), and God, as the source of their blessings, or their misfortunes. Good and evil come alike from God, the weli, the ancestor; and the jinn, for there are good genii as well as evil.[3] A jinn, as we have seen, can make the ill well, and the well ill.[4]

Now, if we can find what is the custom regarding sacrifice, always and everywhere, we may be sure that the same has been the custom back to the very beginnings of the history of the Semites. Or if, in other words, a feast at which the saint was the host, was the customary idea of sacrifice in primitive times, it should be the customary idea now. If we find another element in sacrifice dominant among those Syrians, Arabs, and Bedouin who are nearest the condition of primitive life now, we may be certain that the same element was dominant in the primitive history of the Semites. The data

[1] See p. 65. [3] P. 94.
[2] P. 124. [4] P. 92.

furnished in ancient literature, from which the critics conclude that the sacrificial meal was the pre-eminent element in sacrifice, are inadequate for a satisfactory induction; those which exist to-day are abundant. After the researches which I was enabled to make last summer, I think there can be no question as to what our conclusion must be, if we carefully consider the facts which I have detailed.

Again, if the mass of modern Semites—and I speak now of those who are not under the influence of Islam and Christianity—look upon misfortune as an evidence of sin, and as an indication of the displeasure of some being to whom, practically, they assign the value of God, whether he be weli, ancestor, or jinn, then our view of the most important element in sacrifice must be different. We are not to go to these people for anything but usage. They may be able to give an explanation of that usage as it may occur to them at the moment, or there may be folklore which represents the effort of the generations to explain certain phenomena. Of such folk-lore I have found little or nothing which has a bearing on the explanation of sacrifice.

It is true that sacrifice may be regarded as a gift on the part of the suppliant, which is designed favorably to dispose the being, who is God to him, in some undertaking on which he is about to enter; or to remove his anger. It may be something like a bribe to blind the eyes of deity, a *keffareh*,[1] so that the divine being who is displeased may overlook the offense on account of which he is angry.

Connected with the sacrifice, there may be a meal, at which all is hilarity. Before the sacrifice was made, or the vow was paid, there might be a sort of uneasy feeling

[1] P. 210.

on the part of the worshiper, but when the promised gift has once been made to the weli, what a weight is rolled off from the man! The sheep, goat, calf, bullock, camel that was vowed has changed owners. It is no longer the property of the man who gave it, but has become the property of the saint or divine being. Now it is to be spread before the man who offered it, and his friends, as the saint's bounty. All is well, care is banished, there is a feast. Why should not the light-hearted Bedouin, Arab, or Fellahin eat, sing, dance, and be merry? Many times, in all parts of the country, I have sought to learn whether the saint were regarded as actually present at such a feast. I have hardly been able to discover any such idea.

But another notion has been set forth with a strange and surprising unanimity, in all parts of the country, among Bedouin, Arabs, and Fellahin, as well as among fairly intelligent Moslems and Christians, namely, that the "shedding of blood," the "bursting forth of blood," is the essential element in sacrifice.[1] As to the accuracy, as well as the emphasis, of this testimony, there can be no question. An aversion to the teaching of the Scriptures with reference to the blood atonement, or a predilection in its favor should have no place here. There can be no scientific research if we come to such an inquiry with our minds made up as to what the result should be. Here, if anywhere, an open mind is absolutely essential. It is clear that the necessity for shedding blood does not exclude the character of sacrifice as a gift, nor does it exclude the feast which follows it. When the sacrifice is made, then, as has been affirmed, men and women may be glad. But it is a very serious question whether the term "sacrificial meal" is not a misnomer.

[1] See chapter XVI.

THE SIGNIFICANCE OF SACRIFICE 223

In what does the sacrifice consist? Is it in giving a certain animal? It seems that this is not so. Young animals are sometimes given to a weli, and are not sacrificed for months. It is clearly recognized that the animal thus given so fully belongs to the weli that even if blemishes develop in it the man who gave it ceases to be responsible for them. While the man could not sacrifice such an animal if it had lost more than a third of its ears or tail,[1] now that the animal belongs to the weli, his responsibility ends. But though he gave it to the weli, and it belongs to the weli, it does not become a sacrifice until he, or the butcher, throws it on its left side, with its head toward Mecca, if he be a Moslem, or toward Jerusalem, if he be a Christian, or toward the shrine of Mar Jirjis, if he sacrifices to St. George in his own village, and cuts its throat. The consummation of the sacrifice is in the outflow of blood. The feast which follows adds nothing. It may be affirmed with emphasis that to the large majority it means nothing except good cheer. If any proof were wanting in support of this statement, it is abundantly furnished by the fact of the great *dahhiyeh* sacrifices in the Valley of Muna, which were adopted by Mohammed from the heathen rites which attended the festival at Mecca. Not only the kissing of the sacred stone by the Moslems at the Kaaba is a primitive rite, but also the sacrifices. At the Valley of Muna there is no feast whatever, the victims are buried, or the Arabs are permitted to come and take them away.[2] It is

[1] Hedaya, London, MDCCXCI., Vol. IV., p. 79.

[2] Cf. Burckhardt, Travels in Arabia, London, 1829, p. 276: "The act of sacrifice itself is subject to no other ceremonies than that of turning the victim's face towards the Kebly, or the Kaaba, and to say, during the act of cutting its throat, 'in the name of the most merciful God ! O Supreme God !' . . . . Any place may be chosen for these sacrifices, which are performed in every corner of Wady Muna; but the favorite spot is a smooth rock on its

clear, with respect to these sacrifices, that the sacrificial act consists in the outflow of the blood of the victims.

It may not be so easy to determine the value of the sacrifice. Does it possess in any degree a substitutionary or vicarious character? Let us pass some of the facts already cited in review. Such a sacrifice is at least thought to insure good luck, but wherein does the good luck consist? There are certain facts which seem to point toward a substitutionary value in sacrifice. Such are the formulas, already mentioned in the preceding chapter, employed for announcing a death in Syria or Palestine: "Abdullah is dead, but your life is redeemed," or "Abdullah is dead, may God give you his life"; that is, "You have a better chance of living on account of his death." An Arab is almost broken-hearted at the loss of a pet mare, whom he loves more than his wife, but a fellow clansman seeks to comfort him by saying, "Do not mourn for her; if she had not died, Allah might have taken your life." So, if a beloved son is cut down in the flower of his youth, the father is comforted by the same assurance, that, had his son not died, he might have lost his own life. This is clearly a substitutionary idea.

So, too, when the minister of the "Chair" at Zebedani, said, "Every house must have its death, either

western extremity, where several thousand sheep were killed in the space of an hour." Burton, Personal Narrative of a Pilgrimage to Al-Madinah and Mecca, London, MDCCCXCIII., Vol. II., p. 218: "It is considered a meritorious act to give away the victim without eating any portion of its flesh. With respect to sacrifices slain for an incomplete performance of duty, Burton remarks, ibid., p. 140, note 3: "The victim is sacrificed as a confession that the offender deems himself worthy of death: the offerer is not allowed to taste any portion of the offering."

Ahmed Hindi of Damascus, who has made three pilgrimages to Mecca, says: "At the age of fifteen, every man and woman must offer a sheep. . . . . . They do not eat the sheep, but put it in a hole in the ground. If any one desires to eat the carcass he may. Journal VIII.

THE SIGNIFICANCE OF SACRIFICE 225

man, woman, child, or animal," it is evident that when the owner slaughters an animal as a sacrifice for his house, it is with the understanding that the being whom he fears will now spare him and his family, because he has offered it up a subsitute in their stead. This came out clearly when a Protestant, Mr. Jabur in the Syrian Desert, yielding to the entreaties of his neighbors, Moslems as well as Christians, cut the throat of a sheep at the entrance of his house to secure the safety of his family. The thought of his neighbors, if clearly expressed, would have been, "If you slay a sheep, your family will be safe; if you do not, one of them will be in danger." Thus the sacrifice which is offered when a bridal couple make their home in an old house, or when a family moves from one house to another, has really a substitutionary character. So, too, the people of Kerak, when they occupy a cave during harvest, insure their lives by killing a victim who takes the place of all of them, as a sacrifice to the jinn who is landlord of the cave. Doughty was definitely assured that the blood of an animal was put on the corner of a house, which was building, to protect the workmen;[1] that is, the animal died that they might live. It was this passage which I found in Doughty[2] a year ago last summer that first suggested to me the substitutionary character of such sacrifices. The reader may well imagine my sensations on the first great interview which I had in Syria with the servant of the "Chair," when he announced, "Every house must have its death."

Other expressions are found for the same idea of vicarious sacrifice, as "head for head," "spirit for spirit," where the head of an animal, or its spirit, is said to

[1] Cf. p. 191.
[2] Travels in Arabia Deserta, Cambridge, 1888, p, 136.

226 PRIMITIVE SEMITIC RELIGION TO-DAY

take the place of the man, woman, child, family, or group for which it dies.

One of the most thrilling discoveries was in regard to the existence of blood-sprinkling at the present day, upon doors, door-posts, and lintels. I do not claim that this was an original discovery, for it had been observed by a young Englishwoman in the Druse Mountains, who mentioned her observations to me; and such a case is cited by Dr. Trumbull, as seen by Dr. Washburn, of Robert College, Constantinople. But this fact has been so emphasized by the number and range of my personal investigations as to have, perhaps, the value of a new discovery.

Some Bible students may be tempted to conclude that in this custom we have an imitation of blood-sprinkling in connection with the institution of the Passover festival, when the destroying angel passed by the houses of the Israelites. At first blush, this would seem probable. But I am confident that a closer view of the subject, a more careful weighing of the facts, will show, that in the institution of blood-sprinkling we have a primitive Semitic custom which long antedates the Passover festival. The use of blood mentioned in Ezekiel, where the priest is to take the blood of the sin-offering and put it upon the door-posts of the house (temple), and upon the four corners of the ledge of the altar, and upon the posts of the gate of the inner court, resembles the usage which we find to-day among Bedouin who never came into contact with the Old Testament.[1] These Arabs, Bedouin, and Fellahin, who are so little influenced by Islam, have evidently not derived the custom from that faith; for as

---

[1] Palmer, The Desert of the Exodus, New York, 1872, p. 218: "We saw no blood upon the door-posts, or on the tomb itself, as is usual in desert welis; but the reason assigned for this by the Arabs

we have seen, orthodox Moslems consider such a use of blood highly reprehensible. Besides we have noticed that the same custom existed among the ancient Babylonians.[1]

What is the object of putting blood on the doors of private houses? In the case of the Israelites, it was that, when the destroying angel went through the land of Egypt to slay the first-born of the Egyptians, he might spare the first-born of the Israelites. If this account were to be translated into the thought and terminology of the ignorant modern Semite, the destroying angel would be an "Afrit," such as the people of Hamath, after they have annually repaired their largest water-wheel, seek to propitiate by causing the blood of a victim to run down into the sluice.[2]

At Hamath, as we have learned, the Christians in the time of cholera put blood, brought from the slaughter-houses on the doors of their houses in the shape of a cross. This is not good Semitic usage, because the blood was not that of victims. But it is founded on good Semitic usage because it represents the idea that blood is the all-important thing in sacrifice, and that there are malignant powers of the air who must be placated, and turned away by the sign of a surrendered life in substitute blood.

It is more difficult to understand the significance of blood, or of semn and henna, placed on a door-post and lintels of a shrine. Perhaps the object is to remind the saint of the blood of the victim that has been slain. It may be sprinkled on the shrine in the same way that the

---

was that on the occasion of sacrifice they placed two stones by the door to receive the blood, and that these are afterwards removed, in order that the tomb may be kept pure and clean."

[1] P. 54, n. 2.   [2] P. 198.

ancient Arab was said to have smeared blood on the sacred stone which was regarded as *bet Allah*, or the house of God.[1]

Whether it involves the idea of a covenant between the one bringing the sacrifice and the saint, as a Protestant deacon suggested to Dr. Henry H. Jessup, in connection with the shrine at Tell Abu en-Neda, is not clear; it may. There can be little doubt that when blood is sprinkled on the sacred stones of a shrine, and upon those who bring the sacrifice, we have an ancient Semitic parallel with the conclusion of the covenant on Mount Sinai, where Moses sprinkled part of the sacrificial blood on the altar and part on the people.

Whether I have given a correct interpretation of the facts gathered, the student must decide. It seems to me, however, that these facts shed much light on the true significance of sacrifice as a primitive Semitic institution.

[1] W. Robertson Smith, op. cit., p. 184.

CHAPTER XVIII

THE PLACE OF SACRIFICE, AND THE ORIGINAL ALTAR[1]

We have already seen that there is no evidence among Syrians and Arabs of the existence of burnt-offerings. Has an ancient rite faded from their memory? If the position taken be true that usage now, among ignorant Syrians and among Arabs, is likely to represent primitive usage, then it seems probable, as has been observed in a preceding chapter, that the original element in sacrifice was not its consumption by fire, but in its being presented to God, and if it were an animal, in its blood being shed.

Let us approach this discussion from another point of view, namely, that of the altar. The Biblical student cannot well conceive of an altar, apart from incense, or one of which the main design was not the offering up of burnt-sacrifices to God. There are also well-attested examples among other Semitic peoples of altars which were used millenniums before Christ for sacrifices made by fire. We might, therefore, be tempted to conclude that an original institution had perished from the memory of the modern Semites, on finding that altars for fire-offerings date back for thousands of years among the Assyrians and other peoples. Yet we must remember that some of the most ancient institutions are still preserved among peoples living in the twentieth century, but who have been unaffected by the progress of the ages in their social and religious customs.

[1] Cf. Appendix F.

If, as we seem to have found, primitive sacrifice consists wholly in the shedding of blood, the place where the sacrifice is slain becomes simply the place of slaughtering, or the place of sacrifice. This conclusion is confirmed by the etymology of the oldest words for altar, both in Arabic and Hebrew. We may be sure that in the form of these words we shall get the primitive idea.

As all Semitic scholars are aware, there is a large class of nouns formed by prefixing the letter *m* to the verbal root. Such nouns signify, either the place where a thing is done, the instrument by which it is done, or the embodiment of the action. The verbal root in Arabic which signifies "to sacrifice," is *dhabaha*. Lane renders this:[1] "He slaughtered [for food, or sacrificed] an animal, or a sheep, or a goat, or an ox, or a cow in the manner prescribed by the law, [that is by cutting the two external jugular veins] or by cutting the throat from beneath at the part next the head . . . . *dhabaha anhu*, he slaughtered or sacrificed for him by way of expiation." The word *dhibh* signifies an animal prepared for slaughter or sacrifice; that is, an intended victim . . . . for example, it is said in the Koran, xxxvii. 107, 'And we ransomed him with a great victim' "; that is, Abraham. Remembering that a noun formed by prefixing *m* may mean the place where a thing is done *madhbah* signifies, "A place where victims are immolated; altar, slaughterhouse."[2] As will be seen, there is no hint in this expression of burnt-offerings, nor in another derivative *midhbah*, (slaughtering-knife). On the other hand, the etymology of the word *madhbah* bears unequivocal testimony to the

[1] Arabic-English Lexicon, *sub voce*.
[2] Wortabet and Porter, Arabic-English Dictionary, Beyrout, 1893, *sub voce*.

THE PLACE OF SACRIFICE 231

fact, that slaughtering an animal by the shedding of blood was the primitive idea of sacrifice.

Let us examine the Hebrew verb signifying "to sacrifice," *zabah*, which is almost identical with the modern Egyptian pronunciation of *dhabah* as *zabh*. This word, too, means originally to slaughter, and *mizbeah* also "place of sacrifice"; so in Biblical Aramaic *madhbah*, "altar," comes from *dĕbah*, which signifies "to slaughter" and then "to sacrifice."

Where were such sacrifices offered? Evidently in connection with some habitation, either of God or man. Among the Bedouin such a habitation is a tent, even when they term it house (*bet*), and describe the pitching of the tent by their women as the building of a house. The entrance of such a tent is on the east. As an emir testified, "Ever since God (*Allah*) created the Arabs, the east has been the front of the tent." Here, then, is the proper place to slay the animal.

But if possible, many sacrifices should be taken to some shrine. If the saint or weli is conceived of as residing in a sacred tree, or as revealing himself there, then at that tree would be the place of slaughtering; if he is at a gigantic grave under the open heavens, plastered over, or in the ordinary Moslem grave covered with stones, and with gravestones at the head and feet, and in both cases surrounded with a low wall, then outside such a shrine would be the place of sacrifice. If in a fountain, as at Ain Fowar, or at Zerka Main, the victims are to be brought to the place. If the weli is thought of as in the little building, usually with a dome, known as a *makam*, *mezar*, *zeyareh*, or by whatever other name, the victim should be slain at the building.

But where is the place of sacrifice? Some say anywhere in the court, around which houses are built, but it is clear that correct usage among Bedouin and Syrians places it at the entrance. There are some definite testimonies with respect to this.

As we have seen, the sacrifices offered to the jinn or the weli of a cave are at the entrance.[1] It is there that the blood falls. The east side, or entrance of a tent, is the proper place for sacrifice. Occasional sacrifices, in payment of vows, brought to Nebi Daud in Jerusalem are slain either before the doorstep of the court, or before one of the doorsteps of the dwellings inside the court. The late Rev. John Zeller, of Jerusalem, relates that he saw the blood of the victims killed at the feasts of circumcision before the doors of Nebi Musa near the Dead Sea.

Abdu Khahil, the head native master of the Boys' School in connection with the Irish Presbyterian Mission at Damascus, says: "It is common to kill a sacrifice at the threshold." Musa Khuri has twice seen in Rasheya, once among the Greek Catholics and once among Syriac Catholics, a lamb slaughtered over the doorstep as fedou. They believe that if they build a new house and neglect to do this some one of the family will die.

Mrs. Dale, daughter of President Bliss, of the Syrian Protestant College, Beirut, saw a sheep killed among the Greek Catholics at Ras Baalbek. They cut its throat on the doorstep and they made the sign of the cross in blood over the door.

There are many examples of the threshold as the place where the sacrifice is slain. We have already passed the various kinds of sacrifices in review. The one for the pilgrim who returns from Mecca, or from Jerusalem, or for a soldier, or prisoner, who comes back to his home, is on the threshold of the entrance to that home. There the butcher cuts the throat of the victim.

[1] P. 184.

THE PLACE OF SACRIFICE 233

The following incident, related to me in Homs, with reference to the use of a threshold in sacrifice, seems most significant in this connection: "If a man has bought a new house, and the inhabitants have been unlucky, that is, have had ill health or death, before moving into the house, the owner makes some change, and offers a sacrifice. The change usually consists in taking up the old stone on the threshold and laying a new one in its place. Then the sacrifice is offered on that threshold. They call it presenting a *keffareh*, in order that no evil may befall them."

So when the sacrifice is made for a new house, a similar ceremony is observed. This is the custom in northern Syria and the Syrian Desert. At Kerak, and on the east side of the Dead Sea, the victim is taken upon the flat roof and its throat is cut so that the blood runs down over the lintel.

Among Moslems and the so-called sects of Islam, as Nusairiyeh, Ismailiyeh, and Druses, it is common to immolate victims on the doorsteps of shrines. The same custom is to be found among the Christians, including the various sects, such as Copts, Jacobites, and others. At a wedding among Syrian members of a Greek Church in New York City, a sheep was sacrificed in the street, probably before the door of the house which was to be the home of the bridal pair, in the month of November, 1901.

In this connection Dr. Henry Clay Trumbull's learned monograph, The Threshold Covenant, is of great value. There can be no question that the sacrifice at the entrance of a tent, a cave, or at the threshold of a house, represents primitive Semitic usage, and that this is the place of sacrifice, so far as that term means the place of immolation, or the pouring forth of blood. It may also be considered the original altar, so far as we understand by that term the place where the blood of the victim is poured out. I have seen conspicuous examples of this usage in the Druse Mountains and in other places.

The next step in the use of an altar is in the employment of a rude stone upon which the victims are slain. Such was the place where the sacrificial blood fell, when the Israelites slaughtered sheep and oxen after their victory over the Philistines between Michmash and Ajalon.[1] We should also remember in this connection that the favorite place at which the Moslems slaughter their victims in the Valley of Muna, is on a smooth rock, which may be regarded as a rude altar.[2]

It is reported that such rude stone altars are still used among the Arabs. The Rev. James B. Nies, Ph.D., of Brooklyn, New York, saw such an altar at Yazuz, in the land of Gilead, under a sacred terebinth tree. It is a rectangular stone, from an old Roman ruin, about three feet long by two feet wide, and about two feet high, with cup-holes and channels for blood, which were probably cut by the Arabs.

There is an Arab graveyard near the sacred trees. Here, then, is a most interesting combination of sacred trees, and probably, if the truth could be learned from the Arabs, a grave where repose the mortal remains of a weli, the saint of a clan, and a stone used as an altar for the victims immolated upon it.

Dr. Nies also points out another illustration of a sacrificial stone in a demi-dolmen, which is thus described by Major Conder:[3] "The cap-stone measures thirteen feet east and west by eleven feet north and south, and the mean thickness is about twenty inches. A curious sys-

[1] 1 Sam. xiv. 33-34.   [2] P. 223, n. 2.
[3] The Survey of Eastern Palestine, London, 1889, Vol. I., p. 20.

SACRED TREES AT YAZUZ, AND ROCK ALTAR OF ARABS UNDER THE TREE ON THE RIGHT.

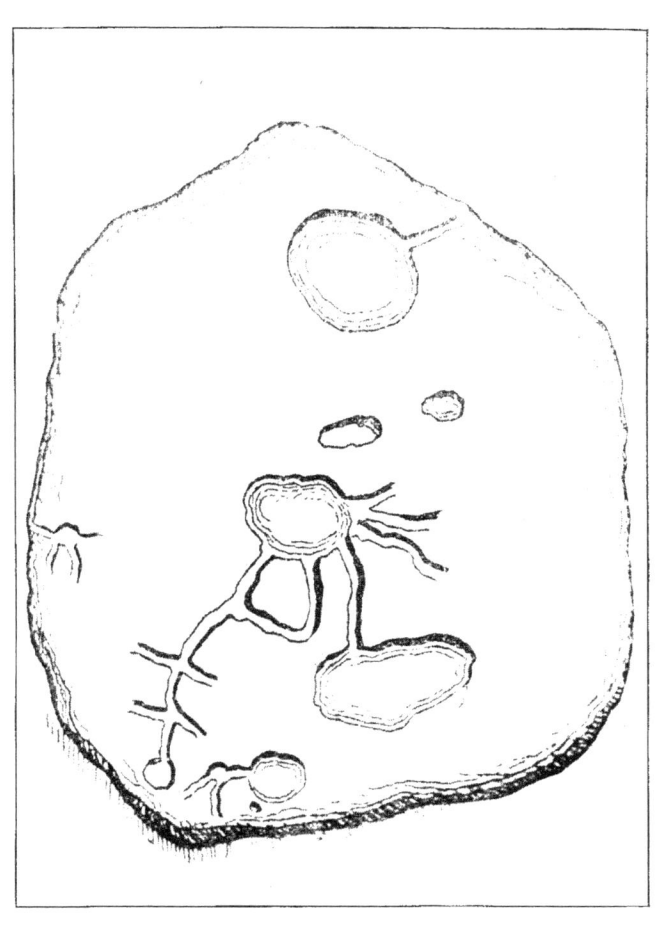

DOLMEN ALTAR, WITH HOLLOWS FOR BLOOD.
AFTER MAJOR CONDER.

DOLMEN NEAR ZERKA MAIN.

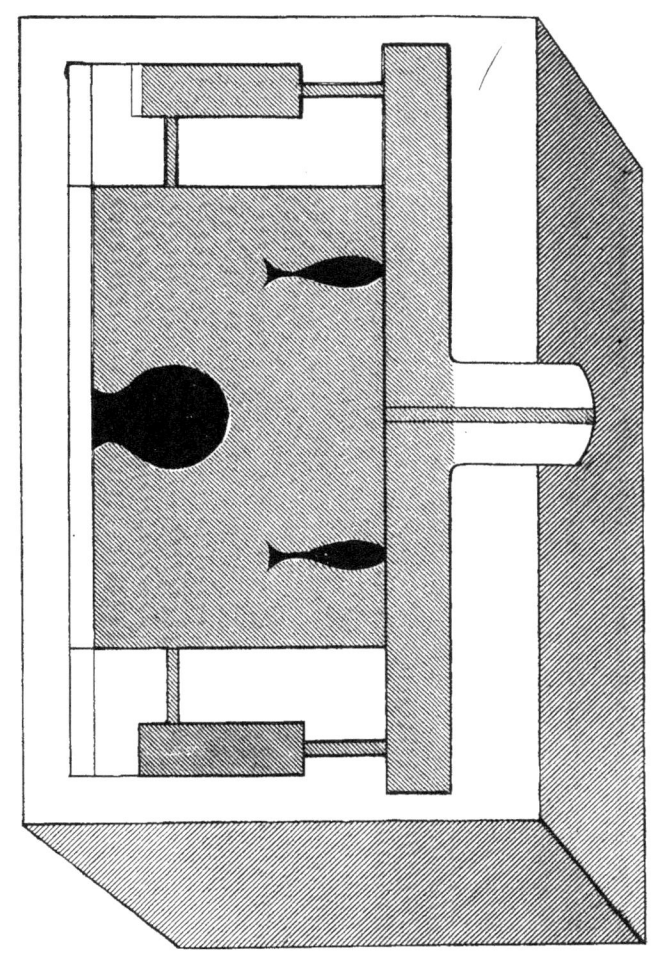

ALTAR AT GIZEH MUSEUM

After a drawing by Dr. Nies

The red color represents surface and channels for the blood

tem of channels and hollows was noticed in the capstone. . . . . Near the middle of the stone is a hollow twenty-six inches by twenty inches and twelve inches deep. Near the west end, which is the highest, is a hollow one foot square." The channels connecting these hollows can be traced from the diagram. Dr. Nies sees in the hollows on the cap-stone of the dolmen artificial depressions made by Arabs in order to receive the blood of their sacrifices. He says that the Gizeh Museum, in Cairo, affords hundreds of altars for the immolation of victims, having on the upper surface round and square holes for receiving the blood.

Perhaps the most important confirmation of the use of a rock as the place of sacrifice among the Bedouin is found in a communication from Dr. Schumacher, of Haifa.[1]

A conspicuous example may be found in the high place at Petra, which I described in the Quarterly State-

---

[1] HAIFA, 30th January, 1902. *My Dear Professor Curtiss*— Your letter of the 4th inst. was just received, and I hasten to reply to it, briefly, as I am to start for a journey to the interior and begin archæological excavations at Taanach and Megiddo.

1. I do not know of any rock altars used by the Bedouin, but of ancient columns and similar large stones, and have come across some at El-Hawi near Ras Birkish in Ajlun, also near Beisan at the shrine of El-Halaby; at Shejarat el-Arrifije ("the tree of the sorceress" vid. my Northern Ajlun p. 106), also in Ajlun and in other places across the Jordan.

2. They are nearly all in connection with sacred trees and shrines.

3. The stones are hollowed on the top and have circular holes of 3 inches to 6 inches diameter and 2 to 4 inches depth.

4. The character of such "altar" holes is for the reception of blood. I have been present at several similar [sacrificial] ceremonies of the Bedouin. In order to fulfil a vow, the family members of a tribe . . . . gather at a shrine under a tree; a sheep or a goat is brought thither, the khatib or priest lays it across the "altar," with the body on the stone and the head and neck hanging down. Then with the

ment of the Palestine Exploration Fund, for October, 1900.

There seems to be a combination in this illustration of the altar of burnt-sacrifice and a table or altar for slaying victims. The latter is eleven feet nine inches long from north to south, sixteen feet six inches wide, and is ascended by four steps in the northeast corner.

On the top of the platform is a remarkable and suggestive feature with reference to its probable use in the preparation of victims for the sacrificial fire. This consists in two circular and concentric pans with vertical sides, cut out of the rock, with a conduit leading from the lower pan which may have served to carry away the blood of the victim. The larger pan is three feet eight inches in diameter, its depth is three inches; the second or lower pan is one foot five inches in diameter, its depth is two inches. The conduit is three feet two inches long, two inches wide, and three inches deep. This platform corresponds to the simple altar of the Arabs, as described by Dr. Nies and Dr. Schumacher, and is combined with the altar of burnt-sacrifice, which arose in the development of worship at a much later period. We have a sim-

---

words: *bismillah, rahman, er-rahim** (in the name of God the merciful of the merciful) he cuts the throat of the animal with a knife, and the Bedouin gather the blood and sprinkle it over the grave of the Muhammedan saint buried at the shrine which is near by. In doing so they call the dead saint to witness that they have fulfilled this vow. The animal is cooked afterwards and eaten.

The sprinkling is generally done with a tassel made of goat hair, which is hung over the shrine after the ceremony is over. The graves of saints or shrines are therefore generally covered with blood . . . . N. B. I find in my notes on northern Ajlun that the Shejarat el-Arrifije (or Shejarat Barakat or Baruka) may be a rock altar. The spot is greatly venerated by the Bedouin and Fellahin of the district. The place, a heap of ruins, and rude, large stones is, however, considered a shrine. . . . . "

*This, of course, differs from the formula in the Koran, C.

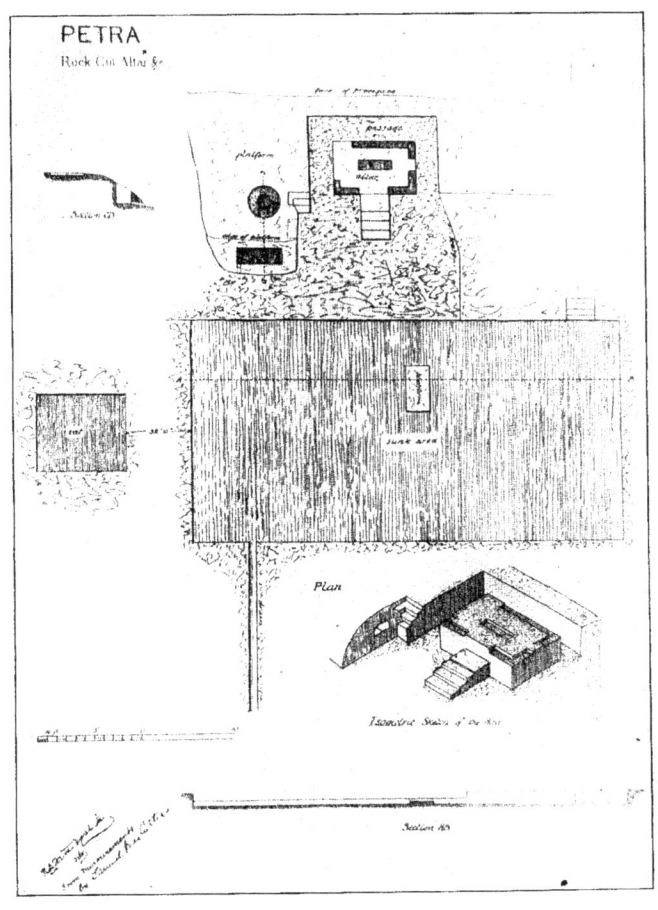

GENERAL PLAN OF HIGH PLACE AND ALTAR AT PETRA.

ANCIENT PLACE FOR SLAUGHTERING SACRIFICE AT PETRA.

AFTER PROFESSOR GEORGE L. ROBINSON.

NOTE.—The observation of the High-Place and Altar at Petra by Professor George L. Robinson, in the spring of 1900, has all the value of a new discovery. The place, though seen and partially described by Mr. Edward L. Wilson, an American, in his SCRIPTURE LANDS, London, 1891, p. 104, remained unrecognized by the learned world, until Dr. Robinson found it, as he thought, for the first time. The writer keenly regrets, that through misinformation as to the thoroughness of Dr. Robinson's researches, he should have anticipated him in the pages of the Quarterly Statement in the announcement and description of a find which is one of the most important made for the history of Semitic worship during the nineteenth century.

THE PLACE OF SACRIFICE 237

ilar combination in Ezekiel, where, in the description of the temple, eight tables are mentioned as used especially for the slaughter of the victims, and four tables of hewn stone for the reception of the burnt-offerings.[1]

When we consider all these examples together, it is easy to trace sacrifice back to a time when it consisted chiefly in shedding the blood of the victim. It was slain at the entrance to the tent, or cave of the earliest Semites; and later, when they lived in houses, on the threshold; and still later, on a rock where, like the Arabs to-day, they hollowed out places to receive the blood.

[1] Ezek. xi. 39-43.

CHAPTER XIX

CONCLUSION

There are three views which may be held with reference to the origin of Israel's religion, as set forth in the Old Testament. One is that of the naturalistic interpreter, who conceives that we have in it simply the record of a human development, from which the idea of God is excluded, except as God may be conceived of as being in all things.

Another is that of those who may be designated as traditionalists, for lack of a better name, who conceive of the worship of ancient Israel as instituted by God himself on new foundations. This view is favored, as the critics affirm, by the historian of the Priests' Code.

A third view recognizes the fact that the religious institutions of ancient Israel, at their beginning, are an outgrowth of those of the primitive Semites, yet not merely through natural development, but through the power of God's Spirit coworking with men.

Let us examine each of these views a little more in detail. The first adopts the principle of natural development, of an advance from the most rudimentary religious conceptions of God and man, and their relations to each other, to those which are complex and spiritual. I think no student who weighs the evidence can question the fact of development in the religion of Israel from elementary ideas, such as are characteristic of the childhood of the race, to those which we find in the most spiritual utterances of prophets and psalmists. This fact can be as truly demonstrated as the development of the eagle

CONCLUSION

from the egg, and the egg from the parent germ, or of the mighty oak from the acorn. None who admits the facts can dispute such a conclusion. But among the modern, as well as among the primitive Semites, the egg stage, or that of the eaglet which has just picked its way out of the shell, has not been passed; the mighty oak has not got beyond the acorn, or the tiny plant which the goat, the enemy of all forests, can crop off. This, as we have seen, is the case among Arabs, Bedouin, and Syrians whose lives have not been affected by positive religion. Whenever positive religion has come in from without, there has been a change. Mohammed saw and promulgated the great idea of "no god, but God." But he did not arrive at this idea through any natural evolution. The Arabs from whom he sprang were where the Arabs had been for millenniums before him, who, while recognizing God as the author of all things, were adherents of the most superstitious rites. There is not the slightest evidence that Mohammed rose on the shoulders of an Arab religion which had been climbing during the millenniums to a grand conception of God.

While he developed individually, his coreligionists still remained in their old heathenism, and had not furnished the soil for his development. Though his mind rose to a worthy conception of God, he was still in the grip of ancient Semitism, in the lust of beauty which he inculcated as a means of sensual indulgence, and the lust of conquest by which he sought to win and hold the Arabs. Besides, his rejection of the revelation of the Father through Jesus Christ, the Son, made the doctrine of the mediation of the saints, and a practical deification of them, a necessity. Islam is in no sense the product of a development from ancient Semitism. On the contrary, it is still fettered by a compromise with old heathenism, by the adoption of the ancient rites at its pilgrim festival, and kissing of the stone at the Kaaba. It is bound by fate; it presents no worthy aim in life; woman's face is veiled that man may not lust after the beauty of his neighbor's wife; continence is secured through license, which is legalized immorality; the zeal of the faithful is stimulated by prospects of plunder; converts are made by the sword; and paradise consists of a garden of sensual delights. This the mass of Moslems believe, and have no place for the spiritual joys of the Christian heaven. We may therefore affirm with emphasis, that Islam, in its doctrine of God, is not a natural development from Semitism. Its noblest teachings have come from Judaism and Christianity. Mohammed was not the product of his own people. Indeed, the old Semitism had power to fetter him and his teaching in the observance of their low standard of morality; and by the tyranny of unchanging custom to confine Islam in a prison house, whence there is no hope of release. Usage, then, which is like a law of the Medes and Persians, that cannot change, has stopped all moral and religious progress in the Moslem world.

No one will, of course, presume to say that Christianity is a natural evolution from ancient Semitism. The facts are too patent to admit of such a supposition. It was because Christianity had become so corrupted and debased in the ancient Syrian world, originally beginning as a pure institution, that Islam, as in some respects a superior faith, was able to choke it out.

If any proposition can admit of an easy demonstration, it is that those characteristics which are noblest and best in these systems, are not a natural evolution from the Semitic mind. Semitic custom, through the compromises which it demanded of Islam, on behalf of heathenism, sensuality, and the love of plunder, has left its brand upon the Moslem religion. Semitism has been able to say to Islam, "Thus far shalt thou go, and no farther." Semitism, so far from producing Christianity, was able to devitalize it, to bring its adherents under the influence of the superstitions of heathenism.

The theory of the traditionalist, that the teachings of the Old Testament are new revelations direct from God, without relation to past customs and institutions, is not borne out by facts. While it is often man's method to break entirely with the past, even in innocent habits and modes of thought, and missionaries in the earlier years are said to have illustrated this method, some at times teaching converts from the historic churches that it was wrong to observe Christmas and Easter, or any other saint's days, or to sing any of the old songs, or to maintain any of the old customs; a study of the Bible shows that this is not God's method.

We are thus borne on by a consideration of the facts of primitive Semitic religion to the third theory that the most spiritual conceptions of the Old and New Testaments have been gradually evolved from ancient Semitic conceptions under the guiding and controlling power of God. God must be predicated as a factor in this evolution, if we take into account the fact that among no branch of the Semitic peoples, if we count out ancient Israel, have they been able to rise to spiritual conceptions of deity and worthy ideas of morality.

Men who had the problem to deal with which was present to God when he decided to lead a people out from the bondage of Semitic ignorance and superstition, would have said, "Let us break completely with the past, let us introduce a new order which is radically different from the old." Not so God, in his wisdom. As we have seen, men had certain conceptions of him as a superhuman man. These he did not reject, though so imperfect and unworthy. He adopted these conceptions as a medium of instruction, and so we find the Jehovist treating of God as if he were a man, with something of a man's imperfections, but presenting a higher ideal than that of the unaided, uninstructed mind. This, however, is the lowest stage of the Old Testament representation of God. It rises constantly higher through the psalmists and prophets, through conceptions of Canaan as Jehovah's land, and Jehovah as Israel's God, and the Temple as his abode, to the conception of the God of all the earth, "who does not dwell in temples made with hands," "whom the heaven of heavens cannot contain." For this view, there were powerful political reasons in the experiences of the Babylonian exile. The exile destroyed, for the Israelites, the conception of God as confined to one land, to one city, to one temple, or to one people. While there had been foregleams of the great truth that God is the God of all the earth, the death of the nation's hopes was needed, in order to instill such lessons as we find in the second part of Isaiah, as to mission of the Servant Israel to all the nations, and that the same God is immanent among all nations, as well as in Israel, and at the same time transcendent above them.

We have seen how easily the Semite deifies men, makes the saint his mediator, and for all practical purposes his god. I have shown in another place how there is nothing startling to his mind in the physical fatherhood of deity, that a mortal woman may have a divine husband. Hence there was a prepared people, in these original and natural ideas, for the mystery of the incarnation, which to them was no mystery. That Jesus should be begotten by the Holy Spirit through the Virgin

CONCLUSION

Mary as son of man, and Son of God, was no surprise to the Semitic mind, still believing in the possibility of such a connection even to the point of credulity.

Then such a personal appearance of God among men satisfied the longing of the Semitic mind, and a longing which we find among other minds. God seems so far away, so indifferent, to the simple Semite to-day, that he feels the need of a saint near at hand to whom he can utter his vows and prayers in his extremity. Here, then, was a natural basis for the doctrine of the incarnation as we find in the New Testament.

We have seen how crude was the original conception of sin, as equivalent to misfortune, visited by an arbitrary and capricious despot. This view is not absent, as we have observed, from the Old Testament. During the period of the judges men are continually falling away into idolatry; misfortune comes upon them through the heavy hands of the Philistines, for a time there is an external reformation, and then they fall back again. There is no real consciousness of guilt. God takes this rudimentary conception; he does not at first attempt a radical change in this thought, but he works constantly through lawgivers, prophets, and psalmists, until men see the exceeding sinfulness of sin, before misfortune has struck them down, so that David could cry:

"Against thee, thee only, have I sinned,[1]
"And done that which is evil in thy sight."

And under the visitation of God's judgment, and his rebukes, Job no longer saw the hand of a capricious

[1] Ps. li. 4. It seems to me that psychologically this Psalm fits David's experience after his sin with Bathsheba, and his murder of Uriah. The last two verses could not well have been from his hand, and were doubtless added at a much later period. Such additions were almost as common in ancient psalmody as in modern hymnology.

tyrant, as was once the case,[1] but had such spiritual views of Him as to say:

"I had heard of thee by the hearing of the ear;[2]
"But now mine eye seeth thee,
"Wherefore I abhor myself, and repent in dust and ashes."

Men see visions of God, like Isaiah, so that they are led to exclaim:

"Woe is me! for I am undone;[3]
"Because I am a man of unclean lips,
"And I dwell in the midst of people of unclean lips;
"For mine eyes have seen the King, the Lord of hosts."

There are indeed other cries in the Semitic world, as we see from the Babylonian Penitential Psalms,[4] which indicate a consciousness of sin, on the part of a few select souls, far deeper than anything we find in primitive Semitism.

But the Babylonian worshiper is still fettered by the conception that sin and misfortune are one; that since the heavenly powers are very angry his sins must be very great. He has indeed reached a higher stage of development than we find among Bedouin, Arabs, and Fellahin, so far as these researches have extended. There does not seem to have arisen anywhere in the world a consciousness of sin as guilt, without the revealing power of God's Spirit.

Again, the original idea of sacrifice seems to be one derived from experience in the East, if not in the West, that "every man has his price." Hence the gods have their price. If God has brought misfortune upon man,

[1] Job. ix. 30, 31.
[2] Job. xlii. 5.
[3] Is. vi. 5.
[4] Zimmern, Babylonische Busspsalmen, Leipzig, 1885, pp. 61 ff.

he can be bought off; if he demands a human life, the price may be paid through a substitute; if the price is the "bursting forth of blood before the face of God," then the blood of sheep, goat, bullock, or camel, the best that a man has of animal life, may avert the misfortune and cover the sin. This is indeed a crude idea. There are many stages between it and that contained in the musings of penitent Israel concerning the vicarious sufferings of the Servant, which strike through every Christian heart with love and sorrow, so that we read them with the same solemn hush, and sometimes with falling tears, as if we stood with Mary and John beneath the cross of Him who bore our sins in his own body on the tree, and whose Christian interpretation has broken some Jewish hearts:

" All we, like sheep, have gone astray,[1]
We have turned every one to his own way,
And Jehovah hath made to light on Him, the iniquity of us all."

It is not natural development which leads up from the most rudimentary conceptions of sin as misfortune, and sacrifice as a gift or substitute offered to a capricious tyrant, to those conceptions which we have in the representation of the Servant, or to a conception which we find centuries before in Hosea.[2]

" How can I give thee up, Ephraim?
How can I deliver thee up, Israel?
How can I make thee as Admah?
How can I set thee as Zeboim?
Mine heart is turned within me;
My compassions are kindled together;
I will not execute the fierceness of mine anger;
I will not return to destroy Ephraim:
For I am God, and not man."

[1] Is. liii. 6.   [2] Hos. xi. 8, 9.

No naturalistic evolution can account for such a conception of the Divine Father as we have in the parable of the Prodigal Son, or in his love message to the world through Jesus Christ, or in the depths of tenderness which we have in Christ, who came to do the Father's will by his ministry of suffering, and by laying down his life for us. In this we see how the divine wisdom has been doing a greater work than in creating worlds, by being the Teacher, the Lover, and the Saviour of the race.

But in no way is the divine love, patience, and condescension more manifest than in its method of reaching down to the ignorance and superstition of a group of Semitic families, to teach the lessons needed, until the fullness of the times should come, when He who was to be the mediator of the love, mercy, and justice of God should be revealed.

APPENDIX A

QUESTIONS ON THE SURVIVALS OF ANCIENT RELIGION IN BIBLE LANDS

I.

CONCEPTIONS OF GOD.—1. What conceptions do people have of God? (*a*) As a supernatural being; (*b*) as a superhuman man. 2. Do they seem to have derived them from the relations of tribal life? (*a*) Do they think of him as moral? (*b*) Do they consider him holy? 3. Is the worship of the saints (welis) a moral force among the natives in your part of the country? 4. Why do the people fear the saints (welis) more than they do God? 5. Are there any indications of the idea that God (the saint, the weli), is the physical father of a tribe or people? 6. Are there any usages or expressions that indicate God as a procreator? (*b*) Do women ever regard the saints (welis) the physical fathers of their children? (*c*) Do they ever speak of a woman, or the representation of a woman, as "the bride of God," or is there any similar idea? (*d*) Is licentiousness ever a feature in the worship at the shrine? (Cf. Hos. iv. 12-14.)

II.

DIVINE REVELATION.—I. *The Place.* 1. Where are tekkes, zeyarehs, makams, welis, mezars placed in your part of the country, and which of these designations is employed? 2. Are altars or a substitute for them ever used? 3. Do you know of any ancient altars or high places? Where? 4. How far are there sacred trees or groves in connection with the shrines? 5. Is the body of a saint (weli) put under a kubbeh, or under the open heavens? How is the place arranged? II. *The Manner.* 1. Names of sacred waters with which you are acquainted, fountains, rivers, streams, wells, etc.; anything especially characteristic of them? (*a*) Do people bathe in them to get healing? (*b*) or barren women to get children? 2. Sacred fish or animals? 3. Sacred trees? (*a*) Are they ever regarded as having a spirit residing in them? (*b*) Are vows ever made to them? Food hung upon them? (*c*) Do people ever receive healing by being under them? (*d*) What is the significance of the rags on trees? What virtues do the natives attribute to them, and what use do they make of them? 4. Sacred stones or pillars. (*a*) Do you know of any stone through which a spirit is supposed to reveal himself, or through which cures are wrought? (*b*) Have you ever seen such a stone in or before a shrine? (*c*) Is it ever anointed with oil, or sprinkled with blood? (*d*) Have you ever heard of a bridal pair passing between such stones? Relate any ceremonies in connection with them. 5. Sacred caves. (*a*) Do you know of any caves said to be inhabited by spirits? (*b*) Do barren women ever go to them for children?

III.

MAN'S RELATION TO GOD (*or the saints*).—I. *Sin.* What is the ordinary conception of sin? 1. Is it regarded as guilt or misfortune? *e.g.*, according to old ideas are murder and theft crimes? 2. In what is the evidence that a man has sinned. II. *Sacrifice.* 1. What is the mode of sacrifice in your district? 2. Does the term used for it signify simply slaughtering, or does it involve something more? 3. Is any part of the victim burned (on an altar or a substitute for an altar)? 4. How is the flesh of the animal commonly disposed of? 5. In what sense do the natives regard fowls, sheep, goats, bullocks killed in payment of vows as sacrifices? III. *Shedding of Blood.* 1. Relate any customs that you have observed, or of which you can learn, in connection with the shedding of blood. 2. Do the natives give any explanation of its significance? 3. Is there any connection between the use that is made of a mixture of semn and henna and blood?

IV.

THE LIFE AFTER DEATH.—1. How far do the people have any idea of a future life? 2. Do they fear death? 3. Do they deem any special preparation necessary for it?

V.

THE SPIRIT WORLD.—1. Have you any original information regarding the jinn? 2. Do people offer sacrifices to them? 3. Do they offer sacrifices to the dead or for them?

VI.

MISCELLANEOUS.—1. Give any useful information about religious customs not covered by the preceding questions. 2. Is there a religious significance in the character of any tattoo marks?

APPENDIX B

Outline of Journeys in Syria, Palestine, Egypt, and the Sinaitic Peninsula, including the time spent at special centers.

NOTE. — The modes of travel throughout Syria and Palestine, except from Jaffa to Jerusalem, and from Beirut to Damascus, which are connected by railroads, was by horses; in visiting various points of interest in Egypt, was by donkeys; and in the Sinaitic Peninsula, by camels. In connection with most of the trips, the expense is indicated, and some particulars are given with respect to the temperature at different points, although no careful observations were taken except on the tours made in the summer of 1900. The report of these observations appears in a separate table.

I. TOURS, 1898-1899

1. Headquarters in Beirut.
   July 9th—July 16th.
2. Journey through the Lebanon (with two tents, which were loaned, with a dragoman and two muleteers; expense, $5.00 a day); Zahleh, Niha (ruined temples), Baalbek, Lake Yammuneh, The Cedars, Jebel Makmal, Bsherreh, Ehden, Hasrun, Ard Akluk, Afka (source of the Adonis), Natural Bridge, Jebel Sunnin, Zahleh, Baruk and Cedars, Der el-Kamar, Aleih, Beirut. Temperature comfortable all the way; very cool at the Cedars.
   July 16th—August 6th.
3. First Conference of Christian workers at Brummana. Temperature pleasant.
   August 9th—August 14th.
4. Visit with the Rev. George C. Doolittle, of Der el-Kamar. Temperature pleasant.
   August 15th—August 22d.
5. Mount Hermon and the sources of the Jordan (on horseback, with the Rev. W. K. Eddy and children, without tent, Mission Stations). Jezzin, Jedeideh, Shiba, Hermon (over night), Merj Ayun, Mutelleh (Jewish Colony), Dan (Tell el-Kadi, chief sources of the Jordan), Cæsarea Phillippi (Baniyas, source of the Jordan), Hasbeya, and Hasbani (first source of the Jordan), Tell Ijon, Der el-Kamar. Temperature comfortable; snow on Mount Hermon, and very cold at night.
   August 22d—August 31st.

250 PRIMITIVE SEMITIC RELIGION TO-DAY

6. Beirut to Tripoli (along the sea coast, on horseback, native hotels); Beirut, the Dog River (inscriptions inspected), Juneh, Gebal, Batrun, Tripoli. Temperature very warm; but fine breeze from the Mediterranean.
   September 6th—September 9th.

7. Northern Syria (companions, the Rev. F. W. March and the Rev. W. S. Nelson, D.D., of the American Presbyterian Mission, and Mr. C. W. Wisner, Jr., of the Syrian Protestant College. We put up in the houses of native helpers and in churches. I slept, as in all other journeys, unless otherwise mentioned, on a portable iron bedstead). Tripoli, Minyara, Beinu, Amar, Kalat el-Hosn, Monastery of St. George (chief seat of his worship by all sects of Moslems and Christians), the Sabbatic fountain, Safita, Meshita, Musyaf, Mehardeh, Hamath, Homs. Temperature pleasant. The first thunderstorm of the season after March occurred at Safita in the night. There was a very heavy fall of rain.
   September 10th—September 29th.

8. Homs to the Syrian Desert (companions, Turkish soldier and Butrus, my cook and muleteer); Homs, Lake of Homs, Tell Nebi Mendeh, Riblah (the natives pronounce it Rubleh, just as they pronounce Kibleh, Kubleh), where we were entertained over night by the sheik of the village, Shemiyeh, Hasya, Hafar. Temperature "quite hot . . . but a nice breeze."
   October 1st—October 2d.

9. Syrian Desert (companion, the Rev. J. Stewart Crawford; houses of native helpers). Hafar, Hawarin, Karyaten, Hot Baths of Solomon, Hafar, Nebk, Yabrud, Malula, Sednaya, Bludan. Temperature very comfortable; cool nights.
   October 2d—October 12th.

10. First visit to Damascus.
    October 12th—October 17th.

11. First visit to Jerusalem during the sojourn of the German Emperor. Temperature very warm.
    October 23d—November 24th.

12. On a Syrian housetop in Damascus. Rainy season, but much pleasant weather. Cold at night, but no fire necessary when there was sunshine.
    November 28th—February 4th, 1899.

13. Egypt. Port Said, Alexandria, Cairo, Pyramids, and Sphinx, Sakkara, Cairo to Luxor (by sleeping-car), Karnak, Thebes, up the Nile on one of Cook's steamers (Ramses III.) to Assuan, Philae. From Assuan to Cairo by train.
    February 7th—March 11th.

APPENDIX B 251

14. Sinaitic Peninsula (companion, the Rev. J. S. Scotland, of Newport, Scotland; dragoman, Joseph M. Shaar; cook, and seven Bedouin from four different tribes. There were ten camels, and the total expense of the journey for both was $600). Cairo, Suez, Ayun Musa, Wadi Werdan, Wadi Gharandel, Ras Abu Zenimeh, Maghara, Firan, Wadi Selaf, Monastery of St. Catharine (two days and a half in a tent), Jebel Katherin, Jebel Musa, Ras es-Safsaf, return journey: Wadi Barak, Wadi el-Beda, Wadi Tal, Wadi Gharandel, and so back over the same course as going. Weather very pleasant, but very cold at the end.
March 12th—March 30th.

15. Beirut. End of rainy season. Powerful showers every day.
April 1st—April 7th.

I. Tours alone; made with two muleteers and a tent. (Expense, $3.60 per day.)

16. Phœnicia, Galilee, and Samaria to Jerusalem. Sidon, Nabatiyeh, Castle of Belfort, Der Mimas, Castle of Baniyas, Castle of Hunin, Castle of Tibnin, Tyre, Alma, Dibl, Nebi Shema, Kadesh Naphtali, Kafr Birim, Jebel Jermak, Meiron, Safed, Tiberias (across the lake to Gamala and Kalat el-Hosn back to Tiberias on horseback, and fording the Jordan at the southern end of the sea of Galilee), Tiberias to rapids of the Jordan at the north end (returning in a boat by moonlight), Mejdel, Wadi el-Hamam, Jebel Hattin, Nazareth, Tabor, Sepphoris, Plain of Battof, Acre, Mount Carmel (Pross' Hotel), Esfiyeh, el-Muhraka, (traditional place of Elijah's sacrifice), Tell Kasis, Jenin, Dothan, Sebastiyeh, Nablus, Gerizim, Ebal, Shiloh, Sinjil, Jerusalem.
April 7th—May 16th.

II. Tours with a companion east of the Dead Sea. (Companion during this and the remaining tours, Professor Gilroy of the Semitic Department in the University of Aberdeen, Scotland).

17. Jericho, Dead Sea, bridge over the Jordan, Heshbon; Medeba, Jebel Neba (Nebo), Main, Dibon, Jebel Shihan, Rabbath Moab, Kerak, Arab encampment; return journey over the same route, spending a night on Jebel Neba.
May 17th—June 2d.

18. Beersheba and Philistine Cities. Bethlehem, Tekoa, Engeddi, Hebron, Beersheba, Gaza, Ascalon, Ashdod, Yebna, Ekron, Tell es-Safi (Camp of Dr. Fred Bliss), Tell, Zakariya, Valley of Elah, Bet Jibrin, Husan, Pools of Solomon, Jerusalem. Temperature always comfortable; sometimes with refreshing breezes.
June 5th—June 16th.

19. Esdraelon and the Maritime Plain. Anathoth, Ain Fara, Geba, Mickmash, Betin, Nablus, Sebastiyeh, Sanur, Jenin, Jezreel, Shulem, Little Hermon, Nain, Endur, Meggido (Lejun), Mount Carmel (at the Monastery), Athlit, Dor (Tantura), Summarin (Jewish colony), Cæsarea, Jaffa, Jewish Industrial School, Lydda, Modin (Mediyeh), Lower Beth Horan, and Upper Beth Horan, Jerusalem. Temperature always comfortable; the night we reached Jerusalem was cold.
June 20th—July 1st.

20. Jerusalem.
July 1st—July 11th.

21. The Jaulan and the Hauran. Jericho, Arak el-Emir, Wadi es-Sir, Rabbath Ammon, es-Salt, Jebel Osha, Wadi Zerka, Jerash, Suf, Ain Jenneh, Ajlun, Kalaat er-Rubud, Arbela (Irbid), Capitolias, Gadara, Hot Springs (forded the Yarmuk three times; the ascent to Fik was steep and almost dangerous). Aphek, el-Merkez, Tell el-Ashary, Edrei, Bosra, Sheik-Miskin, Damascus (by rail.) Temperature, with the exception of sirocco, when the thermometer stood at ninety for six hours, at Jerash, was very pleasant.
July 11th—July 27th.

22. Jerusalem. The return home was by steamer from Jaffa to Beirut; from Beirut and Smyrna to Constantinople, to Athens, and by train to Patras, and by steamer to Brindisi, and from Brindisi by train over Milan and Basle to Paris and London. Temperature in Jerusalem comfortable at night, and in the shade during the day.
August 3d—August 17th.

II. TOURS, SUMMER OF 1900

Companion, Mr. A. Forder, of Jerusalem, missionary to the Arabs. Expense of journey, $7.50 per day; traveled with a tent; landed at Beirut June 11th. [For a record of the temperatures see special tables below.]

1. South Country (Negeb) and Gadis (Kadesh Barnea). Jerusalem, Mar Saba, Bethlehem, Pools of Solomon, Hebron, Kurmul (Carmel), Main, Yutta, Dahariyeh, Beersheba, Khalasa, Ruheiba (Rehoboth), Biren, Gadis; returning Biren, Rasisi, Sbeta, Wadi Dhega, Asluj, Kurnub, Wadi Milh, Hebron, Jerusalem.
June 18th—June 30th.

2. Jerusalem to Petra (Wadi Musa). Jericho, Medeba, Meshetta, Zerka Main, Machaerus, Wadi Mojib, Kerak, Tafileh, Shobek, Petra (Wadi Musa), Tomb of Aaron. We returned by the same route.
July 2d—July 20th.

APPENDIX B   253

3. Jerusalem to Damascus. Jerusalem, Nablus, Beisan, Irbid, Muzerib (by rail to) Damascus.

   July 26th—July 29th.

4. Damascus to Palmyra (victoria, drawn by three horses; total expense, $65.00). Damascus, Kutefeh, Nebk, Hafar, Mahin, Karyaten, Beda, Palmyra. We returned over the same route, including Der Atiyeh.

   July 31st—August 10th.

5. Damascus to the Druse Mountains. Damascus, Negha, Brak, Suwaret el-Kebireh, Smed, Umm ez-Zetun, Damet el-Alia, Kanawat, Mayim, Sahwet, Ayun, Salkhad, Orman, Tell Shaf, Busan, Shoba (Philippolis), Umm ez-Zetun, Suwaret esh-Shaghireh, Suwaret el-Kebireh, Brak, Merjaneh, Der Ali, El-Kisweh, Damascus. The temperature, with the exception of one day of sirocco weather, was delightful.

   August 13th—August 23d.

III. TOURS, SUMMER, 1901

1. Headquarters at Damascus (including visits to Bludan and Ain Fijeh).

   June 5th—June 20th.

2. Damascus to northern Syria, the Nusairiyeh Mountains and Ladikiyeh (companion, the Rev. J. Stewart Crawford. We took our own beds; entertainment mostly in native houses; expense, $3.50 a day). Damascus, Kutefeh Nebk, Kara, Hesya, Homs, Hamath, Mehardeh, Abu Obeda, Ain Kurum, Jebel Dhahr esh-Sh'ar, Matwar, Snobar, Ladikiyeh, Kadmus, Musyaf, Mehardeh, and back to Damascus by the route already indicated.

   June 21st—July 20th.

3. Bludan to Mount Hermon (companion, the Rev. J. Stewart Crawford ; expense, $2.50 per day). Bludan, Rasheya, Mount Hermon, Kafr Miski, Burj en-Nebi, Nebi Safa, Ain Shirsha, Der el-Ashair, Bludan.

   July 26th—August 2d.

4. Second Missionary Conference at Brummana.

   August 13th—August 18th.

5. Visit to Abbas Effendi at Acre. Beirut to Haifa and return.

   August 20—August 24.

REMARK.—The temperature during the summer of 1900, as will be seen from the following record, was comfortable; at times it was very cool. And during the summer of 1901, with the exception of heat and humidity at Ladikiyeh, it was pleasant.

SUMMER TEMPERATURES
1900

Place.	Date.	Time of Day.	Degrees Fahr.	Remarks.
Jaffa	June 14th	7:30 A. M.	72	
Jerusalem	June 15th	6:30 A. M.	60	"Strong breeze."
"	June 16th	7:15 A. M.	58	
"	June 17th	7:45 A. M.	62	
"	"	8 P. M.	60	
Mar Saba	June 18th	8:30 P. M.	71	
"	June 19th	5:30 A. M.	67	
Hebron	June 20th	6:30 A. M.	55	"Breath of morning delicious."
Dahariyeh	June 21st	6 A. M.	59	
Beersheba	"	5:30 P. M.	81	
"	June 22d	5 A. M.	59	
Ruheibah	"	4:30 A. M.	70	
Biren	June 23d	2 P. M.	93	"In the tent."
"	June 24th	7:30 A. M.	75	
"	"	2:30 P. M.	92	
"	June 25th	4 A. M.	59	
Sbeta	June 26th	12 M.	65	"Under Terebinth."
Jericho	July 2d	5 P. M.	98	"Thermometer in the shade, but on the wall."
"	July 3d	12 A. M.	84	
Medeba	"	6 P. M.	76	"Nice breeze, heat not oppressive."
"	July 4th	5 A. M.	61	
Zerka Main	July 5th	1 P. M.	92	"In the shade."
Machaerus	July 6th	4:30 A. M.	67	"Beautiful day for traveling."
Wadi Mojib	July 7th		Warm	"Deep ravine."
Kerak	July 9th	4:15 A. M.	71	
Tafileh	July 10th	5:35 A. M.	61	
Shobek	July 11th	5 A. M.	53	
Petra	July 13th	6:30 A. M.	67	"Treasury of Pharaoh."
"	"	5:30 P. M.	72	"Temperature fell in ten minutes to 65°."
Tafileh	July 14th	5 A. M.	52	
"	"	5:45 P. M.	71	"Beautiful breeze all day."
"	July 15th	7:45 A. M.	58	"Cold in the night."
Kerak	July 17th	9:30 A. M.	69	
Wadi Mojib	July 18th	3:30 A. M.	77	

APPENDIX C

THE SEVEN WELLS AT BEERSHEBA

JOURNAL V. Gaza, June 11, 1899. — "We had a most interesting experience at Beersheba. I arose at 4:15 A.M., and went to inspect the wells. One was near the place where we camped. It is about ten feet in diameter. The stones are hewn square, and joined with much regularity. I should think the well might be fifty or sixty feet deep. Water is drawn up in a large skin, by a camel, by means of a windlass, and runs from thence into a stone reservoir, after it has been emptied by a couple of Arabs, and then into a trough for the animals. A second well is of about the same dimensions, and with the same arrangement for drawing water. A third is about six feet in diameter, and of about the same depth. The stones lining the well are hewn, and are quite regular. The water is raised in skins, of smaller size than that at the large well, two or three men pulling up each separately. [This is the usual method of drawing water in the South Country.] The ropes have worn grooves in the soft limestone rock which lines the wells. A fourth well is being opened. The old stones which were used in lining it, and which had been thrown out, are irregular, and evidently from an ancient period; some of them used for lining the well at the top bore the marks where the rope had worn grooves. The superintendent told me there were three other wells which had been closed. It was one of the most fascinating sights I have seen, (if not the most fascinating) to behold the camels, donkeys, sheep, goats, and horses gathered at these wells. It was a matter of the deepest interest to see these characteristics of patriarchal life in a district entirely without houses, but where there are many tents. The country reminds me of a western prairie in its level character around Beersheba, and especially from Beersheba to Gaza. It seems to be well adapted for the growing of grain and the pasturage of flocks. I must have seen several hundred camels at Beersheba and other points. Camels are watered once in two days in the regular course of things, although in the Sinaitic Peninsula they go without water four or five days. Horses can endure if they have water once a day."

JOURNAL VI. Beersheba, June 21, 1900. — "We arrived at Beersheba at 12:30 P.M., after a ride of five and a half hours from Dahariyeh. We could have made the journey in five, but our guide being old was not able to keep up, so we gave him a ride two or three different times on our animals. . . . When I visited Beersheba a year ago four wells had been opened; now there is a fifth. The site of two others not very far from the chief well was pointed out, so that seven wells are accounted for."

APPENDIX D

THE PROSE VERSION OF THE STORY OF 'ARJA

The name of the heroine of this story was Fatima. She was lame in her right leg, and was therefore called 'Arja. She and three other girls lived in a village where there was no water. They each belonged to a patron saint.

One day the four girls went to the well from which they were accustomed to draw water, and found their respective saints sitting around it; but they did not recognize them as such. The four saints began to jest with the girls.

One of them to whom the best-looking girl belonged said, addressing her, "Would you not like to become the disciple of our sheik?" naming another to whom she was not devoted. She refused to abandon her sheik, and passed on, and let down her jar into the well, it came out intact.

Another, to whom the girl who was next in good looks belonged, said, "Take such a sheik," naming one besides himself. She replied, "I will not abandon my sheik." She filled her jar, and it came out whole. There remained two girls. The third was attractive. Her sheik, whom she did not recognize, said, "Take a sheik." She replied, "I have one," mentioning him. He said, 'He's no good." She answered, "I will not abandon him." She, too, filled her jar, and it came up unharmed. The fourth girl remained. Her sheik asked her, "Have you a saint?" She replied, "Yes," though she, like the others, did not recognize her saint. He said, "He's no good; take such an one; he will help you bring up your pitcher; it will come out safe; but your saint will break your pitcher for you." She refused to abandon her saint; so the other three saints said to her saint, "Will you permit us to break her jar?" She lowered her jar, and there came up only the two handles. She began to cry. Her companions had filled their jars and had gone. The saints said to her, "Did we not advise you to take such an one as saint, and you would not heed our counsel, but adhered to your patron, and he has broken your jar."

After her companions had been gone nearly half an hour, the saints took pity on her; so her patron saint leaned over the well, and said, "In the name of God, the merciful and compassionate," and brought up her jar whole and full of water. He told her "Take your jar and go; there are your companions." She swore by the life of her saint she would not go. She said, "I must know who you are. He told her who they were. "Now," said her patron, "you know our names, go." She replied, "You must first give me the gifts of the good." [*i. e.*, the wine of those who are good, the brotherhoods are formed through the cup.] The sheik gave her to drink, and she became a holy woman—a sheika. She then said, "I am not going; you see I am lame." He replied, "I am not a surgeon." She responded, "The man who restored my jar can cure my leg." He then said, "We used to be potters, now we have become physicians. Oh, God, cure her leg!" She began to walk like a gazelle. He said, "Take your jar and go." She said, "How can I go? I am bald." The sheik said, "No, by G—, that is an affliction; we began as potters; we continued as surgeons; now we have become physicians," and prayed, "Oh, God, give her long hair." It came. He then bade her go, but she said, "One of my eyes is bad." He named the name of God over her, put one of his hands on her eye, and it was restored. He urged her to go with her companions. She refused to go because she was naked. He prayed God, who sent down upon her a green robe like silk from the truth. She then asked for money. He said, "We do not seek for property; you can turn up the carpet. We go; the property remains." She turned up the rug, and found a river of gold and of silver. She did not take any, as he advised her not to do so. He and his followers do not seek wealth. They are allowed to beg. He said, "I do not come for gold. Are you better than your saint? Let it go on flowing under the carpet!"

He told her to go. She said, "I am afraid to go; you must bring me to the girls." He told her to turn her back; he named the name of God; he pushed her, and she landed by the side of the girls; he pushed her again, and she was in front of the girls; he pushed her a third time, and she was beyond them. The girls did not recognize her, because she was so changed from her condition when she was lame, bald, blind, and naked. Finally they recognized her face, and asked how it had happened. She replied, "These were our four sheiks; it was my saint that broke my jar, and who gave me all this." She then spent the rest of her life in going about.

When she came to die she abode at the place now called the "Mother of Pieces." She is under the stones, where women who make vows to break jars, in case they receive the blessings for which they ask, break them. The father of the priest of the "Mother of Pieces" sought to build a shrine for her. He spent a night at the place, and dreamed that he struck his pickaxe into the ground and hit the neck of a woman. The religious men whom he consulted told him it was evident she did not wish that he should build her a shrine.

The women now break jars in fulfilment of their vows because her jar was broken. She used to have great power in preventing any one from taking anything from the trees; but recently she seems to have lost some of her power, for two or three trees have been dug up.

APPENDIX E

HIGH PLACES AND SACRED SHRINES

On my return from a visit of fourteen months in Syria, Egypt, the Sinaitic Peninsula, and Palestine, I had an opportunity to consult the literature of the subject with reference to sacred shrines. I found, in Conder's Tent Work in Palestine, an interesting confirmation of results which I had reached independently, through my own researches as well as some new information. I quote the most important passages:

"The professed religion of the country is Islam, . . . yet you may live for months in the out-of-the-way parts of Palestine without seeing a mosque or hearing the call of the Muedhen to prayer. Still the people are not without a religion which shapes every action of their daily life. . . . In almost every village in the country a small building surmounted by a whitewashed dome is observable, being the sacred chapel of the place; it is variously called Kubbeh (dome), Mazâr (shrine), or Mukâm (station), the latter being used in the Bible for the 'places' of the Canaanites, which Israel was commanded to destroy 'upon the high mountains, and upon the hills, and under every green tree.' (Deut. xii. 2.)

"Just as in the time of Moses, so now, the position chosen for the Mukâm is generally conspicuous. On the top of a peak, or on the back of a ridge, the little white dome gleams brightly in the sun. Under the boughs of the spreading oak or terebinth, beside the solitary palm, or among the aged lotus-trees at a spring, one lights constantly on the low building, standing isolated, or surrounded by the shallow graves of a small cemetery. The trees beside the Mukâms are always considered sacred, and every bough which falls is treasured within the sacred building. . . . The typical Mukâm is . . . a little building of modern masonry, some ten feet square, with a round dome carefully whitewashed, and a . . . prayer niche on the south wall. . . . There is generally a small cenotaph within, directed with the head to the west, the body being supposed to lie on its right side, facing . . .

Mecca. . . . This Mukâm represents the real religion of the peasant. It is sacred as the place where some saint is supposed once to have 'stood' (the name signifying standing-place), or else it is consecrated by some other connection with his history. It is the central point from which the influence of the saint is supposed to radiate, extending in the case of a powerful sheik to a distance of perhaps twenty miles all round."[1]

My next quotation regarding the shrines is from Clermont Ganneau, from his monograph on The Arabs in Palestine:

"The tenacity with which old religious customs have been kept up is another remarkable circumstance. Not only have the Fellaheen, as Robinson conjectured, preserved, by the erection of their Mussulman kubbehs, and their fetishism for certain large isolated trees, the site and the souvenir of the hill sanctuaries and shady groves, which were marked out for the execration of the Israelites, on their entry into the Promised Land, but they pay them almost the same veneration as did the Canaanite kooffars, whose descendants they are. These makoms, as Deuteronomy calls them, which Manasseh rebuilt, and against which the prophets in vain exhausted their invectives, are word for word, thing for thing, the Arabic makams, whose little white-topped cupolas are dotted so picturesquely over the mountain horizon of central Judæa.

"In order to conceal their suspicious origin, these fellah sanctuaries have been placed under the protection of the purest Mohammedan orthodoxy, by becoming the tombs or shrines of *Sheykhs, welys,* and *nebys* (elders, saints, or prophets), deceased in the odor of sanctity. But there are numerous indications of their true origin beneath this simple disguise. For instance, the name given to them is often the same as that of the locality, and is not merely a simple name, but a personification, or deification if I may so say, of the place itself; for many legends show that in the eyes of the peasants the neby, or prophet, has given his own name to the place.

"This close connection of names and places is found in the Phœnician and Canaanite mythology, which is remarkable for the number of its local divinities, and it helps to explain why Moses, not content with ordering the destruction of the Pagan sanctuaries, insisted upon the abolition of the names (Deut. xii. 3). . . . Another point of religious resemblance is the worship of

[1] Tent Work in Palestine, London, 1895, pp. 304, 305.

female divinities, which we know was common among the Canaanites and is still practised, many modern kubbehs being consecrated to women. In certain cases there is duality, the wely or the neby being venerated in connection with a woman, who passes generally for a sister or his daughter. This relationship, originally conjugal,[1] which has been changed by the Mussulmans into one of consanguinity offers an equivalent of the sexual symmetry of these Phœnecian couples so clearly brought to light by M. de Vogüe."[2]

For the Sinaitic Peninsula I can cite no better authority than the lamented Professor Palmer, whose attainments in colloquial Arabic were so marvelous.

The following is his general characterization of the shrines with which he became so familiar. In his chapter on Feiran, he writes: "Here, too, is a burial ground with several nicely kept graves. . . . This cemetery, as usual, contains a 'Weli,' the tomb of Sheik Abu Shebíb, the patron saint of the district. It is a small stone building. . . . The cenotaph in the center is actually covered with a *kisweh*, or a cotton pall. . . . The Peninsula of Sinai is divided into so many districts, each of which has its own private saint. In every 'parish' an acacia (or shittim) tree is consecrated, and is not mutilated by having its branches rudely lopped off to feed the flocks withal, the fate of every other tree of the species. The pods are shaken off when ripe, as they form a favorite and nutritious food for the camels; but even for this the saint's permission is formally asked at his tomb. The Arab regards his patron with as profound a reverence as that with which an Italian peasant looks upon his little copper Janarius. He appeals to him for help on every occasion of difficulty. . . . Abu Shebíb himself is reported to have appeared in answer to the prayers of a hunter who had broken his leg on Jebel el-Benát, and to have conveyed him safe and sound to his own home. True, however, even after death, to his Arab instincts, the saint stipulated for a handsome *bakhshish*, a white-faced sheep to be offered once every year at his tomb."[3]

[1] There is an example of such conjugal relationship at the shrine of Job, at El-Merkez, the capital of the Hauran. His cenotaph and that of his wife were pointed out to Dr. Schumacher, of Haifa, but the old sheik who showed me the cenotaphs assigned one of them to Job's son, which would be more in accordance with Moslem ideas.
[2] The Survey of Western Palestine, Special Papers, pp. 325, 326.
[3] The Desert of the Exodus. New York, 1872, pp. 139, 140.

APPENDIX E

In this connection I present Burckhardt's account of his sacrifice in Wadi Musa in sight of the tomb of Nebi Aaron. "The sun had already set when we arrived on the plain; it was too late to reach the tomb. . . . I therefore hastened to kill the goat, in sight of the tomb, at a spot where I found a number of heaps of stone, placed there in token of as many sacrifices in honor of the saint. While I was in the act of slaying the animal, my guide exclaimed aloud, 'Oh Haroun, look upon us! It is for you we slaughter this victim. Oh Haroun, protect us and forgive us! Oh Haroun, be content with our good intentions, for it is but a lean goat! Oh Haroun, smooth our paths; and praise be to the lord of all creatures.' This he repeated several times, after which he covered the blood that had fallen on the ground with a heap of stones; we then dressed the best part of the flesh for our supper."[1]

[1] Travels in Syria and the Holy Land, London, 1822, p. 430.

APPENDIX F

THE SAMARITAN PASSOVER

The following description was given by an eye-witness, Dr. Daud Katibah, Nablus, July 26, 1900. I have preserved the language of the communication without essential change.

"The observance is celebrated on the fourteenth of Nisan, which varies according to the lunar year. When Saturday falls on the fourteenth, they celebrate the Passover on the preceding Friday.

"They go to the top of Mount Gerizim, at least a week before the feast, pitch their tents, and there they remain two weeks. They observe the feast seven days.

"In the Samaritan community there are forty men; including women and children, the whole number may be estimated at one hundred and fifty or two hundred. [Baedeker, Palestine and Syria, Leipzig, 1898, gives the number at 170.] They all attend the festival, even though they are ill; *e.g.*, a man went up this year (1900) who had not recovered from pneumonia.

"They reckon each day from sunset to sunset. The observances on the day of the Passover are as follows: They begin at sunset with singing, in which all take part. As a rule they kill the lambs needed for the congregation at sunset. These are white, one year old, without blemish. Should Saturday fall on the fourteenth of the month, they kill at noon on Friday, and eat at sunset. As a rule they eat the lambs late at night.

"All the people are dressed in white, and they begin with prayer and singing. There are several priests to kill the animals with special knives. The knife must be put in under the larynx. If an animal is not properly killed they call it unclean, and give it to the Moslems or the Christians. During the slaughtering they sing (shout) in Samaritan.

"While slaughtering the animals they make a fire ready in two places. One of the fires is prepared for burning the wool, the hoofs, the horns, and the entrails. Everything that is not eaten is burned. They do not remove the skins of the animal. They scald

APPENDIX F 265

them and pull off the wool. Two men then hang the lamb on a pole by its hind legs, placing the pole on their shoulders. Then the priest opens the belly of the animal and removes the entrails, the liver, and the fat on the kidneys. These he burns with fire.

"The other fire is prepared a long time before the sacrifices. They dig a pit, ten or twelve feet in depth, and in this they make the fire five or six hours before they sacrifice. A special priest feeds the fire all the time. When the lambs have been made ready by the priests, they put the poles through the animals from end to end. At a signal from the priest they quickly put the lambs, seven or eight in number, into the pit. All the while they are singing in the Samaritan language. Then they cover the pit with a network of wood, and afterwards cover it with earth. No air gets inside, so there is no conflagration, only heat. The lambs remain in the pit three or four hours.

"After they have placed the lambs in the pit, they all go to a special place on the mountain, including men, women and children, and kneel in rows. The priest has the law of Moses. When he prays he has a special mantle on his shoulders. They repeat their prayers by rote, with their faces toward the south, and assume different attitudes.

"When the time comes for removing the sacrifices, the priest approaches the pit and makes a brief prayer. Then the people remove the covering from the top of the pit, and afterwards lift up the poles, on which are the lambs, one by one. Sometimes the poles get burned, and a man who has covered up his face and hands is let down with ropes or by their hands, and he takes up the lambs.

"By this time the people are very hungry. None can eat of the lambs but those who are circumcised, and who are (ceremonially) clean. Each family, and those who are reckoned with them, take a lamb and put it in a basket, and sit around it in a circle. The priest begins with a short prayer and song. After this, standing, they eat the flesh of the lambs in haste with unleavened bread and bitter herbs. None of the Moslems and Christians who are watching this ceremony may partake of the lamb, though some of the generous Samaritans offer them unleavened bread and bitter herbs."

APPENDIX G

ALTARS AND SACRIFICES IN THE PRIMITIVE ART OF BABYLONIA

BY REV. WILLIAM HAYES WARD, D.D., LL.D.

An attempt is not made in this paper to cover the literary material bearing upon the use of sacrifices and the nature of the altars in the worship of the early East. That would require a study of texts beyond what I have leisure to make. I simply attempt to gather from the art of early Babylonia the representations of altars and sacrifices, and discover the religious ideas so far as they may be involved therein. A very large part of the material must come from the seal cylinders, which have preserved much the larger part of the art of Babylonia, in contracted, though fortunately permanent, forms; and to these cylinders I have given minute study for many years.

Babylonia was not a mountainous region, and yet the early art often suggests familiarity with the region of mountains. Gilgamesh sometimes fights the swamp-buffalo, and sometimes the wild bull of the forests. The sun-god appears rising above the eastern mountains, which suggest Elam. There are ibexes or oryxes which seem to suggest the hills of Arabia. There are different types of faces, front view and profile, which seem to suggest different origins. We seem to find two utterly different races, indicated by their languages, Sumerians and Semites, going back to the earliest times, not to speak of the "black heads" and the evidence of a primitive negroid race. These facts make us suspicious that the Babylonian religion and the Babylonian gods may have become a composite of diverse origins, which perhaps it may yet be possible to separate. But to do this would require a minute study of both the literatures and art, such as has not yet been made. I merely call attention to this point just now as one to be kept in mind in observing diverse customs that may arise.

So far as I can make out, at the very beginning of Babylonian art, two entirely different kinds of altars were in use, one

APPENDIX G 267

of which soon passed out of use. This appears to be a square altar with a single high step or shelf. Its shape may be seen from the example in Fig. 1, taken from a very archaic shell

FIG. 1. SEAL IN THE METROPOLITAN MUSEUM, NEW YORK

cylinder, which, if we can judge from its style, is considerably older than the time of Sargon I., whose date has been usually assigned, on the authority of Nabonidos, to 3800 B.C., although Lehmann and others who follow him believe that this date is perhaps a thousand years too early. The two shelves appear to be used to support vases, cakes, or animal sacrifices.

Before the figure of Bel in a four-wheeled chariot, drawn by a winged dragon, between whose wings stands a goddess holding a sheaf of thunderbolts, stands an altar of this shape. On the top of the altar are what may be two flat cakes, and there is some appearance as if there were a vase on the shelf below.

FIG. 2. METROPOLITAN MUSEUM

268   PRIMITIVE SEMITIC RELIGION TO-DAY

Before the altar a worshiper pours a libation through the spout of a small vase. The libation does not fall on the altar but beyond it. In this case the idea seems to be of a worshiper before what may be a bas-relief of the god, goddess, and dragon.

A second illustration of this very primitive style of altar appears on another archaic seal (Fig. 2) of green serpentine. In this case the seated goddess holds three stalks of grain in her hand, while before her is an altar, on the lower shelf of which appears to be a pile of flat cakes, with a bird above them, while a vase is set on the upper shelf. A second figure holds a plow. A yet more important illustration of this kind of altar is seen in the famous Rich cylinder (Fig. 3), which represents the worship of Gula. Here the

FIG. 3.   THE RICH CYLINDER

altar stands before the goddess, and we seem to see its construction, probably of bricks, although it is equally possible to conceive of it in the form of a table or stand made, as such objects are still made, of stems of the palm. Here on the upper shelf, the top of the altar, are what may be cakes, and on them the head of a goat, probably, which may represent the whole animal. A worshiper led to the goddess carries in his arms a goat, presumably for sacrifice, if we may be guided by the head of the animal on the altar.

Yet another case of this altar with a shelf is seen in figure 4, where a cup with what appears to be a flame arising from it, is seen on the shelf. Here the concave sides are due to the necessity of so drawing them because of the concave surface of the cylinder.

These four seals are the only ones I know which represent the altar of this shape. They are of the highest antiquity, and show offerings of food on the altar, apparently cakes, also apparently a

APPENDIX G 269

bird on the altar, and the head of an animal, also a vase on the altar, with burning oil, also the pouring out of a libation, and farther than this, the actual presentation of an animal before the altar by a worshiper. We have here a pretty full ritual of sacrifice. Several different deities are being worshiped; in one case the seated Gula, in another perhaps the same goddess as the patroness of agriculture, in another case both the god Bel, perhaps in his chariot, and the goddess with the thunderbolts, and in the fourth case an uncertain seated deity. In each case the deity is seated.

A second form of altar apparently quite archaic, is the round hour-glass form. The altar we have been considering with a lower

FIG. 4. METROPOLITAN MUSEUM

shelf, or step, appears to have been of square construction, of brick, if it were not possibly of wood, or rather like the seats framed from stout stems of palm-leaves. This second type is contracted in the middle, not merely by the concavity of the cylinder, but evidently the altar itself was more slender, and of quite a different shape. The oldest cylinder of this type is of the extremest archaic style. This is seen in figure 5. This cylinder, like three of the four previously shown, belongs to the remarkable collection in the Metropolitan Museum of New York, and is of marble. The bird-like heads indicate its antiquity. On cylinders of this type we frequently find the earliest rude forms of the design which gives us what Heuzy calls the coat of arms of Sirgulla, and which we see in its best form in the silver vase of Entemena, an eagle seizing an animal of some sort symmetrically with each of its talons. On this cylinder the altar carries at the

270 PRIMITIVE SEMITIC RELIGION TO-DAY

top what may be two flames, but which look very like two simple branches. We shall see, however, that in the bas-relief from Susa (Fig. 4) the single flame looks very much like a branch. It is impossible, however, for us to imagine that that bas-relief represented the priest as watering a plant in a flower-pot. We have in this archaic design (Fig. 5) one of the earliest representations of a

FIG. 5. METROPOLITAN MUSEUM

worshiper carrying in his arms an animal, always, I believe, a goat, for sacrifice to a god. This is an extremely frequent representation in later times, when the altar in any form almost disappears; and in the earlier times the occurrence both of the altar and of the animal carried in the arms is not usual.

A similar altar, round, and of the hour-glass shape, and also showing the two flames, appears on a cylinder (Fig. 6) in the British Museum. While not as primitive as the last cylinder,

FIG. 6. BRITISH MUSEUM

APPENDIX G 271

it is quite archaic, and it confirms the supposition that it is two flames that are represented between the backs of the two gods: one being the sun-god, rising behind the eastern mountains; and another, repeated for symmetry, a god having the attributes of Nergal.

In Fig. 7, we have an unusually complete and instructive design. Here we see a seated goddess holding a scepter, and be-

FIG. 7. METROPOLITAN MUSEUM

fore her a round altar of the hour-glass shape, somewhat modified. In front of the altar stands a worshiper, carrying on one arm a goat, while with the other hand he pours a libation upon the altar, from which rises a flame. Behind him follow two female attendants, one carrying a pail or basket, and the other some uncertain object on her raised hand.

Considerably more slender in shape are the two almost col-

FIG. 8. METROPOLITAN MUSEUM

umnar altars, which we see on an archaic cylinder, though not of this earliest period (Fig. 8). Here a male deity appears holding a plow and a club, while before him a worshiper pours a libation from a slender vase on the altar.

We have had, in Fig. 7, an altar of this style, in which the upper half of the hour-glass was enlarged. In the cylinder of Dungi (Fig. 9), the upper part is much reduced, and the

FIG. 9. DE CLERCQ COLLECTION

lower part is enlarged. Here the standing god, or goddess, is recognized by the horned head-dress; although the goddess, in her familiar attitude, does not wear the usual flounced dress. The worshiper pours the libation from a vase, and it flows over the edges, the two symmetrical streams ending in the conventional knob. We may suppose that the oil in these two streams is imagined to be in flames; but no flame can well be

FIG. 10. THE LOUVRE

FIG. 11, DE MORGAN.

APPENDIX G 273

represented as rising, since the space is occupied by the action of pouring the oil from a vase.

The slender hour-glass altar, which we saw doubled in Fig. 8, appears in several cylinders of the period of Gudea, of which Fig. 10 is a sufficient example. I take it from Heuzy's copy of an impression of a seal on a tablet in the Louvre, but it is probably not quite correctly drawn; and the two flounced deities, one sitting and the other standing, should probably be beardless goddesses. From the altar rises a flame, and two conventional streams fall symmetrically, one on each side. We get the impression on all these altars of a depression like a cup, cut in the top of the altar, into which the oil is poured, and from which the burning stream overflows to the ground. Yet another admirable example (Fig. 11) is taken from a bas-relief found by de Morgan at Susa. The construction of the altar is well shown, with a raised ornamental band in the middle, the top apparently hollowed to make a basin. A worshiper pours into this basin a libation of oil from a vase with a spout. A flame arises, conventionally drawn so that it resembles a simple plant Two symmetrically arranged pendants, from the bottom of the flame, represent, not fruit, but the overflow of the burning oil (de Morgan, Délégation en Perse, Tome I., Recherches Archéologiques. Paris, 1900, p. 102). This special type of altar, with flames thus arranged, was the usual style in the Gudea period.

I now revert to a period anterior to Gudea. On a bas-relief from Nippur (Fig. 12), appears a deity seated on a seat, the back of which ends in a design like a bird's head. The god holds a vase; behind the god a divine attendant leads in the

FIG. 12. BAS-RELIEF FROM NIPPUR

worshiper, who brings a goat in his arms, another instance from the very earliest period in which this presentation of an animal offering appears. In front of the god is what is evidently a round altar, flaring at the top, so as to be rather of a wine-glass shape than the shape of an hour-glass. Flames rise from the top of the altar, indicating that oil was poured and burned upon it. Unfortunately the fracture makes it impossible to distinguish clearly what were the figures in front of the altar. This design shows what was one of the earliest forms of the round altar, which in the time of Gudea had become a slender hour-glass, and was drawn with the single slender flame and two over-flowing flames. And yet we remember that the first of the round altars we saw (Fig. 5) flared equally at the top and bottom.

I have mentioned one cylinder which I thought imperfectly drawn, belonging to the Louvre. In Lujard's Culte de Mithren, XXVIII. 12, is a cylinder (Fig. 13), credited to the Museum of The

FIG. 13. AFTER LUJARD

Hague, but which does not appear in Menant's Catalogue of The Hague. Before the seated goddess is an altar, and four female figures approach her. On the altar appears to be a cloth, and some objects seem to be above it. But I think it most probable that what appears to be cloth is simply a badly drawn conception of the streams falling from the altar.

There is a very peculiar type of cylinder of quite an early period, although apparently less archaic than the last, on which the seated deity is represented with the body ending in the shape of a serpent. We may presume that this represents the god Siru.

APPENDIX G 275

The corresponding goddess sometimes sits opposite him, but not with a serpent's body; or sometimes a worshiper stands before him. A gate, with or without a porter, finishes the main design. But an altar stands before the god in figure 14.

FIG. 14. BIBLIOTHÈQUE NATIONALE

In figure 15 we have another of the serpent gods. Between the god and goddess is an altar which seems to be a simple upright construction, apparently of bricks, and the flame is represented to be rising from the top. One is at liberty to imagine that this represents a mere open fireplace for warming the hands of the gods, but I think not.

I have shown that a worshiper may be represented as carrying a goat as an offering to a god. He is sometimes led by a divine attendant who takes his hand, and a second worshiper may follow as in figure 7, carrying a pail or basket by the handles. This design,

FIG. 15. COLLECTION DE CLERCQ

with the second figure carrying the pail, which begins to appear at an early, but perhaps not the earliest, period, is more frequently seen without the altar, on the carefully engraved smaller hematite cylinders of the Middle Empire. Among the older examples are some, as in figure 16, where large amphoræ seem to be presented

FIG. 16. THE LOUVRE

to the goddess, and sometimes, as in figure 17, the worshiper presents a drink-offering in a cup.

The nature of the vase from which libations are poured to the god in the archaic period appears in two very old votive bas-reliefs (Figs. 18, 19), figured by Hilprecht, Bab. Exp. I., Pt. II., Pl. XVI., figures 37, 38. Here we may presume that both the ram and the goat were brought as offerings as well as the gifts which another worshiper carries in his hand.

From the representation of these hour-glass altars we gain

FIG. 17. COLLECTION DE CLERCQ

FIGURE 18, HILPRECHT.

FIGURE 19, HILPRECHT.

very little that differs from those which were of the stepped pattern. We do not see any representation of animals on these altars, although we see animals brought in the arms of the worshipers. The altars are used chiefly, or wholly, for libations of oil. No cakes are seen. That it is oil, and not blood, that is poured on the altar appears from the flames. It is noticeable that in no case do we see an animal slain, as we do see it in the contests of Gilgamesh and Ea-bani, with lions, buffaloes, bulls, and leopards. There is no outpouring of blood represented. Yet on the other hand, if the blood sacrificed is not poured out, neither is the thought that of a meal with the god. What we most notice is the good savor of the oil burnt before the god.

INDICES.

I. NAMES.

Aaron, tomb of, 40, 79, 185.
Abbas Effendi, 48, 102, 109.
Abdu Khadir, 205.
"Abdullah is dead," 208, 224.
Abdullah saved by slaughter of 100 camels, 209.
Abraham, birthplace, 81.
Abraham, tribe of, 57.
Abu Ali works himself into a frenzy, 79.
Abu Ibrahim, 189.
Abu Obeida, blood marks, 192, 193.
Abu Rabah, 117.
Abu Risha, 85.
Abyssinia, 189.
Achan, 130.
'Ain Kadis, 182,
'Ain Kurum, 98.
Ali, worship of, 103, 104, 106.
Attonyan, Dr. A. A., 215.
Arabs, Mawali, 201.
Aramaeans, 61.
'Arja, poetical story of, 82; prose account of, 257 ff.
Asfuriyeh, 90.
Assassins, 101.
Assuan, 30.
Atiyeh, Joseph, 209.
Ayeshah, 194.
'Ayun, 187.
Azazimeh, 37.

Baalbek, journey to, 26.
Baalim, 133, 171.
Babites, 96, 108.
Baldensperger, titles of articles, 19.
Babylonian account of Noah's sacrifice, 73.
Barren women, 117, 118.
Barton, 56.

Bashan, 186.
Baudissin, 133.
Beersheba, 36, 255.
Behammra, 100.
Beinu, 17, 139.
Beirut, 12.
Berzeh, shrine of, 81, 171.
Bethesda, 90.
Bliss, President, Daniel, 23.
Bliss, F. J., 32, 61.
Blunt, Lady, 64, 67.
Bozra, 39.
Braigh, 211.
Browne, 96, 108.
Brummana, missionary Conferences at, 26, 48.
Burckhardt, 20, 21, 164, 175, 204.
Busan, 187.
Burton, 173, 175, 176, 224.
Butrus, cook and muleteer, 31.

Cairo, 30.
Calcutta, sacrifice to goddess Kali, 216.
Callirrhoe, 39, 89.
"Chair," minister of, 225.
Chemosh angry with his land, 128.
Church of Redemption, dedication of, 29.
Circassians, 62.
Conder, 260.
Copts, custom at marriage, 204.
Crawford, Rev. John, 29; characterization of Syrian Desert, 40.
Crawford, Mrs. John, 175.
Crawford, Rev. J. Stewart, 14, 21, 28, 199.

Dale, Mrs., 232.
Damascus, 12, 29.

INDICES.

Delitzsch, Franz, 11, 22.
Demishki, Hanna, 162, 181.
Der Atiyeh, 192.
Desert, Syrian, 28.
Dahariyeh, 36.
Dibbash, 207.
Dimitri, teacher of Arabic, 29.
Doolittle, Rev. George C., 25, 26.
Doughty, 21, 66, 92, 178, 189, 190, 191.
Druse Mountains, 35, 40.
Druses, 61, 62, 96, 208.

Ebers, 166.
Eddy, Rev. W. K., 25, 27, 124, 125, 189.
Egypt, journey in, 30.
En Misphat, 38.
Erman, 87.

Feiyad, 91.
Ford, Miss T. Maxwell, 104, 125.
Forder, 20, 35, 89.
Frazer, 51, 77.

Gadis (Kadesh Barnea) 34, 37, 38, 182.
Gates, Rev. Herbert W., 15.
Gaza, 143.
Geiger, 51.
George, St., 83.
Ghazaleh, Ahmed, 178.
Gilroy, Prof., University of Aberdeen, companion in travel, 32.
Graham, Dr. and Mrs., 31.

Hakim, 107.
Hamath, 90, 197.
Hamed el-Hudefi, 185.
Hanauer, Rev. J. E., 181.
Harding, Henry C., 67, 72, 89, 91, 183, 198, 206.
Hasan, 104.
Haupt, Paul, 210.
Hermon, Mt., ascent of, 27.
Hindi, Ahmed, 175, 224.
Homs, 84, 197.
Hornstein, C., 164.
Hosein, 104.
Hoskins, Rev. Franklin E., 105, 187.
Hughes, 194.
Hunter, Sir W. W., 217.

Ishmael, sacrifice of, 175.
Islam, not a development from ancient Semitism, 240.
Ismailiyeh, religious customs, 60, 202.

Jabur, 61.
Jacob, wrestles with God, 74.
Jebel Kasiun, 30.
Jedaideh, 27.
Jehovistic account of Noah's sacrifice, 73.
Jerusalem, 12.
Jessup, Rev. Henry H., 25, 79, 188, 228.
Jevons, 60.
Jiddah, 186.
Job, misfortunes of, sign of sin, 127.
Johnson, Dr. F., 198.
Juneh, cave of, visited by barren couples, 119.
Juttah, 36.

Kaaba, kissing the stone, 240.
Kadesh Barnea, 38, 182.
Kalat el-Hosn, 84.
Kali, goddess, 216.
Kandhs, 217.
Kazem Beg, 108.
Kerak, 114.
Khalasa, 36, 37.
Khahil, Abdu, 232.
Khuri, Faris L., 84, 191.
Kurmul, 36.
Kurnub, 38.
Karyaten, 85, 91.

Lane, 66, 195, 207.
Lang, 51, 64.
Layard, 186.
Lepsius, 142.
Loba, J. F., 59.
Lyde, missionary among the Nusairiyeh, 100, 106.

Mackenzie, Rev. Wm. Douglas, 15.
Mackie, G. M., 71.
Mahin, 205.
Matthews, A. N., 195.
Masud, Anis, dragoman, 26.
Mar, Sarkis, 139.

INDICES.

Mar, Yehanna, 85.
March, Rev. F. W., 17, 28.
Mecca, 170, 175.
Mehardeh, 201.
Myer, Rev. F. B., 216.
Michmash, 234.
Mina, or Muna, 170, 175, 223.
Mishwat, 190.
Mohammed, traditional saying of, 194.
Muir, Sir Wm., 192, 197, 211.
Musa, guide at Petra, dialogue with, 79.
Musyaf, 101.
Musulleh, 140.
Naaman, 58.
Nebi Safa, 173.
Nebk, 199, 205.
Nelson, Rev. W. S., 17, 25.
Nies, Rev. James B., 234, 236.
Noah, his sacrifice, 73.
Nofel Effendi, 174.
Noorian, Daniel Z., 59.
Nusair, 120.
Nusairiyeh, 60; claim Ali had no children, 107; reckoned as Moslems, 96; secrets of initiated revealed, 97.

Orontes, channels of, 117.

Palgrave, 66, 126.
Palmer, 205, 226, 262.
Palmyra, journey to, 40, 186.
Petra, 39, 183, 235, 236.
Pharaoh, treasury of, 39.
Porter, Professor, 101.
Porter, Rev. J. L., 186.
Post, Rev. George E., M. D., 18, 66, 184.

Ramses II., 86.
Rasheyeh, 83, 214.
Ravndal, G. B., American Consul at Beirut, 100.
Richards, British Consul at Damascus, 186.
Ritschl, Examiner in Hebrew, 210.
Rüppel, 142.
Ruheibeh, 182.

Safa, Nebi, 283.
Safita, 17.
Saladin, 101.
Sale, 170.
Salisbury, Professor of Yale College, translator of the secrets of the Nusairian religion, 97.
Samuel's sacrifice on the High Place, 138.
Sayce, 56.
Schaff, Philip, 22.
Schimper, 166.
Schumacher, 86, 235, 236.
Sell, 170.
Sellum, Anis, 81.
Shammar, Arab tribe, 64.
Sheik, Rihan, 92.
Sheik, Sa'ad, 86.
Sheik, Shadli, discoverer of coffee, 183.
Sherarat, 125.
Shiites, do not use the term fedou, 210.
Sinai, Mt., journey to, 30.
Smith, George Adam, 59.
Smith, W. Robertson, 21, 56, 218.
Snobar, 212.
South Country, 36.
Stade, 61.
Stambul, report to Sultan, 20.
St. Catharine, 30.
St. Rih, 84.
Sterling, Dr., 36.
Stewart, Rev. James S., 78, 100.
Straus, Mr. Oscar, fails to get permission to visit Druse Mountains, 35.
Suleiman of Adana, 47.
Suleiman of Nebk, 69, 72.
Sufsaf, Ras, 30.
Surur, 201, 205.
Syrians, not of pure stock, 62.
Syrian Desert, 40.

Tell el-Kadi, 143.
Tell Abu en-Neda, 228.
Tell Sh'af, 187.
Teyahah, 37.
Thompson, W. L., 63, 84.
Tischendorf, 165.
Tongas, 84.
Tophel, 185.
Towarah, specimen of prayers, 67, 68.

Tripoli, 197.
Trumbull, H. Clay, 35, 57, 177, 233.

Urfa, 214.

VanDyck, Dr. Wm., 91, 93, 97.

Wahabites, most orthodox sect of Islam, sought to crush out worship of welis, 76.
Waldmeier, 90, 162, 189.
Walpole, 167.
Ward, Rev. W. Hayes, 14.
Watson, Rev. Dr., 30.

Wathic, 211.
Webster, H. A., 61.
West, Robert H., 25.
Wheeler, Percy D. 'Erf, M.D., 182.
Williams, 182.
Wilson, Edward L., does not reach Gadis, 35.
Wortabet, Arabic-English Dictionary, 230.

Yadji, Habeeb, 64.
Yuseph el-Hagg, 79.

Zeller, Rev. John, 71, 232.
Zimmern, 49, 53, 54, 196, 205, 219.

II. SUBJECTS.

Afrit, supposed to inhabit sluice, 198.
Altars, built by patriarchs, 133.
"Ancient and Primitive," not synonymous, 50.
Angel, troubling the water, 90.
Angels, sacrifices to, 179.
Animal, cooked, 215.
Arabic, pronunciation of, transliteration of, 15; modern, study of, 30.
Atonement, Babylonian Ritual, 53; doctrine of, 195.

Babylonian exile destroyed monolatry, 242.
Bargain with saint for child, 118.
Baths of Solomon, 116.
Bay of St. George, 24.
Best gowns worn by jinn, 115.
Bible, record of many revelations, 14.
Birth of son, announcement of, 201.
Blasphemy against Mohammed, State offense, 96.
Blessing, 185.
Blood, avenger of, 191; "breaking forth of," 202; bride must step over it among Copts, 204; "bursting forth of," 197, 211, 212, 213; child anointed with, 203; considered defiling by Moslems, 219; covered up, 200; existence regarded impossible at Moslem shrine, 19; used in foundations of buildings, 184; in sluice of water wheel, 198; marks of, at shrine of Abu Obeida, 193; of black fowls on lintels, etc., in Abyssinia, 189; of cock, good for bad eyes, 141; on neck of camel, 183; on the door posts, 181; shed at entrance of cave, 184; used in sign of cross, 198; sprinkled on corner of building, 191; sprinkled on door posts of shrine, 192; stripes of on makam at Nebi Eyyub, 188; used in bathing face and shoulders, 205; used in solemnization of marriage among Aenezes, 204.
Blood-Sprinkling, Babylonian, 54; supposed to propitiate a jinn, 190.
Book, outgrowth of journeys, 17.
Books, sacred, 81.
"Bride of God," 114.
"Bride of the Nile," 114.
Bush, burning, 92.

Calf, offered to St. George, 213.
Camel not good for transportation of traveller's baggage, in Palestine, 31.

INDICES.

Cave, Juneh, 95.
Caves, controlled by a spirit, 94.
Cave of Khuddr, 95.
"Chair of the Companions," 87; servant of, 65.
Child, presented at shrine, 202.
Circulars of inquiry sent, 18.
Conquered races impose their customs on conquerors, 58.
Corpse, borne across a stream defiles it, 200.
Covenant between God and Israel, 214.
Curses of other sects in the Nusairian ritual, 98.
Custom, persistence of, among Orientals, 53, 65, 220.

Death, "Every house must have its death," 196.
Deification of men excluded by Moslem creed, 96.
Desecration of shrine visited with death, 140.
Development in O.T., 14.
Dolmen, channels for blood, 234.
Druse woman interviewed, 214.

East of tent the front, 202.
"Every house must have its death," 65.
Evil, Moslems think it from the devil by God's permission, 68.
Expiation, doctrine of, 194.

"Fail me," "why did you?" 70.
Fatalist, Moslem, 65.
Festival, annual, 215.
"Fire of Hell," 125.
Folk-lore, 78.
Forests in Syria, 99.
Fowls sacrificed by poor, 203.

German Emperor, 29.
Girls in care of flocks, 37.
God, author of good and evil, 68; chief residing in the sun, 67; fate to which all must bow, 68; may lead astray, 69; jealous, 71; he and St. George are brothers, 72; has human organism, 72; worship of him and inferior deities side by side, 64; "God had three sons," 113; shameless conceptions of, 114.

Guards passed at night, 42.

"Hardening the heart," 70.
"Head for head," 207, 227.
Heaps of witness, 80.
Heavenly bodies, worship of, 104.
High Places, 133 ff.
"Holy men," 149.
House, "Every house must have its death," 225.
House of Ivory, 110.
Housetop, home for two months, 29.

Incarnation, illustrated by image of sun in a mirror, 109.
Investigations, place for, 60; success of, 47.
Insane, 189.
Interviewing natives, 20.

Journals, unpublished, used as sources, 13; lost, 41.

Kid, killed over head of a man, 204.

Lawlessness at "Ain Kurum," 98.
Libation of coffee, 183.

Marriage of Joram and Athaliah, 110.
Messages of O.T., why divine? 14.
Misfortune, evidence of sin, 127, 221.
Method of investigation, 20.
Missionaries thought to be possessed of important archaeological information, 34; companions in travel, 20.

Moslems, unlettered, refer to books, 81.
Mt. Carmel, 95; cave at, 203.
Mt Hermon, remains of ashes and bones, 142.
Mt. Hor, visited, 185.
Mt. of Jehovah, 93.
Mt. Serbal, place of worship, 142.

"Not a bone to be broken," 178.

Obscene language avoided in going to a shrine, 75.
Obscenity, 129.
Old Testament, record of many divine revelations, 14.
Origin of Israel's religion, three views, 238 ff.

Palestine Exploration Fund, questions, 19.
Purse, "on account of," 215.
Penitential Psalms, 131.
Phallic worship, possible symbol of, 188; in India, 59.
Phallus, laid across entrance to shrine, 140.
Physical fatherhood of deity, repugnant to Islam, 112.
"Positive religion," 64.
Primitive Semitism furnished forms of speech, 14.
Procreative power possessed by spirits of the dead, 115, 116.
Primitive Semitic Religion, institutions of, medium of revelation, 55; traces of to-day, 49, 50.
Prayer, attitude of Moslems, 145.
Priesthood, portion received from the sacrifices, 147.

Reconciliation of avenger with murderer, 191.
"Redeemed you," 212.
"Redeem soul by soul," 208.
Researches, special, 34 ff.
Revue biblique, article on Dr. Trumbull, 35.
Robbed, 30.
"Rock," Semitic name of God, 88.

Sabbatic fountain, 213.
Sacred Oak, 94.
Sacrifice and slaughtering, Arabic word for them the same, 172.
Sacrifices, animals and fowls used, 174; between the feet, 177; confession one is worthy of death, 176; covers sin; 211; dahhiyeh, uses of, 176; for children, 177; for the dead, 179, 206; for houses, Babylonian, 54; hand put on back of animal, 148; in payment of vows, 172; part which falls to the priest, 173; important part, pouring out of blood, 216; human, 217; in connection with circumcision, 178; place where they may be slain, 211; place of, 229 ff; placed in the ground at Muna, 224; substitutionary character of, 225; that in which it consists, 223; tenth day of Pilgrim month, 170; to jinn, 198.
Sacrificial meal, 170, 218; term, misnomer, 222.
Saints, according to Moslems only mediators, 75.
Saint, called God, 95; real force in the life of the people, 124.
Samaritan passover, 171, 264.
Secrets revealed by Suleiman of Adana confirmed, 97.
Semites, primitive religion of, among Syrians and Arabs, 12, 13.
Semites, modern, 56 ff; no ethical conception of God, 66.
Semitic worship, survival of, 17.
Sheiks, religious, among Arabs, 64.
Shrines, 17.
"Simplicity of our minds," 65.
Sin, not conceived of as guilt, 129, 130.
Singing and dancing, 218.
Sodomites, 149.
Son of God, born of virgin, no mystery to Oriental, 242, 243.
Spirits, evil, in caves, 184.
"Spirit for spirit," 225.
Stones, medium of divine revelation, 84.
Stream, property of saint at Nebk, 88.
Substitution, 208.
Sufiism, basis of Babiism, 109.
Sun temples in Syria, 105.
Syncretism, 124.
Syrian Protestant College, library of, 23.

Table of God, 74.
Theophany, seat of, regarded as shrine, 93, 133, 134.
Threshold, place of sacrifice, 233; renewed when the house has been unfortunate, 233.
"Times of ignorance," 170.

INDICES. 285

Tours in Syria, false idea that it is dangerous to travel in summer, 23.
Traditionalists, 241.
Travels, preliminary, 22 ff; 1898–1899, extent of, 32, 33.
Trees, hung with rags, 91; under which saints rested, holy, 93.

Unspiritual views of the deity, 126.

Vicarious use of green cloth, 140.
Virgin, sacred, 115.
Vocation in travel, first discovered in company with Messrs. March and Nelson, 27.

Vows, payment of, 141.
Voyage from New York to Beirut, 24.

Wages of muleteers, cheaper in Syria than in Palestine, 32.
Walnut tree, sacred in flames, 93.
Water for irrigation in Syrian Desert, 199.
Ways and means, 29.
Weli, invitation to shrine, 81.
Wells in South country, 36.
"Whited-sepulchres," 141.
Writing, Arabs fear it as "black art," 20, 201.

III.—ARABIC AND OTHER SEMITIC WORDS.

Definitions and illustrations may be found by reference to pages.

'Ain Fowar, 89.
Allah, 170.
el-Arab, 63.
Asah, 137.
Bamoth, 137, 138, 143.
Banah, 137.
Bath Zur, 110.
Bedawi, 63.
Bedw, 63.
Benai Elohim, 120.
Bet Allah, 228.
Beth Elohim, 88.
"Bismillah? Allahu akbar," 173.
Bismillah, rahman er-rahim, 236.
Dahhiyeh, 148, 175, 209, 211, 223.
Dakhiel, 214.
Debah, 231.
Dekr, 117.
Dhabaha, 230.
Dhabh, 172.
Dhibh, 230.
Eed Kirbam, 170.
Fada, 195.
Fedou, 178, 195, 196, 197, 200, 202, 205, 206, 209, 210, 232.
Fellahin, 63.
Fidee, 201, 207, 209.
Fidyeh, 207.
Goal, 76.

Hedaya, 170.
Henna, 185.
Id dahhiyeh, 181.
Idu 'l-Azha, 195.
Ilani-ja, 110.
Jan, ahl el-ard, 190.
Jinn, 60, 89, 150.
Kadesh, 149.
Kdsh, 149.
Kedeshah, 149.
Kafara, 53, 210.
Kaffara, 209, 210.
Kalat, el-Kursi, 87.
Keffareh, 178, 209, 210, 211, 221, 233.
Khuddr, 84, 95, 197.
Kibla, 145.
Kipper, 53, 210.
Kis, 172.
Kubbeh, 143.
Kuffuru, 53, 54.
Kursi, 144, 171.
Kursi el-Aktab, 87.
Madhbah, 172, 230, 231.
Makam, 143, 231.
Mar, 76.
Mar Jirjis, 77.
Mar Yehanneh, 141.
Mazzeboth, 88.
Medayfeh, 42, 186.

Mejnun, 150.
Meshhad, 80.
Mezars, 184, 231.
Midbah, 230.
Midd, 162.
Nebi eyyub, 88.
Negeb, 62.
Piastre, 174.
Ramah, 136.
Rotl, 174.
Saraph, 137.
Sayyidat az-Zahra, 154.
Sayyideh, 154.

Semn, 80, 185.
Sheik, 64.
Tannur, 183.
Tezekereh, Turkish passport, 101.
Ulia, 77.
Umm Shakakif, 82, 144.
Weli, 76, 77, 78, 89, 90.
Ya rubb khattiti, 125.
Zabah, 172, 231.
Zabh, 172, 231.
Zeyareh, 213, 231.
Zikr, 164.

IV. SCRIPTURE REFERENCES.

GENESIS.

iii, 21	73
iv, 3-4	71
vi, 1-4	120
viii, 8-10	73
xi, 5	74
xi, 6	72
xii, 2	134
xiv, 13	133
xiv, 14	56
xviii, 1	133
xviii, 20, 21	74
xxi, 33	133
xxii, 14	93
xxvi, 25	133
xxviii, 18, 19, 22	88
xxviii, 20-22	159
xxix, 9	37
xxix, 26	151
xxxi, 13	88
xxxi, 48	80
xxxi, 54	134
xxxii, 24-30	74
xxxv, 7	88
xxxv, 14	88
xliii, 9	130
xlvi, 1	133
xlvi, 1-27	57

EXODUS.

ii, 16-21	37
iii, 1	134

iii, 2-4	92
iv, 21	70
iv, 27	134
viii, 15, 32	70
ix, 12	70
x, 20, 27	70
xi, 10	70
xii, 7	54
xii, 37-38	57
xiv, 4, 8, 17	70
xxi, 6	110
xxii, 7-9	110
xxii, 11	163
xxiv, 4	88
xxiv, 13	134
xxv, 30	74
xxxii, 5, 6, 19	166
xxxiv, 13	88

LEVITICUS.

v, 7, 11,	213
vii, 8, 32, 33	147
xiv, 32	212
xvii, 11	194
xix, 9, 10	163

NUMBERS.

xxi, 29	122
xxii, 41; xxxiii, 4	137

DEUTERONOMY.

i, 1	185
xii, 2	135

INDICES.

xii, 3 88
xii, 11, 12, 17, 18 167
xvi, 22 88
xviii, 1 218
xviii, 3 147
xxiii, 17 . . . . 149, 153
xxxii, 4 87

Joshua.

vii, 1-12 130
xiii, 14 218
xiii, 17 137
xv, 53 36

Judges.

vi, 11, 21, 24 134
ix, 6 134
ix, 13 74
xi, 11 134
xi, 30, 31, 34-36 168
xxi, 19, 21 167

Ruth.

iii, 12 76

I Samuel.

i, 3 146
i, 9-11 157
i, 24, 25 202
ii, 12-15 173
ii, 25 110
ix, 12, 13 135
xiv, 33, 34 234
xv, 2-20 130
xvi, 14-16 23
xvii, 53 130
xviii, 10 69
xxi, 16 74
xxv, 40-43 36
xxvi, 19 71

II Samuel.

v, 24 93
vi, 14 169
xv, 8 159
xv, 30, 32 134
xxiii, 3 87
xxiv, 1 69

I Kings.

iii, 4, 5 135
xi, 7 136

xviii, 30 134
xxii, 39 110
xxii, 43 138

II Kings.

iii, 2 88
v, 12 92
xii, 3; xiv, 4 138
xvii, 9 137
xvii, 10; xviii 4 88
xxi, 3; xxiii, 8, 15 137
xxiii, 8-13 77
xxiii, 14 88

I Chronicles.

xxi, 1 69

Job.

i, 6-12, ii, 1-6 122
i, 13-19 127
ii, 10 69
iii, 13-18 121
iv, 7 128
viii, 6 128
ix, 30, 31 244
xix, 25 76
xxii, 5-10 128
xliii, 5 244

Psalms.

xxii, 25, 26 159
xlv 110
xlv, 12-16 111
li, 4 243
lxii, 2 87
lxxxii, 1 110

Isaiah.

ii, 2 134
vi, 5 244
vi, 9, 10 70
xiv, 9, 10 121
xix, 19 88
xxx, 29 87
liii, 6 245
lxiii, 1 39

Jeremiah.

ii, 20 136
iii, 2 137
xix, 5 137
xxxii, 35 137

EZEKIEL.

xi, 39-43	237
xx, 28, 29	136

HOSEA.

ii, 5, 8, 12	162
ii, 7, 13, 15	137
iii, 4	88
iv, 13	137
iv, 14	149
iv, 12, 13	135
ix, 7	151
xi, 8, 9	245

AMOS.

iii, 6	69
v, 21-23	167

MICAH.

iv, 1	134

MALACHI.

ii, 11	123

MATTHEW.

xxiii, 27	141

LUKE.

i, 39	36
ii, 22-28	202
xiii, 1-5	128

JOHN.

v, 2, 3	90
ix, 1	127

ACTS.

xix, 11, 12	92

HEBREWS.

i, 8, 9	111
ix, 22	194

V. QUOTATIONS FROM THE KORAN.

ii, 258; iii, 61	76	xxii, 35	174
iii, 191, 194	210	xxxvii, 107	230
iv, 59	125	xxxviii, 3-9	125
xvii, 5-7	125	xxxix, 36	210

www.ingramcontent.com/pod-product-compliance
Lightning Source LLC
Chambersburg PA
CBHW050333230426
43663CB00010B/1835